IMAGES
of America

DELAWARE AIR NATIONAL GUARD

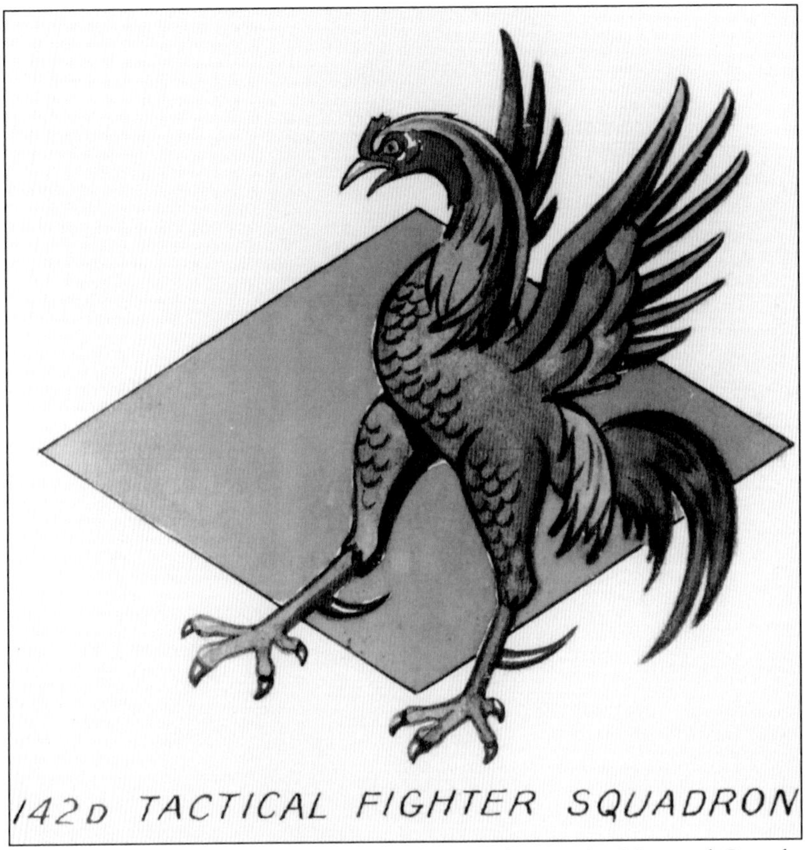

The insignia is shown of the 142nd Fighter Squadron, Delaware Air National Guard, reflecting the Delaware "Blue Hen" mascot, "Diamond State" in blue and gold, the colors of Delaware, and the U.S. Air Force. The 142nd was the heir to the lineage of the 342nd Fighter Squadron, which had flown P-47s and P-51s in New Guinea, the Philippines, and Shima as part of the 348th Fighter Group, 5th Air Force, during World War II. The *Delaware Air National Guard 60th Anniversary Yearbook* records:

> The Blue Hen's Chickens—Name applied to the Delaware soldiers during the Revolution, who from their gallant conduct, were first called by their companions 'game cocks.' The name Blue was derived from their blue uniforms. Some, however, say that it was from one of their most gallant leaders [Capt. Jonathan Caldwell], alleging that every true game chicken was of blue color. Others said that he [Caldwell] had a blue game chicken which he carried with his baggage. Be that as it may, however, the soldiers would say amongst themselves as the gallant Delawareans were killed off, and more were sent to supply their places, in fancy, denominating the state which sent them as the Old Blue Hen, "Here comes some more of Blue Hen's chickens." The name was afterward applied to all Delawareans.

(Courtesy of the Delaware Military Heritage and Education Foundation.)

ON THE COVER: The crew of an early overseas strategic airlift mission to Europe by the Delaware Air Guard in 1963 included, from left to right, M.Sgt. Roger Lambeth, flight engineer; Capt. Jim Moore, pilot; Capt. Mike Reucidlo, pilot; Lt. Col. Elmer Hanselman, navigator; unidentified U.S. Air Force advisor; Larry McBride, loadmaster; John Cheban, loadmaster; George Rittenhouse; and Chester Field, flight engineer. (Courtesy of the Delaware Military Heritage and Education Foundation.)

IMAGES
of America

DELAWARE AIR NATIONAL GUARD

Brig. Gen. Kennard R. Wiggins Jr. (DE ANG Retired)

ARCADIA PUBLISHING

ISBN 978-0-7385-6707-5

Published by Arcadia Publishing
Charleston, South Carolina

Printed in the United States of America

Library of Congress Catalog Card Number: 2008931988

For all general information contact Arcadia Publishing at:
Telephone 843-853-2070
Fax 843-853-0044
E-mail sales@arcadiapublishing.com
For customer service and orders:
Toll-Free 1-888-313-2665

Visit us on the Internet at www.arcadiapublishing.com

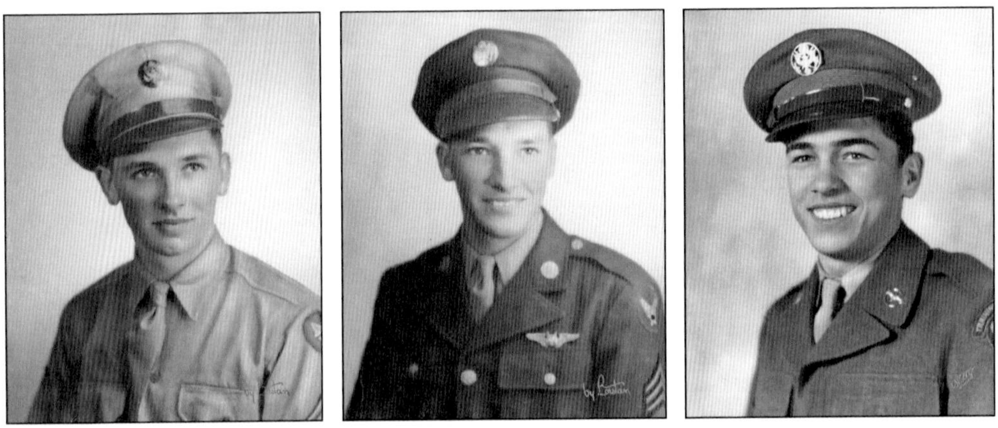

This book is dedicated to the Wiggins brothers: from left to right, T.Sgt. Lawrence E. Wiggins Sr., S.Sgt. Kennard R. Wiggins Sr., both charter members of the Delaware Air National Guard, and youngest brother M.Sgt. Charles E. Wiggins, who served with the unit until his retirement.

Kennard R. Wiggins Sr. said, "One day my brother Lawrence told me they were going to form a fighter squadron at the air base to be called the 142nd Fighter Squadron of the Delaware Air National Guard. I became a charter member. I was with them till the Korean War broke out." (Author's collection.)

Contents

ACKNOWLEDGMENTS

This project was a labor of love for me. It turns out I'm not the only person who bears a special fondness for the Delaware Air National Guard. It is a shared appreciation with several thousand all-volunteer members or former members of this storied organization and their families, friends, and neighbors. Many more than I can count, or find room to name here, have demonstrated their dedication by adding bits to the history of the Delaware Air Guard. They have offered their stories, their photographs, and their very personal experiences over a period of decades to accumulate this history. Their history documents tireless dedication, personal integrity, service before self, and excellence in all they do.

I would like to acknowledge the expert assistance of Edward Blackburn, who taught me that airplanes have individual personalities, as well as Gene Bedgood, Hugh Broomall, Carl Butterworth, Larry Cantera, Dale Dickerson, Ike Guessford, Norm Jackson, Andy Kirchner, Roger Lambeth, Tom Lauppe, Al Lugano, Tom Nale, Walt Powell, Ernie Schwab, James P. Scott II, Dave Speer, and countless other Delaware Air Guard members and retirees who were primary sources of information in identifying the historic images.

I am grateful to the Delaware Military Heritage and Education Foundation for providing access to its historic archival material and supporting this project. I thank the editorial judgment and publishing advice provided by Ben Matwey, Jan Churchill, Rebecca Melvin Johnson, Jerry Dorsman, and Floyd Kemske, as well as moral support from the JBS. A special thanks goes to Mark Giansanti and the cadet/students of the Delaware Military Academy who helped to archive the historic material, especially cadets Nick Bucci, Zak Fisch, Sean Grady, and Amanda Walton. Thanks also to Katie Stephens, my editor at Arcadia Publishing, who was most helpful in seeing this project to completion. Finally, I am indebted to my wife, Liz, and my family for their loving encouragement and support.

INTRODUCTION

It is very difficult to produce a book that encompasses, in a comprehensive way, the entire scope and depth of the Delaware Air National Guard's more than 60 years of service to the nation. In that time, several thousand men and women have taken their turn in the continuum of this storied organization. I am limited here by a finite number of pages. Arcadia Publishing's Images of America series focuses upon historic images, and so the reader will find that I have chosen to highlight the vintage photographs of the unit's very first few decades. Please forgive me for giving short shrift to the later years. One must make choices, and I will leave it to a future historian to pick up where I have left off.

The founding fathers of the Delaware Air Guard were almost all veterans of World War II, many with combat experience. They had earned their stripes through the hard experience of war and were determined to start something that would be of lasting value as they returned to their homes and to their civilian jobs. They were a relatively homogenous group, all fairly young, with a shared experience. They joined for the camaraderie, the chance to fly, and the opportunity to start something big and new. "It was quite a conglomeration," said Rex Riley, charter member. "It was a small unit and everyone knew everyone else. There was party after party. Our maximum strength then was probably not much more than 200 men. It was all of course, very informal. We were all young guys just released from the war. The pilots were a pretty wild bunch."

What started as a veterans' flying club soon got serious with a first test only a few years after its founding. The Korean War sent these veterans back into combat once again, stripping the organization of its manpower. After the Korean War, it was a major effort to rebuild the 142nd Fighter Squadron to its former strength, but the addition of new jets and new recruits reinvigorated the Delaware Air National Guard. The 1950s were a time when the unit began to truly professionalize by standing air defense alert and by applying rigor and discipline to the regime of flying high-performance aircraft. The 142nd Fighter Squadron was still a tight-knit group of about 400 personnel.

With the arrival of the 1960s, the unit got a new airplane, the C-97, and a new mission, to fly strategic airlift at intercontinental range. It also brought a big increase in size as the organization became the 166th Airlift Group, including the 142nd Airlift Squadron and an aeromedical evacuation mission, as well as support functions such as communications, a clinic, engineers, supply, and more. Its personnel strength grew to about 1,000 airmen.

In the fighter days, the airplanes were "in reserve" to be called up in case of war. The focus was on training. The strategic airlift mission was an operational mission, flying (part-time) a real world task of airlifting cargo and personnel worldwide. Delaware Air National Guard planes and crews supported missions in Europe, Africa, Asia, the Pacific, and South America. The unit regularly flew cargo to Vietnam during the conflict there.

The new mission also brought a culture change: from the elite status of the solitary fighter pilot to a "crew" aircraft, which for the first time included enlisted personnel as aircrew members. This had the effect of making the mission more of a team effort, not just on the flightdeck but in all the parts of the newly expanded organization. Everyone had a reason to identify with the mission.

The Air Guard also developed its domestic mission of supporting civil order, providing a resource for natural disasters and emergencies, and playing a positive role in the community through volunteer efforts. They serve the governor of Delaware and have been historically an indispensable asset in that role.

The 1960s and 1970s were decades of turmoil and change. The post-Vietnam Delaware Air Guard found itself no longer relying upon the draft to attract new recruits and had to actively recruit for the first time in a professional way. It hired minorities and women in increasing numbers, reflecting the changes in society.

The C-130 Hercules airlifter replaced the C-97 in 1971, and the mission changed to Tactical Airlift, flying the airdrop of equipment and troops in support of ground operations. The 166th continued to deploy around the world but did so generally in order to fly local missions in support of the combat commands. The airplane and its trained personnel also happen to be an ideal combination for humanitarian relief. Delaware Air Guardsmen have deployed globally in support of relief for hurricanes, earthquakes, floods, and human disasters. Their training discipline and specialized skills are frequently put to this good use.

The unit got a boost in 1985 when it began trading its 1956 vintage C-130A aircraft for factory-new C-130H models, making it much more capable of the future challenges that awaited it.

What had been an all-volunteer force of part-time personnel was activated for Desert Storm and Desert Shield in 1990 and was mobilized for the Gulf War. Not just aircrews but cooks, mechanics, clerks, and cops were part of the effort.

Maj. Dave Prox, a Delaware Air National Guard (ANG) pilot, remembers:

> At 0700 we were awakened by Tom Lauppe, "You're going to Kuwait! You've got one hour to get airborne." We were the first Guard aircraft to land in Kuwait. It was amazing. The burning oil wells and thunderstorms created a visibility problem. Descending into the black clouds was very eerie; everything turned pitch black. As we got lower we would get glimpses of the fires below. It was like flying into hell. It was a great feeling being there first, and representing the State of Delaware.

After the Gulf War, the Air Guard never truly "stood down" to its former part-time status. With the help of its people, it continued to play an operational role in exercises, deployments, and relief missions at a tempo far above its previous level, gradually increasing until 9/11, when it once again mobilized for the nation's security. Today the men and women of the 166th remain in Iraq, Afghanistan, and points all over the world on a rotational basis. There is renewed emphasis on homeland security, and the Delaware ANG plays a role in that arena. It has added Information Operations to its mission list. It would have been almost unimaginable for the founding fathers to predict such growth and maturity in the little unit they started in 1946.

The story revealed in these vintage photographs only gives a hint of the strong foundation the first Delaware Air Guardsmen have built. The real story of the Delaware Air Guard picks up momentum where I have left off, particularly since the Gulf War.

One

FORMATIVE YEARS 1946–1949

The Delaware National Guard was reorganized after World War II as separate battalions of anti-aircraft artillery. But it had added a brand-new element to the force that had never existed before. Mirroring the emergence of an independent air force from the Army Air Corps, the Delaware National Guard added an Air National Guard organization.

Organizational meetings were held at the National Guard Bureau and attended by Brig. Gen. Paul Rinard, the adjutant general, accompanied by Col. John B. Grier, the U.S. property and fiscal officer, as early as March 1946. Their first task was to recruit veterans for this new unit. General Order No. 9, dated July 8, 1946, outlined an organization that included the 142nd Fighter Squadron (32 officers, 127 enlisted men); 142nd Utility Flight of 142nd Fighter Squadron (6 officers, 29 enlisted men); Detachment "C" 208th Air Service Group (Fighter) (8 officers, 1 warrant officer, 168 enlisted men); and 142nd Weather Station (Type A) (3 officers, 5 enlisted men).

On September 6, 1946, the formal federal recognition and activation of Delaware's first Air National Guard unit (142nd Fighter Squadron) took place at a ceremony in the Wilmington Armory. The ceremony was conducted by Brig. Gen. Paul R. Rinard (the adjutant general) and Col. John B. Grier, U.S. property and disbursing officer for Delaware. The unit would begin with 49 officers and 263 enlisted men authorized. Actual strength on founding day was 14 officers, 1 warrant officer, and 36 enlisted men. These original 51 "plank-owners" were commanded by Lt. Col. Wallace A. Cameron.

Shortly afterward, the squadron received its first of 25 fighter planes, F-47N Thunderbolts. In late 1946, two L-5 and two AT-6 aircraft were received to assist in the training of new pilots. The year 1947 brought the addition of several more airplanes, including C-47s and four B-26 target-towing bombers.

The Medical Group has been a part of the Delaware Air National Guard's history since its origin in 1946. The medical section in those days was an army unit comprised of one doctor and three enlisted personnel.

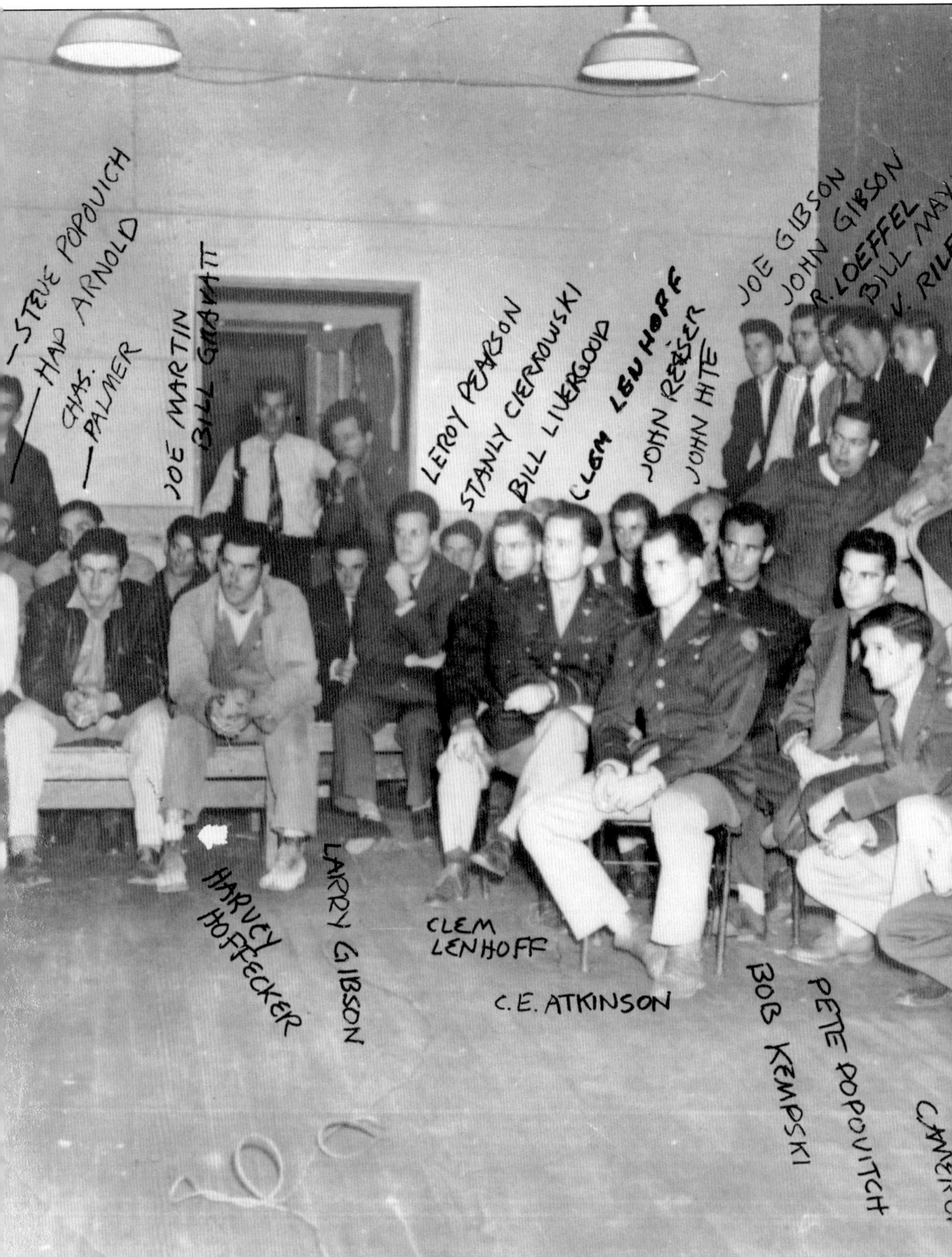
STEVE POPOVICH
HAP ARNOLD
CHAS. PALMER
JOE MARTIN
BILL GRAVATT
LEROY PEARSON
STANLY CIERKOWSKI
BILL LIVERGOOD
CLEM LENHOFF
JOHN REISER
JOHN HITE
JOE GIBSON
JOHN GIBSON
R. LOEFFEL
BILL MAY
V. RILE
HARVEY HOFFECKER
LARRY GIBSON
CLEM LENHOFF
C.E. ATKINSON
BOB KEMPSKI
PETE POPOVITCH

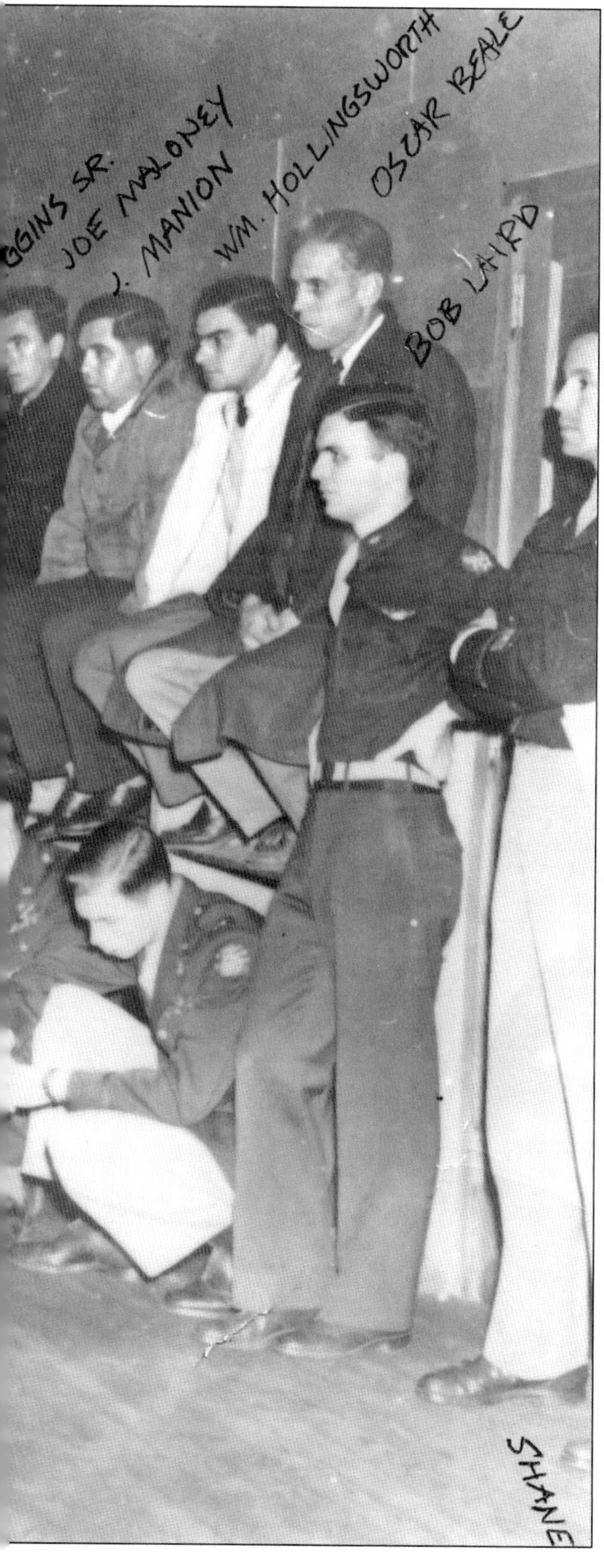

The original Delaware Air National Guard founding fathers are pictured at an organizational meeting in the Wilmington Armory in March 1946. "A friend of mine, Army National Guard LTC Warren Perry, called me up and said they just got a message in from the Pentagon that they're going to start an Air Guard and asked if I'd be interested," said Lt. Gen. Clarence E. Atkinson. "And naturally, I was. So the next Guard meeting that the army had, I was there, and got introduced to everybody, and what was going on. That was in May 1946. Then more people got involved and everything, until September the 6th when we were officially organized and recognized by the Air Force as being a unit." (Courtesy of the Delaware Military Heritage and Education Foundation.)

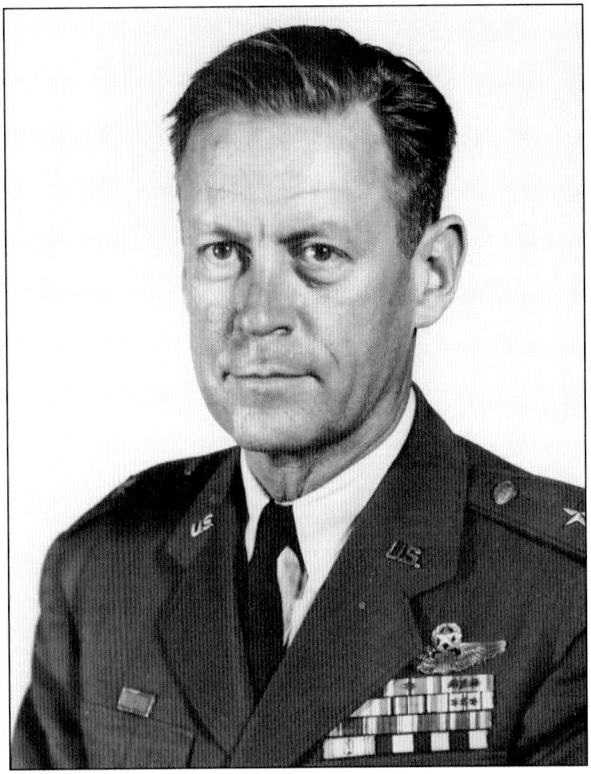

William W. Spruance was a founding member of Delaware Air National Guard and World War II veteran of the China/India/Burma theater, where he "flew the hump" with 362 missions over the Himalayas. He was also a pioneer in developing forward air control tactics and techniques with Gen. George Patton. Brigadier General Spruance noted, "What attracts people is the common interest in the airplanes, and flying a mission and the rewarding effect of getting something done when you're working with a team of people. So I guess that's what inspired me." (Courtesy of the Delaware Military Heritage and Education Foundation.)

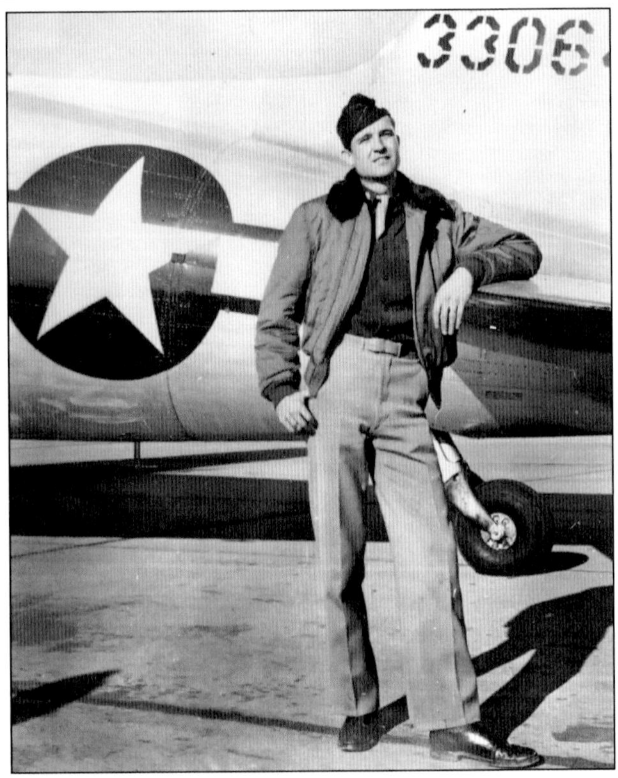

Lt. Col. Wallace A. Cameron, first commanding officer of the 142nd Fighter Squadron, Delaware Air National Guard, is shown here. Cameron was a veteran of World War II, flying P-47s with the 9th Air Force, 48 Fighter Group (FG), 493rd Fighter Squadron. He accepted an active-duty commission and served in the U.S. Air Force into the late 1960s. (Courtesy of the Delaware Military Heritage and Education Foundation.)

Clarence "Ed" Atkinson was a charter member of Delaware Air National Guard. A combat veteran of the Army Air Force in World War II flying bombers in the Pacific, and later a maintenance officer during the Korean War with the legendary 4th Fighter Wing, Atkinson was the original adjutant to the newly formed 142nd Fighter Squadron. He remarked, "I did not get into organizing the unit itself. That was all done by full-time people at the armory. . . . In fact, I was told I was the first man ever contacted about the Air National Guard by COL Warren Perry." (Courtesy of the Delaware Military Heritage and Education Foundation.)

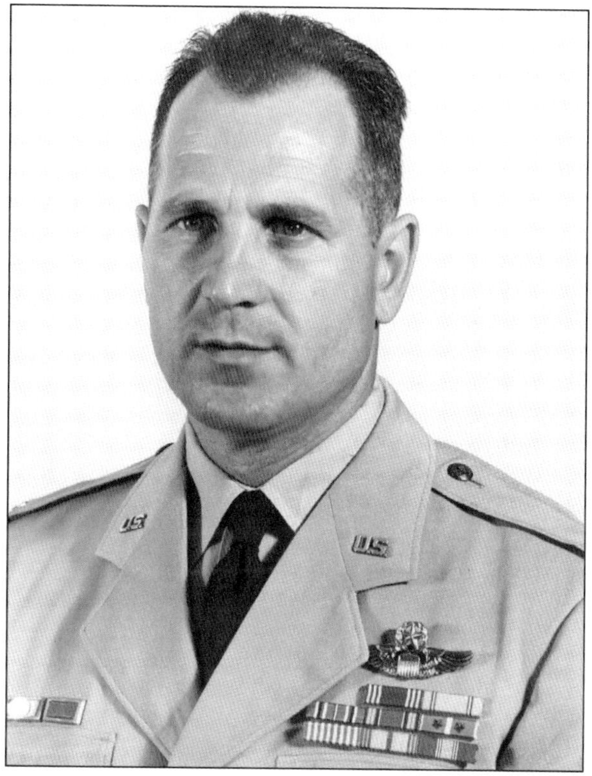

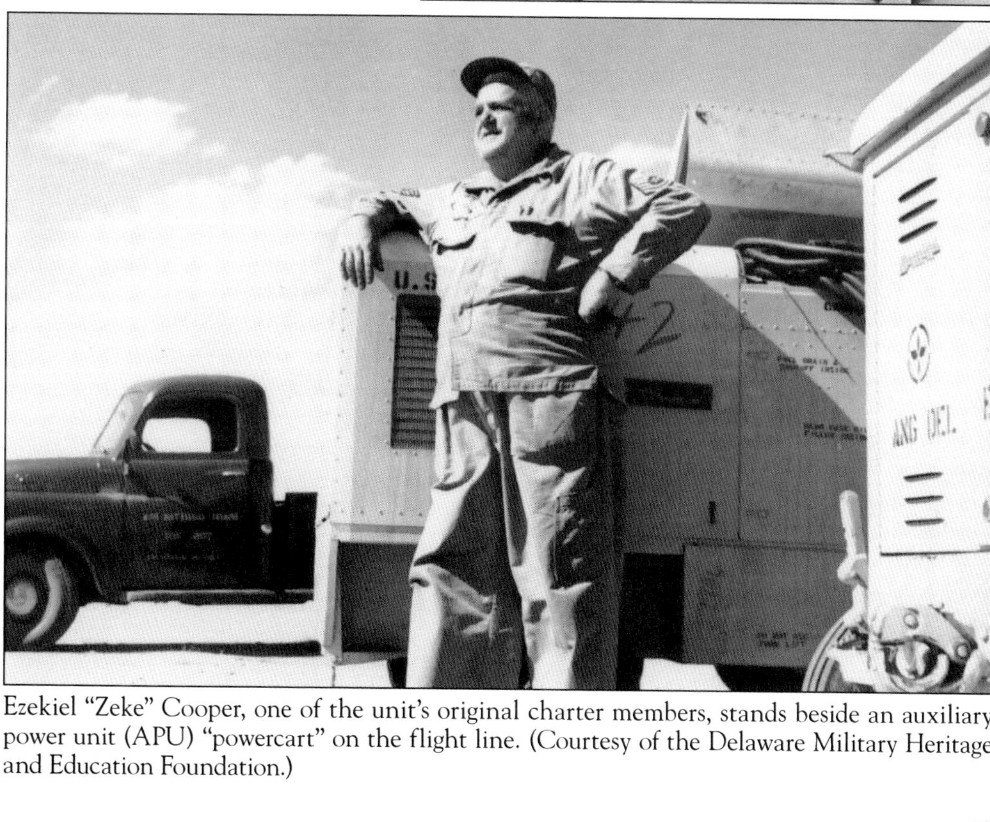

Ezekiel "Zeke" Cooper, one of the unit's original charter members, stands beside an auxiliary power unit (APU) "powercart" on the flight line. (Courtesy of the Delaware Military Heritage and Education Foundation.)

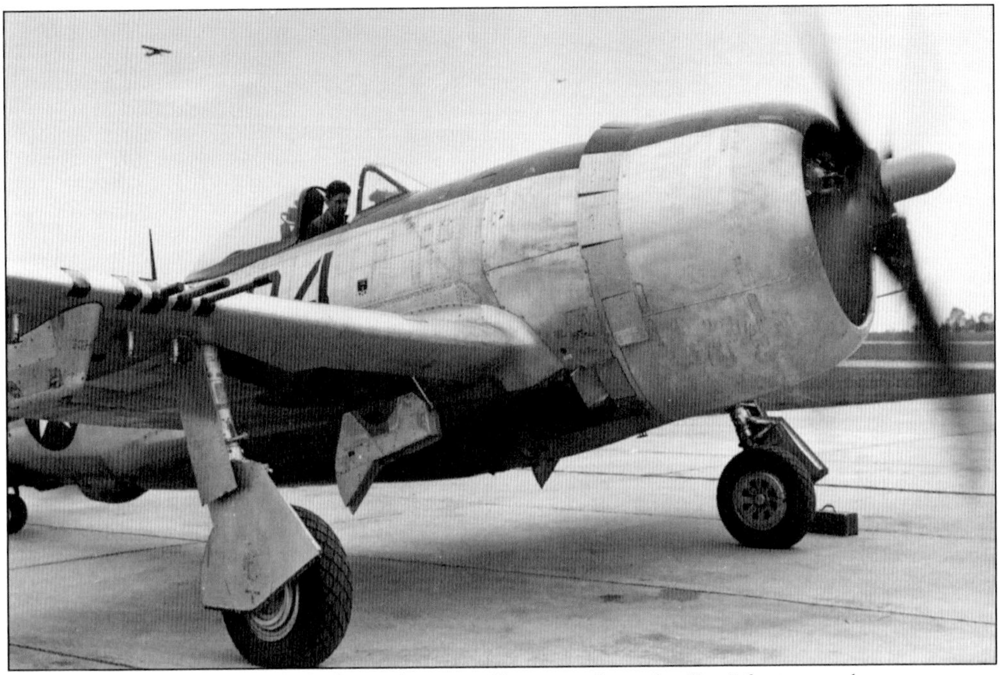

The Republic F-47N Thunderbolt was known affectionately as the "Jug" for its portly appearance. Delaware Air National Guard's first frontline aircraft was assigned to the unit between 1946 and 1950. The Thunderbolt was among the most heavily armed fighters of World War II. The F-47N was a variant designed for long range in the Pacific theater and was the last version mass produced. Over 1,800 were produced between December 1944 and 1945. (Courtesy of the Delaware Military Heritage and Education Foundation.)

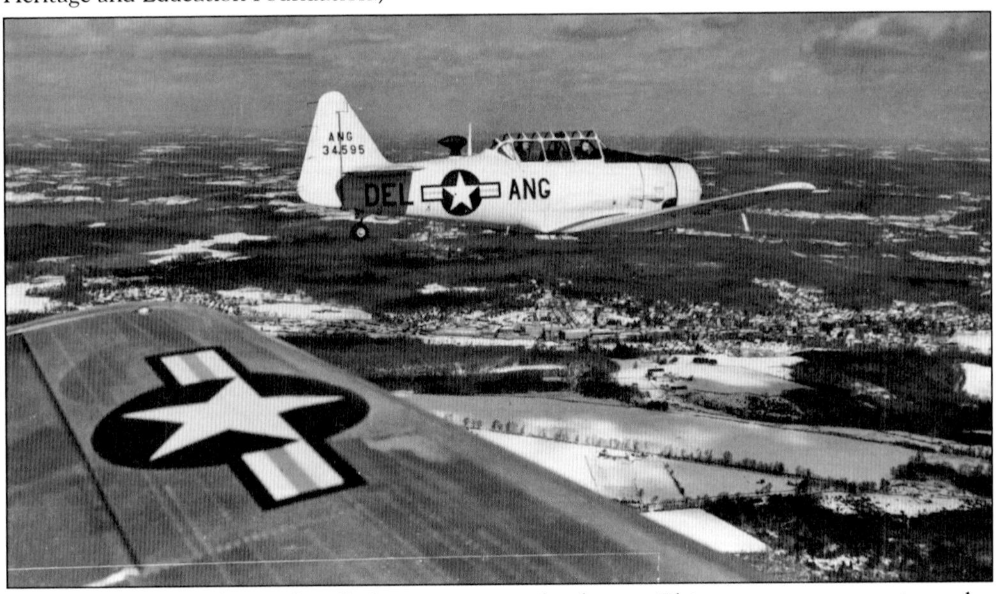

An AT-6F Texan is depicted in flight over a snowy landscape. This was a two-seat trainer, also used as an all–purpose hack. It was among the first airplanes delivered to the new outfit in 1947. Two were originally assigned to the 142nd Fighter Squadron. (Courtesy of the Delaware Military Heritage and Education Foundation.)

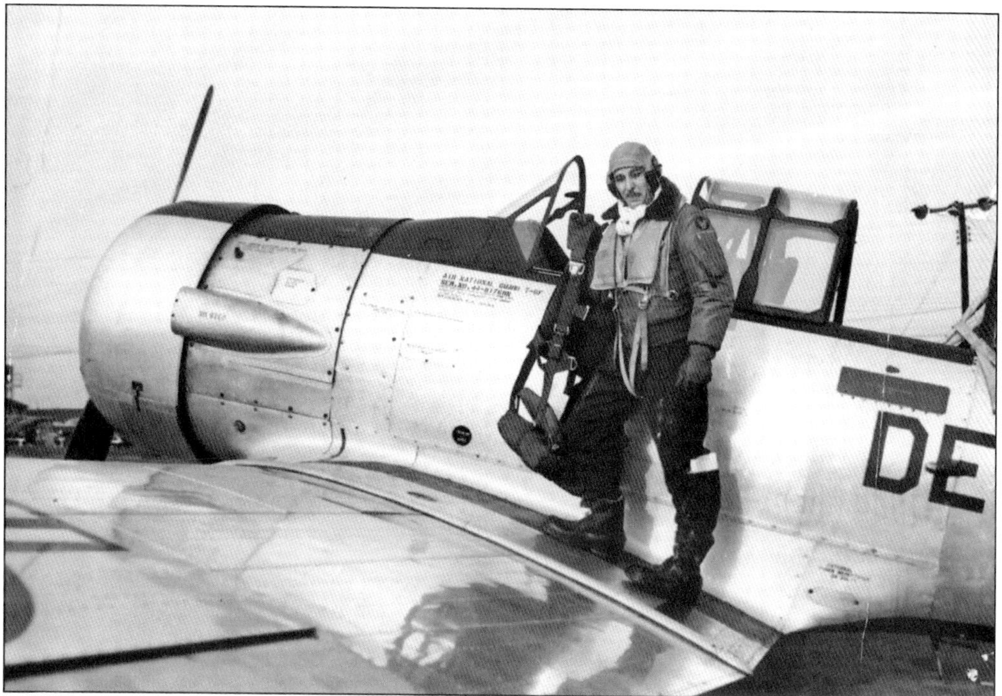

Pilot Harry Stowell stands on the wing of an AT-6 trainer clad in typical flying togs, including a "Mae West" lifejacket and parachute along with a leather flying helmet and a debonair white scarf. (Courtesy of the Delaware Military Heritage and Education Foundation.)

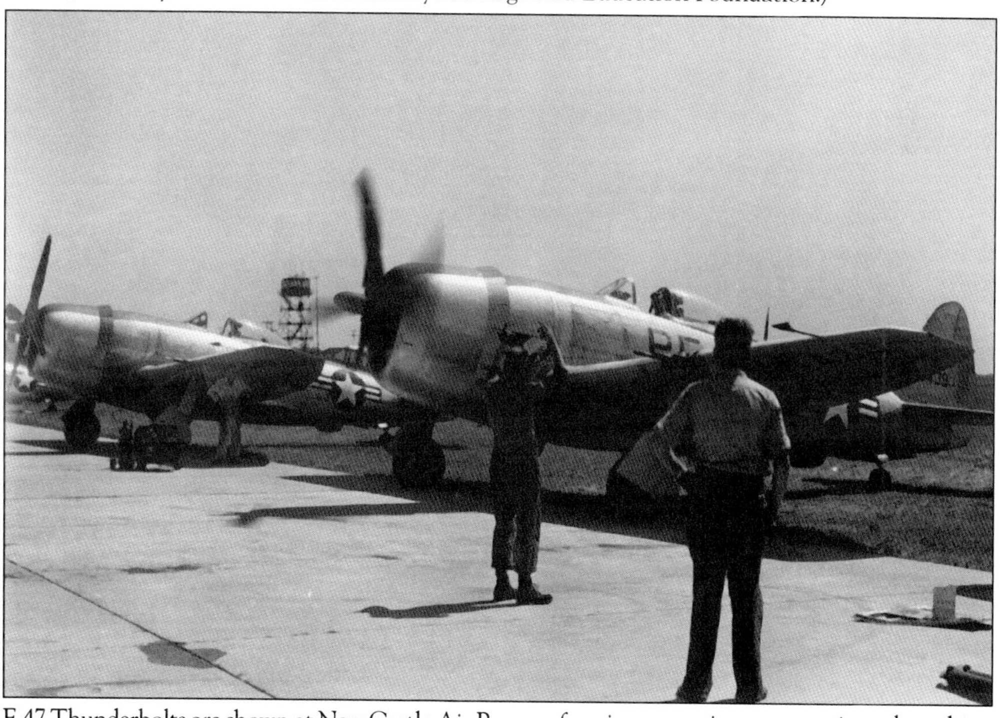

F-47 Thunderbolts are shown at New Castle Air Base performing an engine run-up prior to launching a training mission. (Courtesy of the Delaware Military Heritage and Education Foundation.)

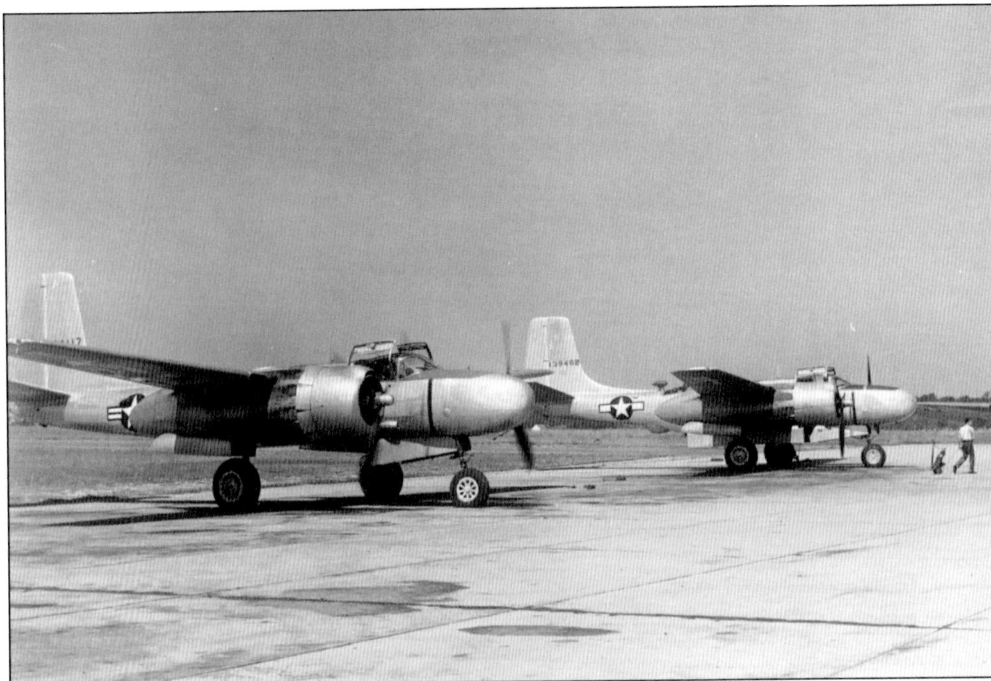

B-26 Invader bombers are parked on the ramp. These light bombers were used to tow targets for the fighter pilots in aerial gunnery. The unit was assigned four of these aircraft from 1947 to 1950. (Courtesy of the Delaware Military Heritage and Education Foundation.)

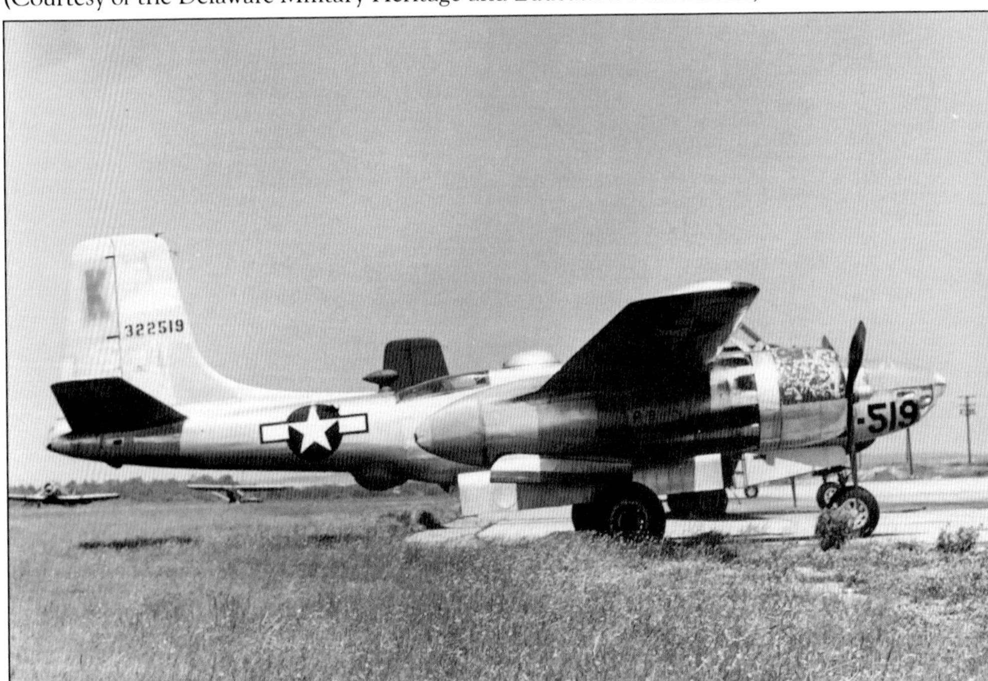

Depicted here is another view of the B-26 Invader with an AT-6 trainer in the background. (Courtesy of the Delaware Military Heritage and Education Foundation.)

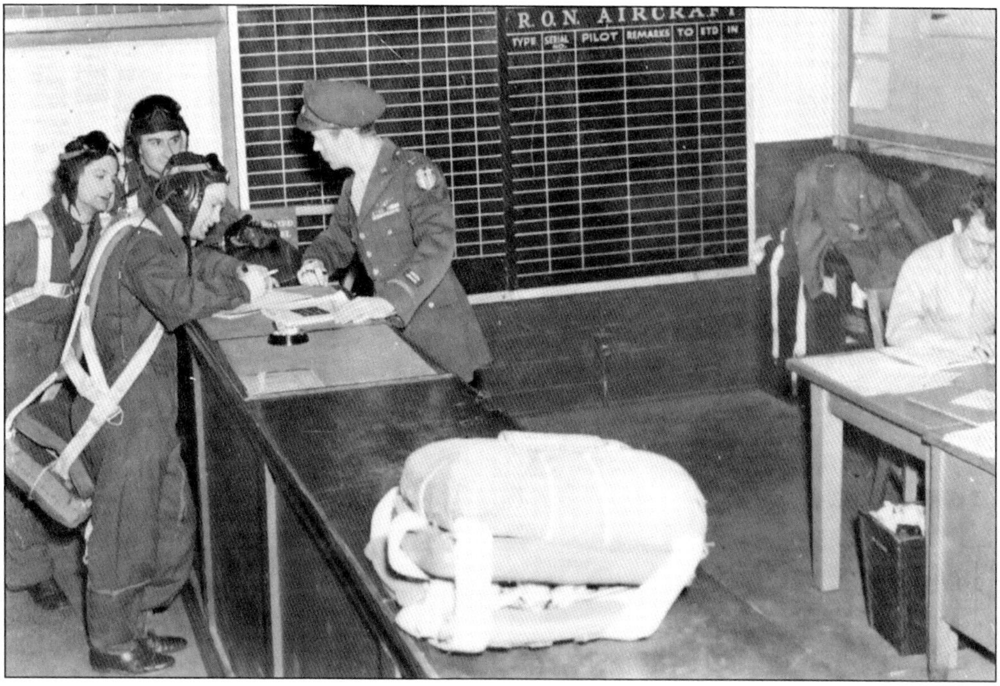

In the pilots' "ready room" is Capt. William Spruance, shown behind the counter, who assigns tasks to unit aviators as they prepare for a mission. (Courtesy of the Delaware Military Heritage and Education Foundation.)

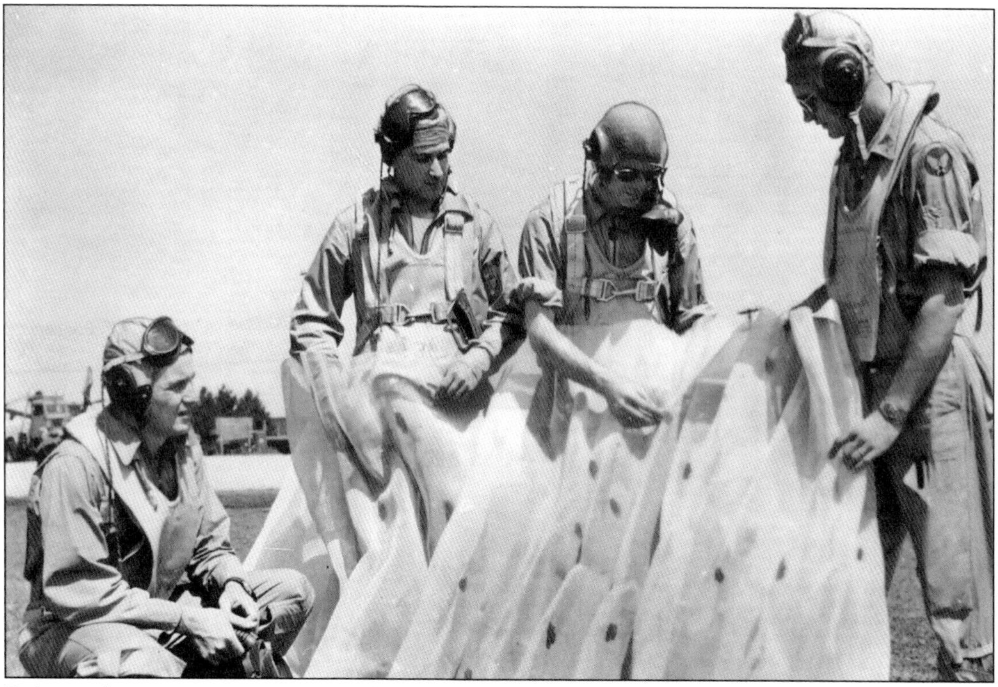

Fighter pilots were eager to assess their scoring in air-to-air gunnery on targets. Each pilot had color-coded munitions so they could gauge their individual accuracy. (Courtesy of the Delaware Military Heritage and Education Foundation.)

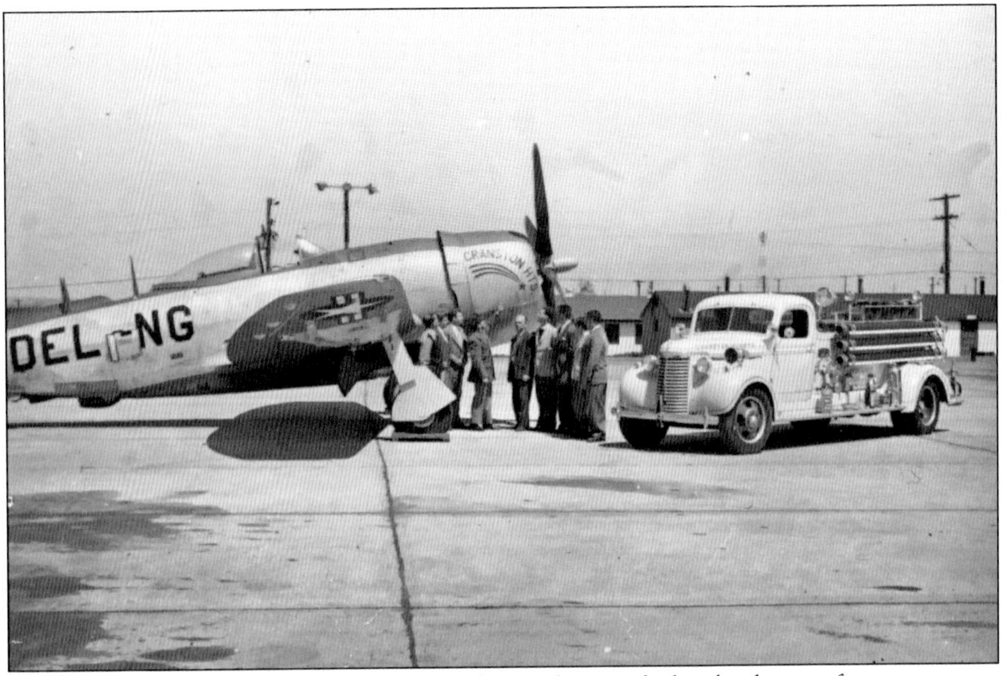

An F-47 fighter is christened "Cranston Heights" in honor of a local volunteer fire company as part of a community recruiting drive. Volunteer firemen and National Guardsmen share many of the same qualities of public service to the community. (Courtesy of the Delaware Military Heritage and Education Foundation.)

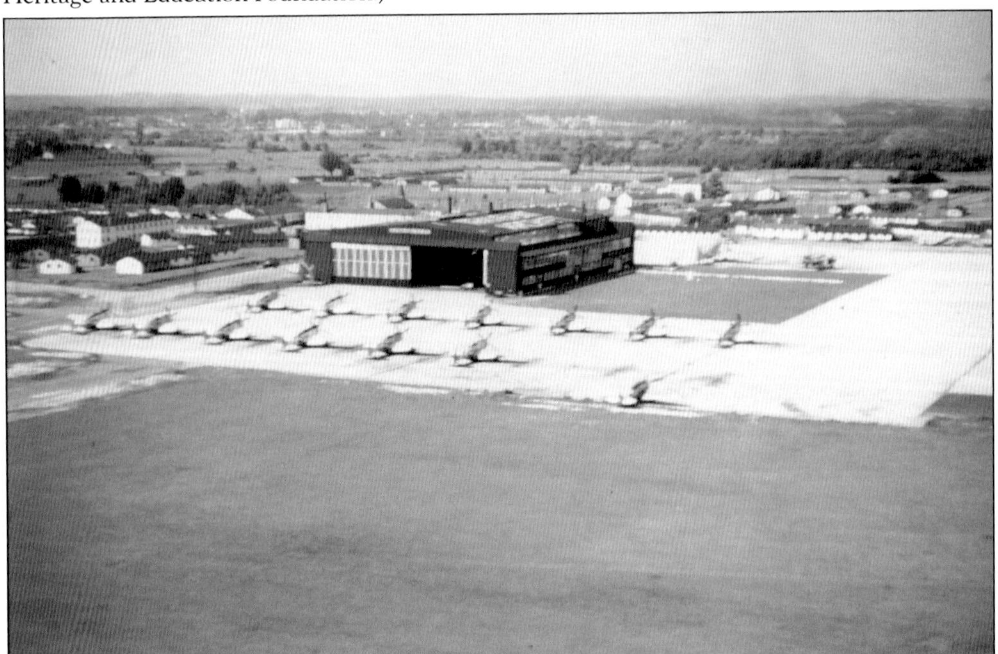

The parking apron and maintenance hangar at New Castle County Airport are shown with 142nd Squadron F-47s arrayed in rows. (Photograph by James R. Shotwell Jr.; courtesy of the Delaware Military Heritage and Education Foundation.)

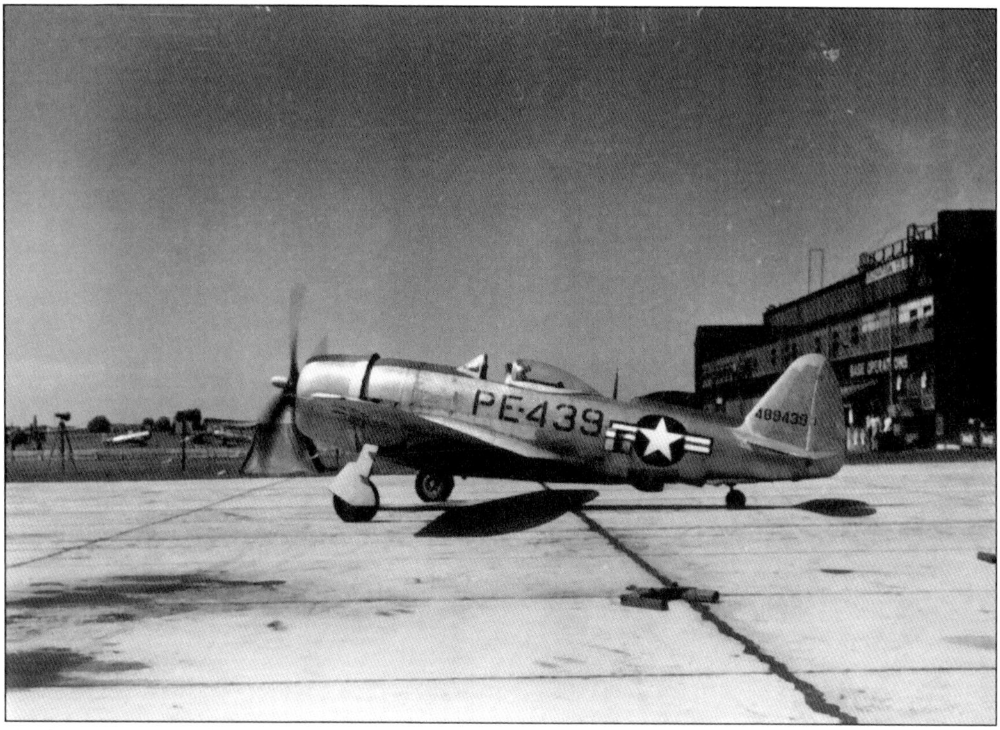

An F-47 taxis on the ramp by the maintenance hangar. (Courtesy of the Delaware Military Heritage and Education Foundation.)

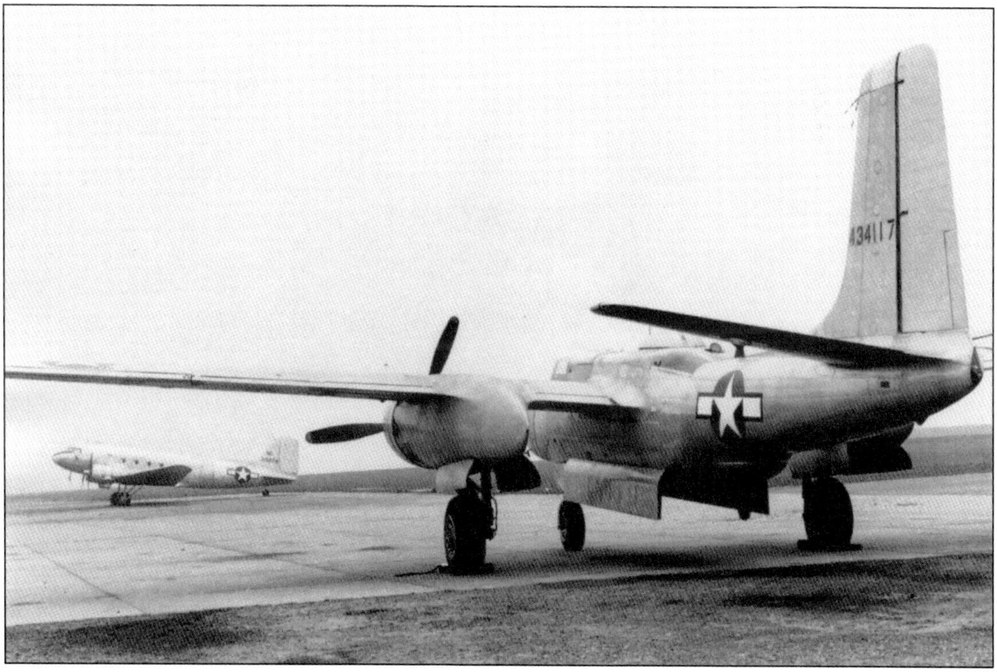

A B-26 Invader attack bomber used as a target tow, in the foreground, stands sentinel over a C-47 used by the squadron as a general purpose transport. (Courtesy of the Delaware Military Heritage and Education Foundation.)

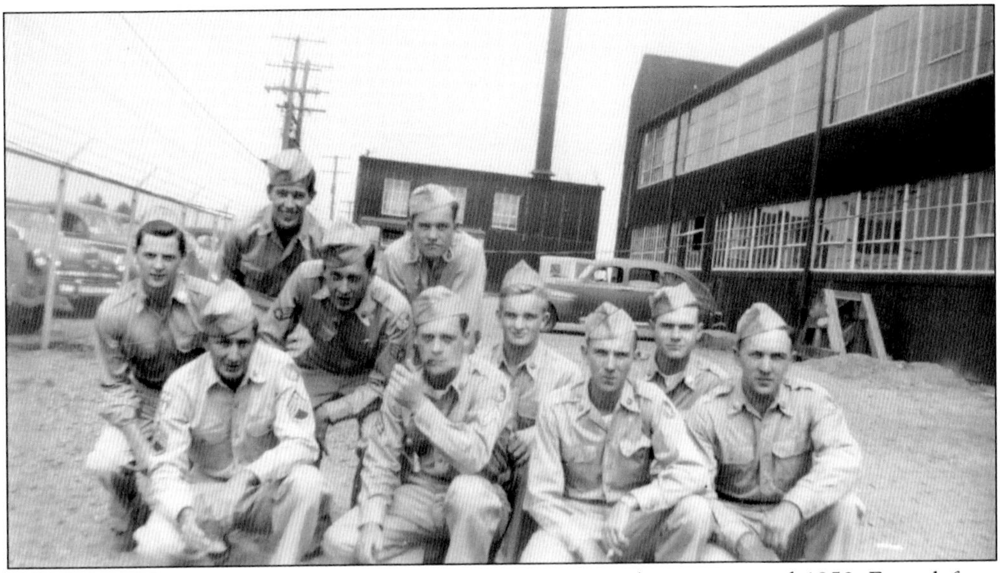

A group of enlisted airmen poses beside the maintenance hangar around 1950. From left to right are (first row) Joseph Beattie, unidentified, Les Bowen, and Phillip Hall; (second row) two unidentified, Joseph Brown, and unidentified; (third row) unidentified and John Harter. (Courtesy of the Delaware Military Heritage and Education Foundation.)

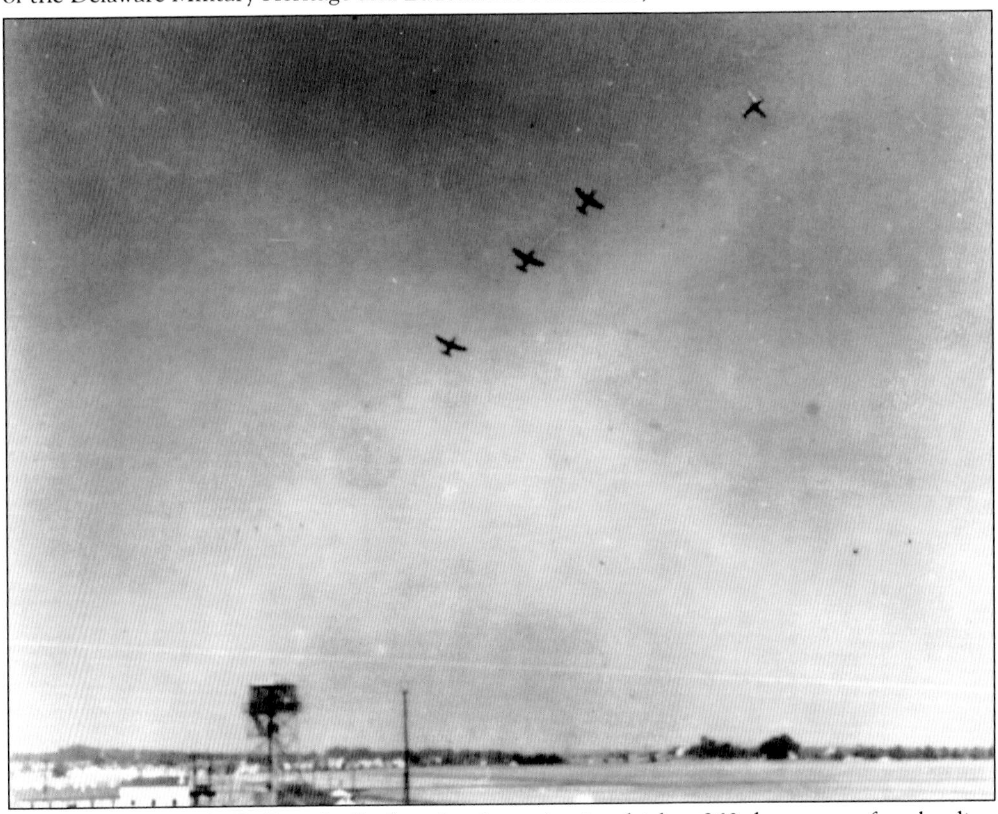

In a combat approach, F-47s peel off a four-ship formation in a high-g, 360-degree turn for a landing at New Castle. (Courtesy of the Delaware Military Heritage and Education Foundation.)

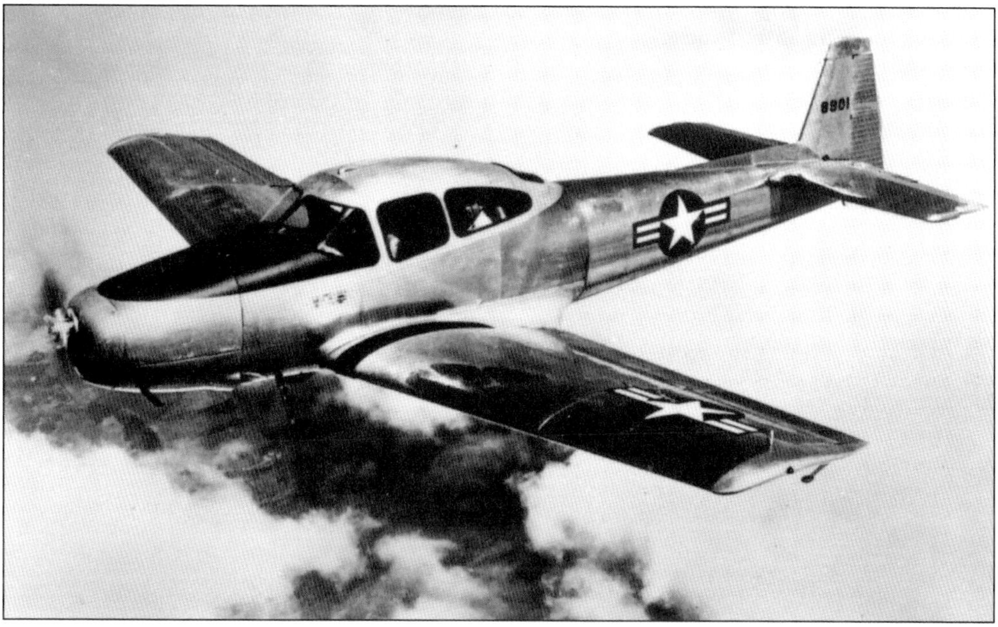

An L-17 Navion ("the poor man's Mustang") liaison aircraft, used by Delaware National Guard for personnel transport, is pictured here. (Courtesy of the Delaware Military Heritage and Education Foundation.)

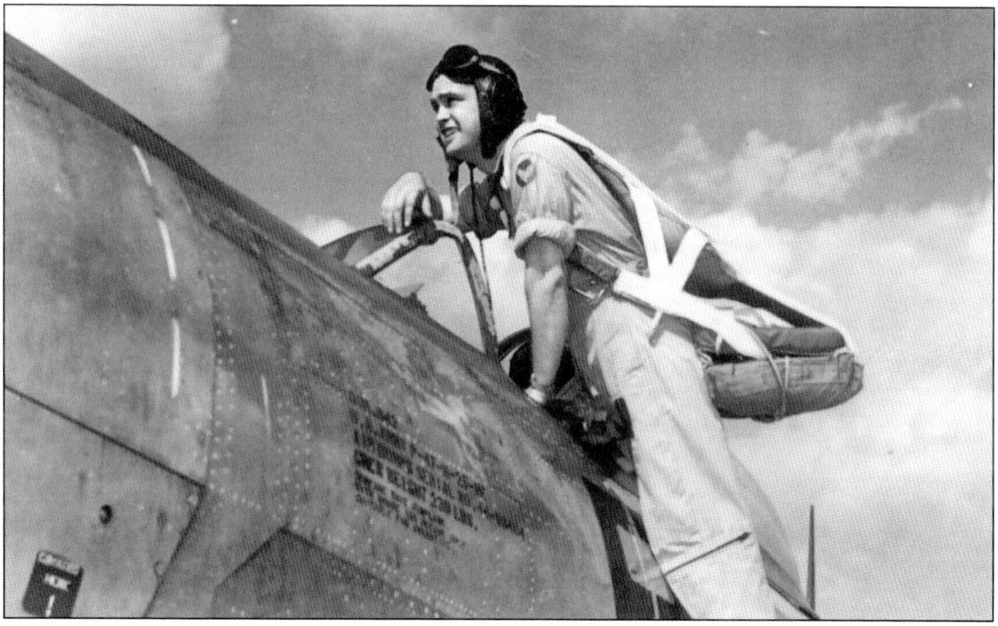

Charter member Capt. William D. Livergood is on the wing of his airplane. On May 13, 1949, Captain Livergood became Delaware's first casualty when his F-47 crashed on final approach to New Castle County Airport. Ed Atkinson described the incident: "If you remember in those days when fighters came in, they'd peel off, do a tight 360 degree three-'G' turn, losing altitude to reduce their speed, and land. He just kept going in the turn and rolled right over, and practically went straight in . . . just about opposite the old entrance." (Courtesy of the Delaware Military Heritage and Education Foundation.)

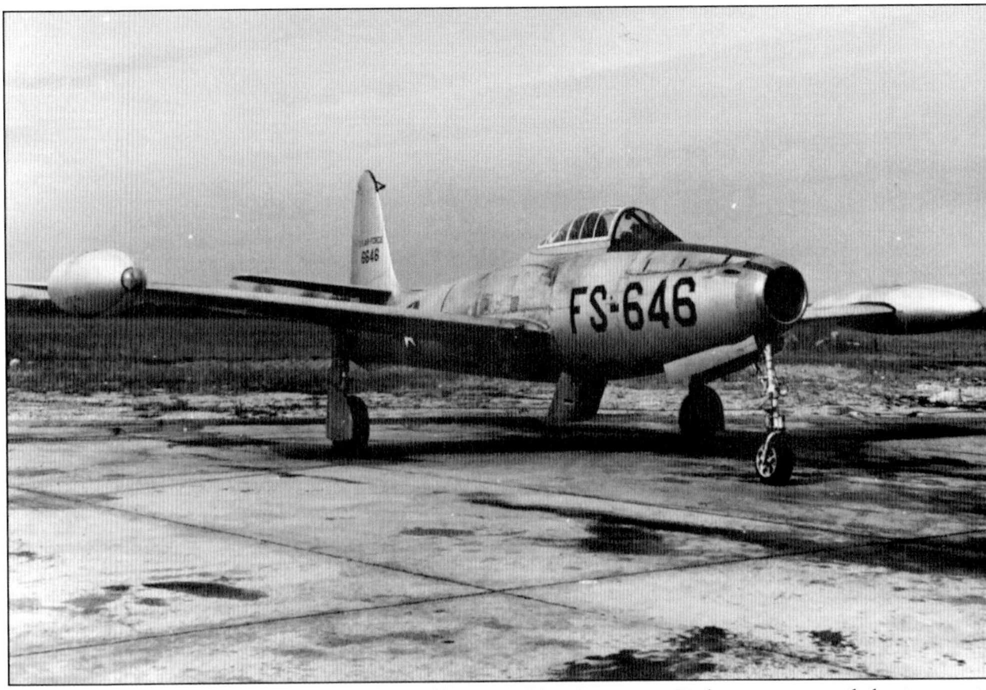

The F-84C Thunderjet was manufactured by Republic Aviation. Delaware entered the jet age in 1949 when they traded their F-47 Thunderbolts for this jet. (Courtesy of the Delaware Military Heritage and Education Foundation.)

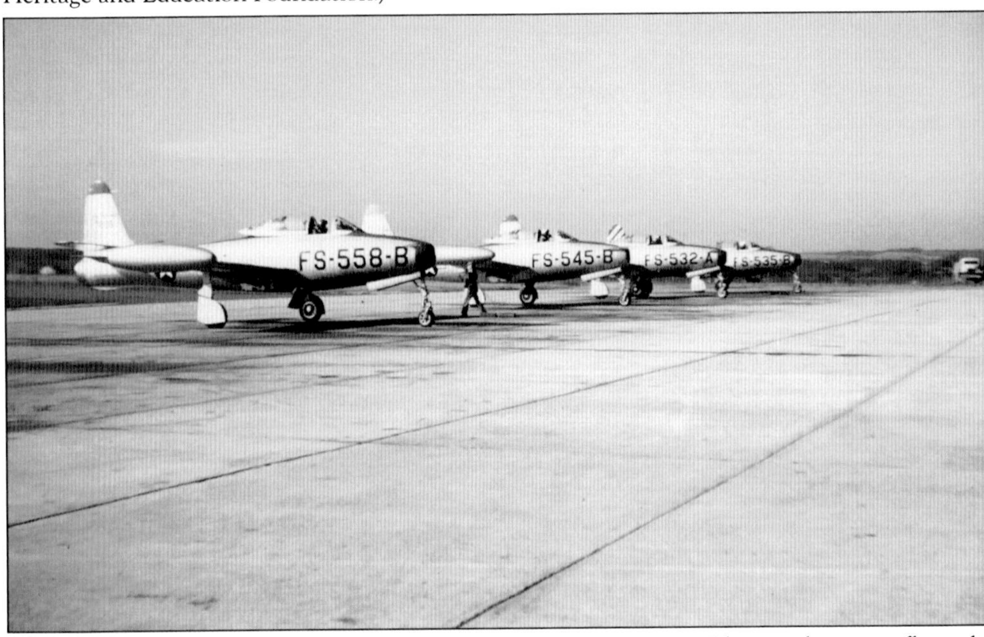

A line of F-84C Thunderjets is preparing to launch on a mission. This airplane was flown by unit members in Korea with the 4th Fighter Bomber Squadron, 49th Fighter Bomber Wing, including Capt. Alvin Thawley, Lt. William F. Hutchison Jr., Capt. John R. Schobelock, Capt. Joseph H. Martin, and Lt. Col. J. Ross Adams. (Courtesy of the Delaware Military Heritage and Education Foundation.)

Two

A First Test

Prior to being mobilized on February 1, 1951, for 21 months of Korean War service, the Delaware ANG received their first jets: F-84s. Although the unit was mobilized in place and most Delaware ANG members served at New Castle, many individuals were reassigned to the combat theater and elsewhere in the U.S. Air Force. In February 1951, Colonel Spruance was assigned the task of reorganizing the air section of the state staff and establishing the headquarters of Delaware Air National Guard. On May 17, 1951, the unit was redesignated the 142nd Fighter-Interceptor Squadron, and in September 1951, the unit exchanged its Republic F-84 Thunderjets for the Lockheed F-94 Starfire aircraft to fit the unit's new continental air defense mission. They stood five-minute runway alert duty seven days a week around the clock for over a year, guarding the mid-Atlantic states against surprise attack by Soviet long-range bombers. When the unit was released from active duty, the F-94s remained with the U.S. Air Force, so the unit had no mission aircraft until it was given F-51s in 1952.

Charter member Charles Palmer recalls, "Bob Loeffel and I were up in New England and we got a call to return to New Castle. Although everyone was activated, only the pilots and selected specialists were actually sent to Korea. Many stayed behind to furnish a manpower pool. Some were disappointed that we didn't go as a unit, but were used piecemeal as individual replacements. Later in the war, we received as part of the Air Defense Command, F-94s, one of the most advanced fighter/interceptors of the time. When we returned to inactive duty status we got P-51s—obsolete relics of World War II. Most of the older guys were World War II veterans and took the call-up in stride."

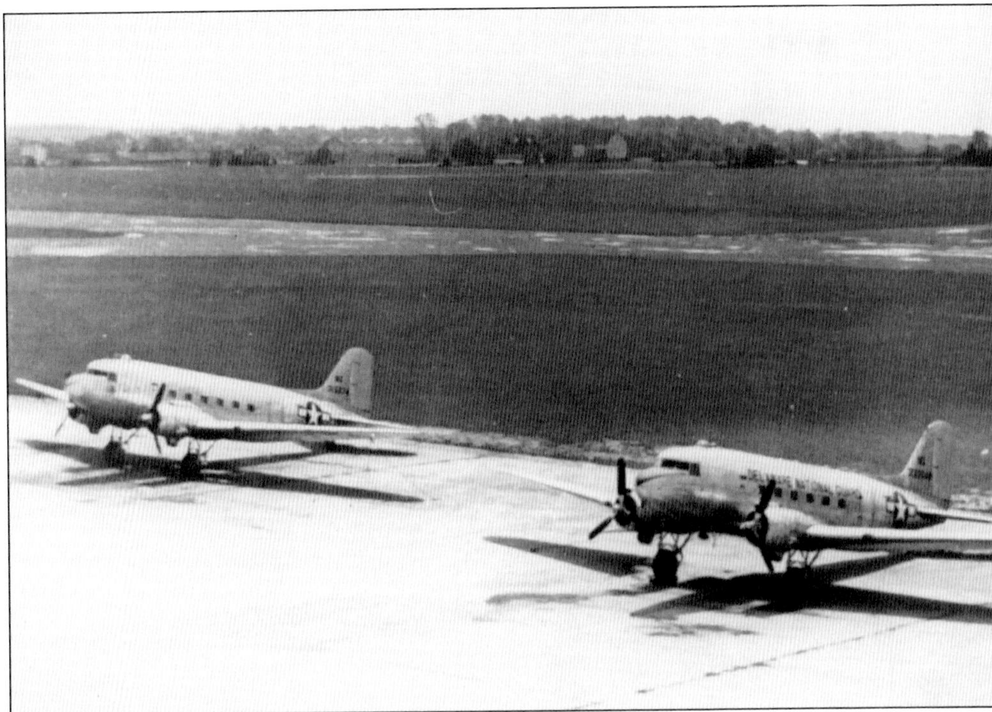

These C-47 Gooneybirds were used as general transports from 1947 to 1960. (Courtesy of the Delaware Military Heritage and Education Foundation.)

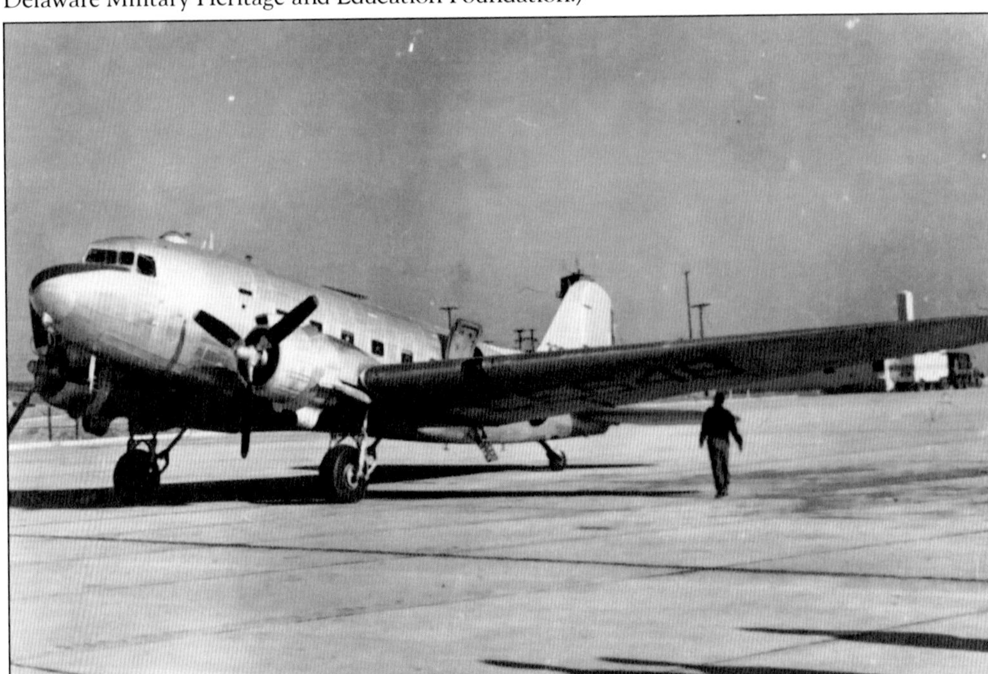

The C-47 was used to transport men to training, to pick up spare parts, and as a transport for fighter wing or national conferences and meetings. (Courtesy of the Delaware Military Heritage and Education Foundation.)

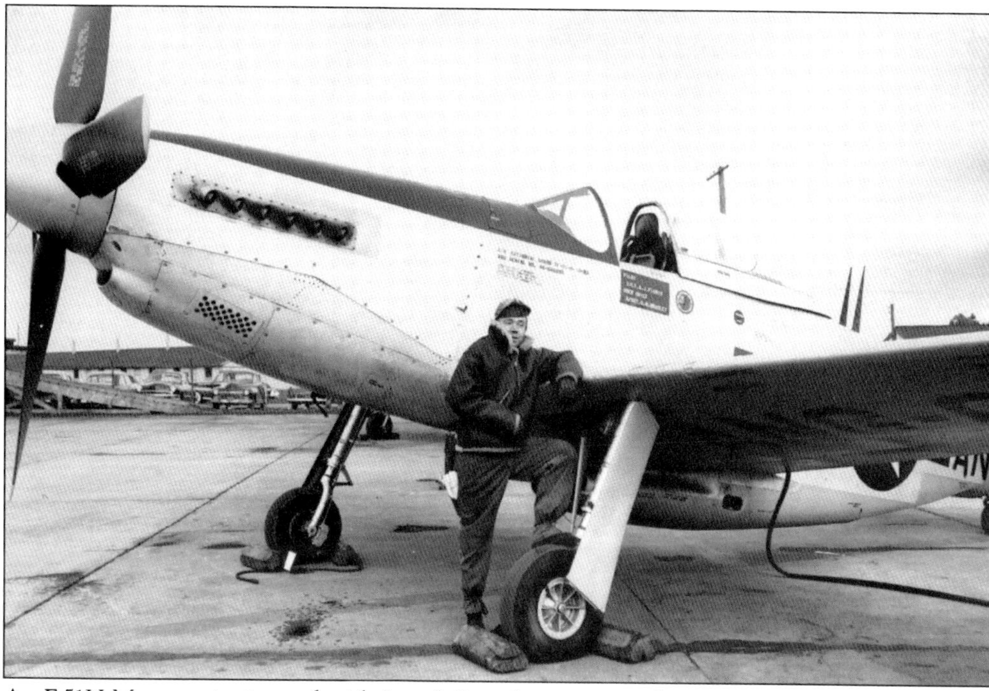

An F-51H Mustang is pictured with Joseph Jenecke posing at the wing root. The pilot assigned to this airplane was 2nd Lt. A. J. Florio, and the crew chief was S.Sgt. G. M. Bradley. (Courtesy of the Delaware Military Heritage and Education Foundation.)

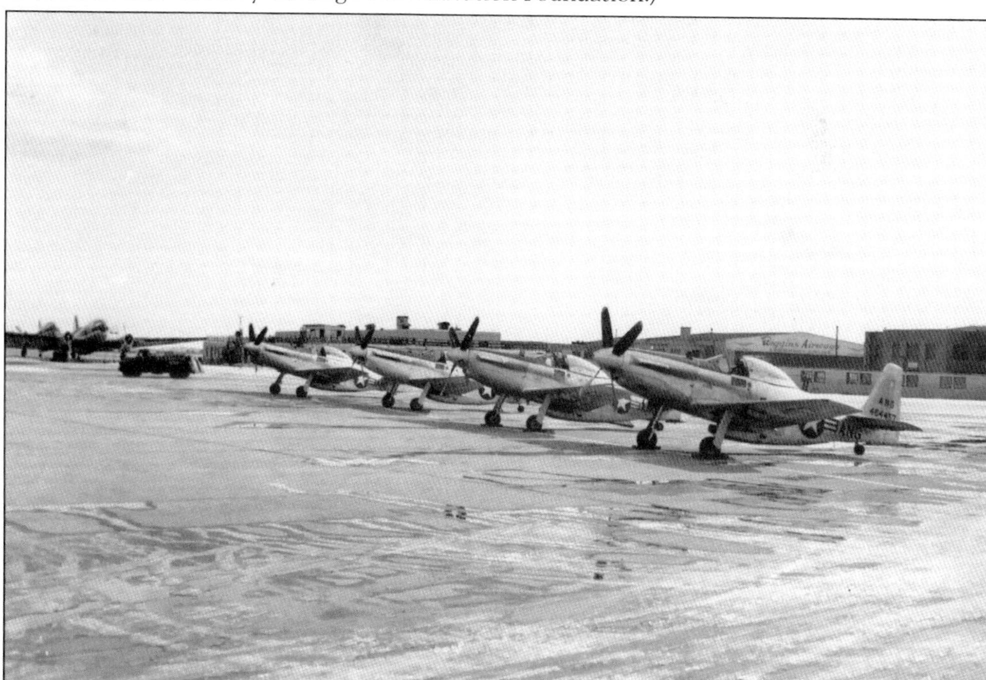

Delaware Air National Guard F-51H Mustangs were deployed to Logan Field, Boston, Massachusetts, on a training mission around 1952–1954. (Courtesy of the Delaware Military Heritage and Education Foundation.)

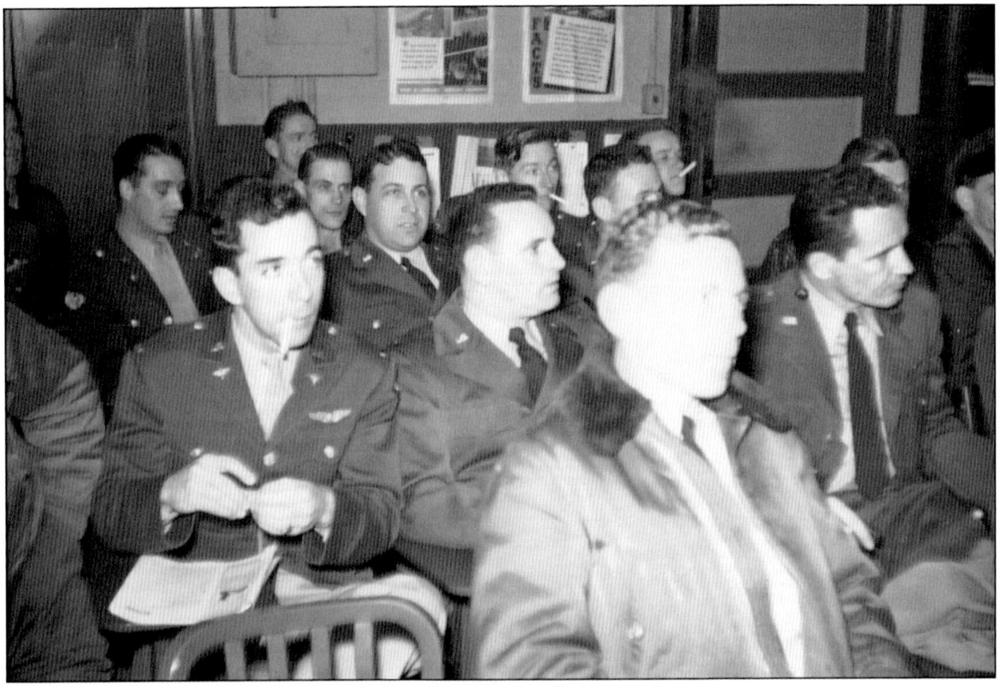

The Pilots' Briefing Room is where aerial missions are briefed. Note the variety of uniforms typical of the postwar "flying club." (Courtesy of the Delaware Military Heritage and Education Foundation.)

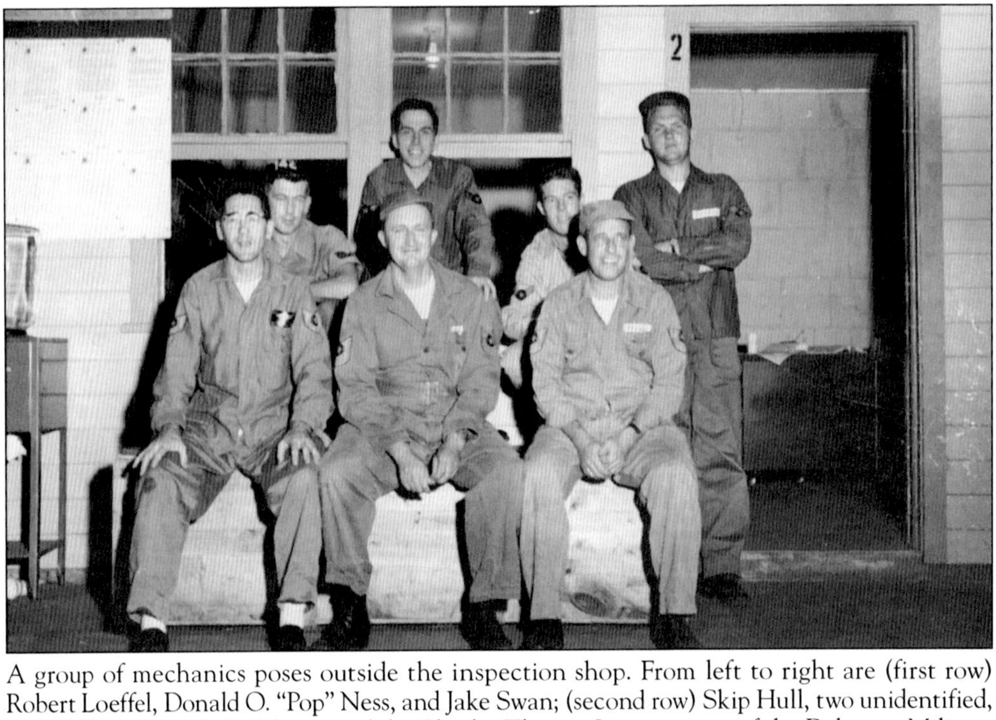

A group of mechanics poses outside the inspection shop. From left to right are (first row) Robert Loeffel, Donald O. "Pop" Ness, and Jake Swan; (second row) Skip Hull, two unidentified, and William Campbell. (Photograph by Charles Thomas Lee; courtesy of the Delaware Military Heritage and Education Foundation.)

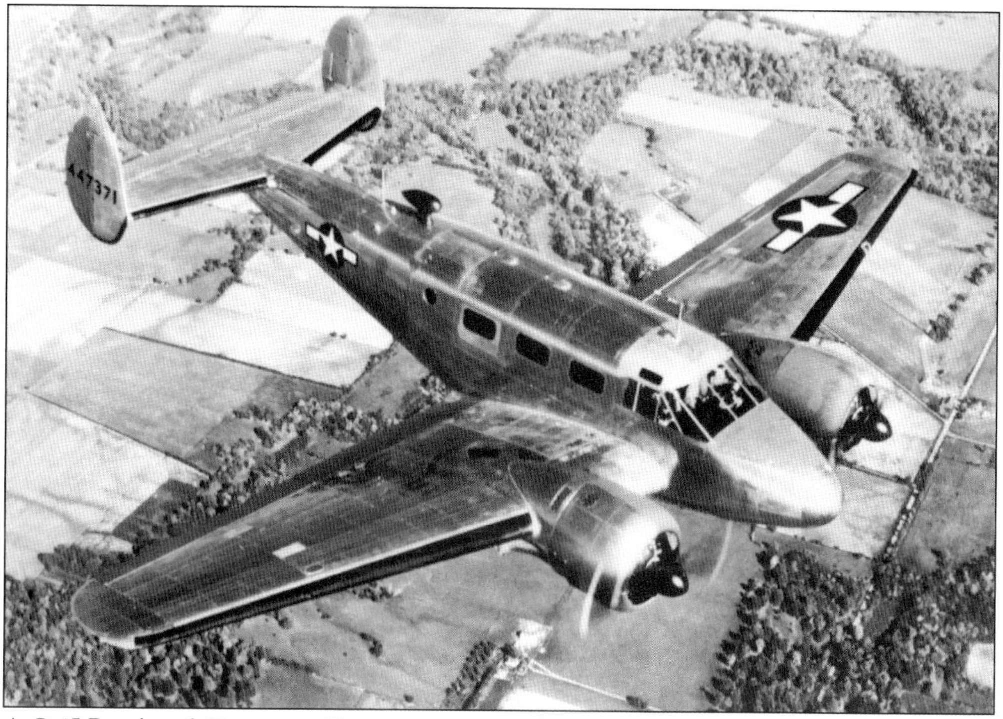

A C-45 Beechcraft Kansan staff transport was used a general utility trainer and transport from 1952 to 1960. (Courtesy of the Delaware Military Heritage and Education Foundation.)

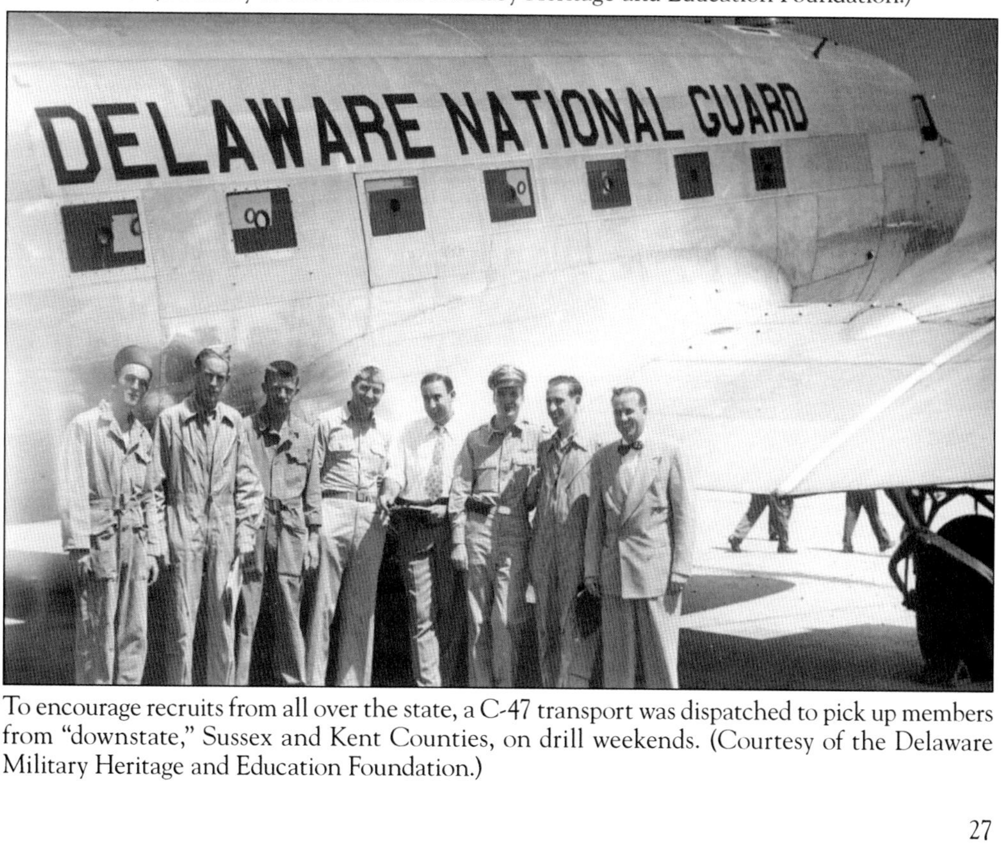

To encourage recruits from all over the state, a C-47 transport was dispatched to pick up members from "downstate," Sussex and Kent Counties, on drill weekends. (Courtesy of the Delaware Military Heritage and Education Foundation.)

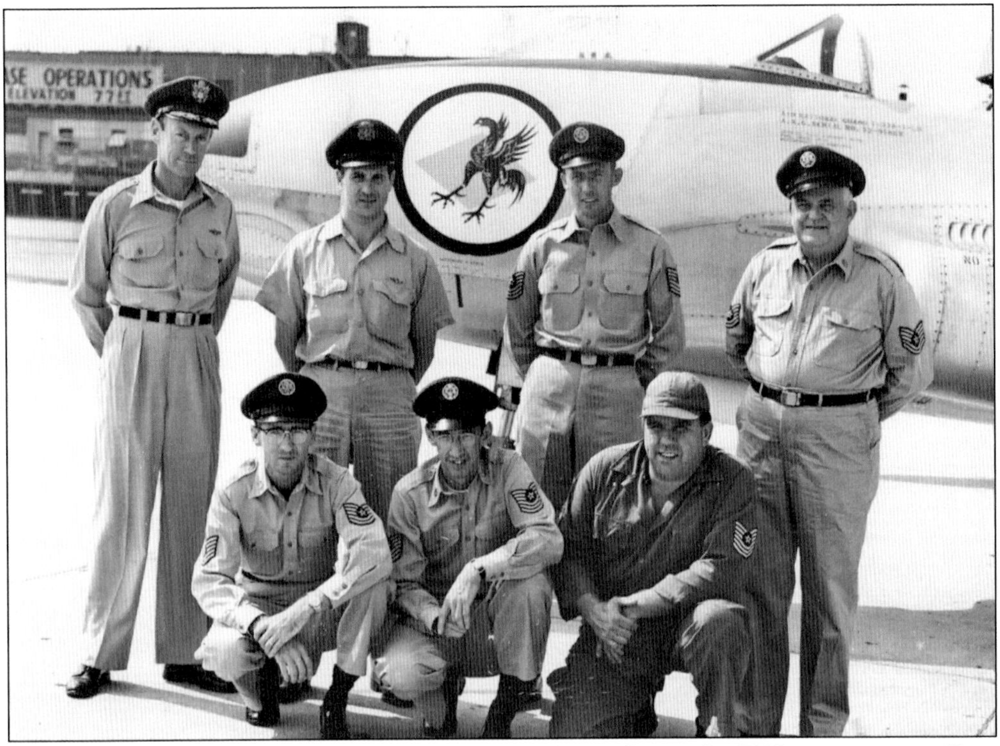

The remaining original "founding fathers" in 1956, in front of a T-33 jet trainer at Base Operations, were, from left to right (kneeling) T.Sgt. Robert F. Loeffel, M.Sgt. Charles Palmer, and M.Sgt. Joseph L. Manion; (standing) William W. Spruance, Clarence E. "Ed" Atkinson, M.Sgt. Vincent L. "Rex" Riley, and T.Sgt. Ezekiel "Zeke" Cooper. All seven were presented the Medal for Military Merit by Gov. Caleb Boggs to mark the 10th anniversary. (Courtesy of the Delaware Military Heritage and Education Foundation.)

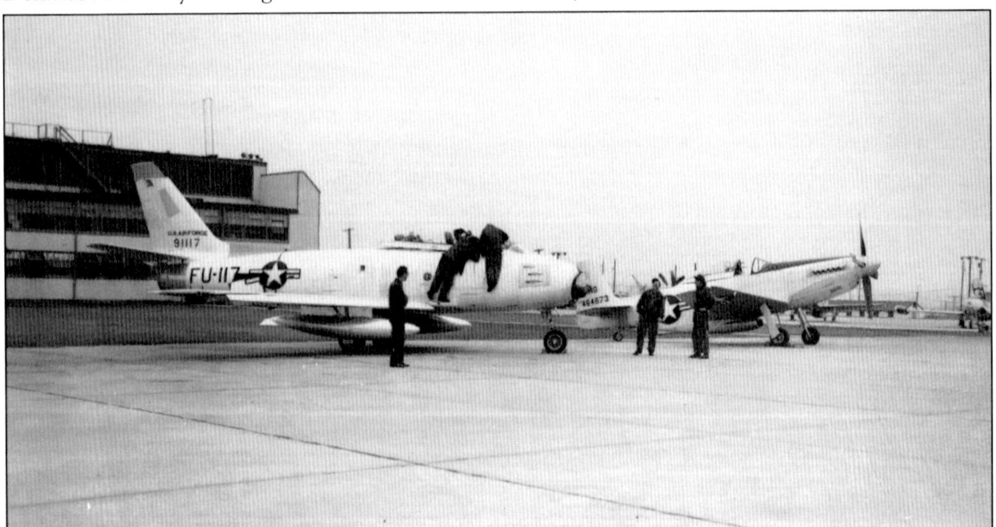

The Delaware Air Guard 142nd Fighter Squadron transitioned from the F-51H Mustang to the F-86A Sabrejet at New Castle Air Base. (Courtesy of the Delaware Military Heritage and Education Foundation.)

Three

Sabres over the Brandywine

On November 1, 1952, the 142nd Fighter-Interceptor Squadron was released from active duty in Korea and reorganized as the Delaware Air National Guard. On December 1, 1952, the unit was redesignated the 142nd Fighter-Bomber Squadron and reverted to propeller-driven aircraft, the F-51H Mustang. The unit suffered a high loss of personnel as the men mustered out after their activation. So the first priority was rebuilding the manpower base through increased recruiting efforts.

In 1954, a brand-new T-33, the trainer version of the F-80 Shooting Star, was received by the 142nd Fighter-Bomber Squadron, and later that year, the unit received F-86 Sabrejets, replacing the F-51H Mustang. This aircraft made the Delaware Air Guard a first-string unit operating advanced equipment.

The Air Guard faced a dim future unless it acquired definite wartime missions, integrated into U.S. Air Force missions on a daily basis, and met the same tough training standards as the active force. The Air Guard also needed more full-time manning. It had to be ready for combat the moment it was called into federal service.

Evidence of this new, improved Air National Guard was provided in July 1956, when Maj. David F. McCallister (142nd Fighter Bomber Squadron commander) set a fighter record by flying his F-86 Sabrejet 1,922 miles in three hours, 30 minutes, to win the Earl T. Ricks Memorial Trophy.

On November 10, 1958, the unit was redesignated the 142nd Tactical Fighter Squadron and was reassigned from the U.S. Air Force's Air Defense Command to the Tactical Air Command.

Flying high-performance single-engine fighters was a dangerous business. On June 4, 1961, Col. David F. McCallister (still commander of the 142nd) and Brig. Gen. William W. Spruance (assistant adjutant general for air) were flying a T-33 jet trainer out of Scott Air Force Base when the aircraft lost power and crashed. Colonel McCallister died, and General Spruance received serious injuries. A total of eight airmen were lost in aircraft accidents during the unit's first 15 years of operation.

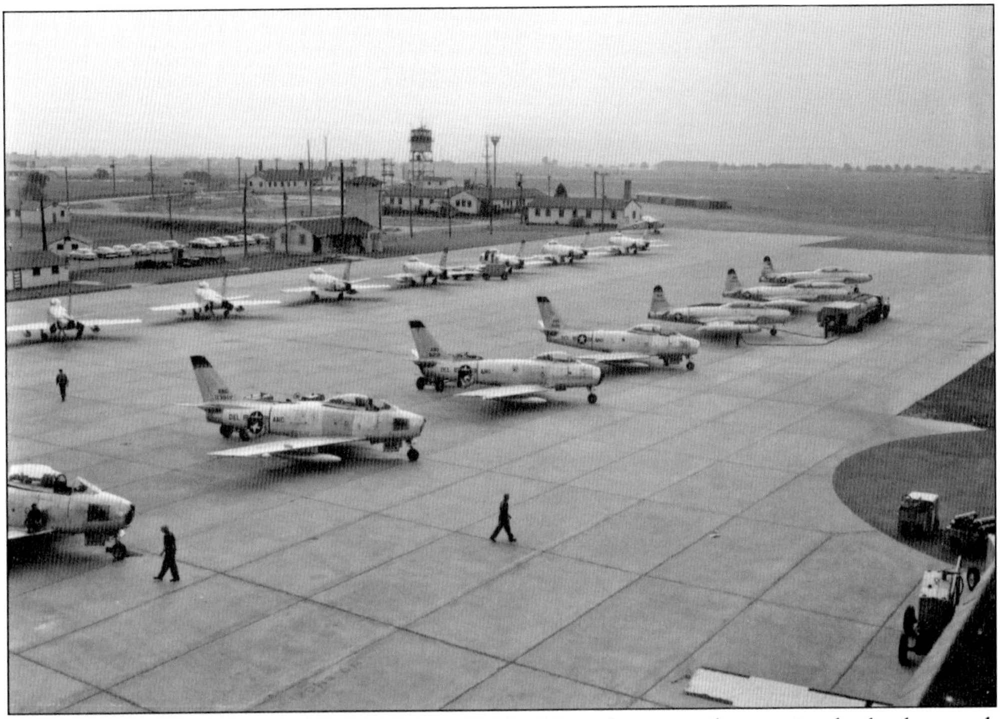

The ramp at New Castle is filled with new F-86s. Note the control tower in the background. (Courtesy of the Delaware Military Heritage and Education Foundation.)

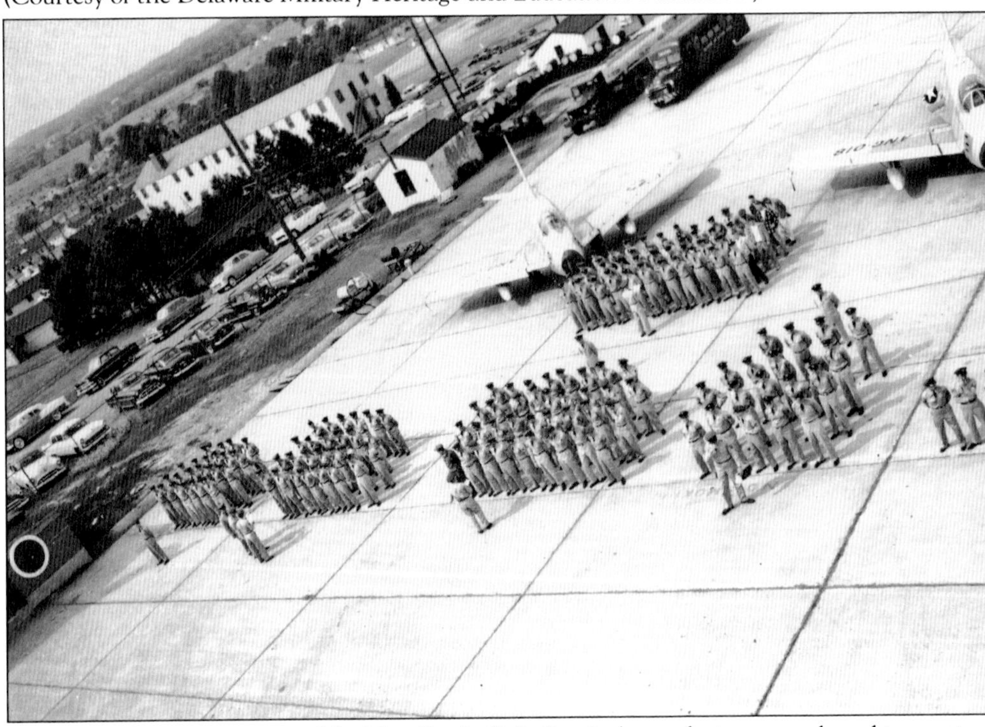

An overhead panoramic view of the New Castle flight line is shown during a parade and inspection. (Courtesy of the Delaware Military Heritage and Education Foundation.)

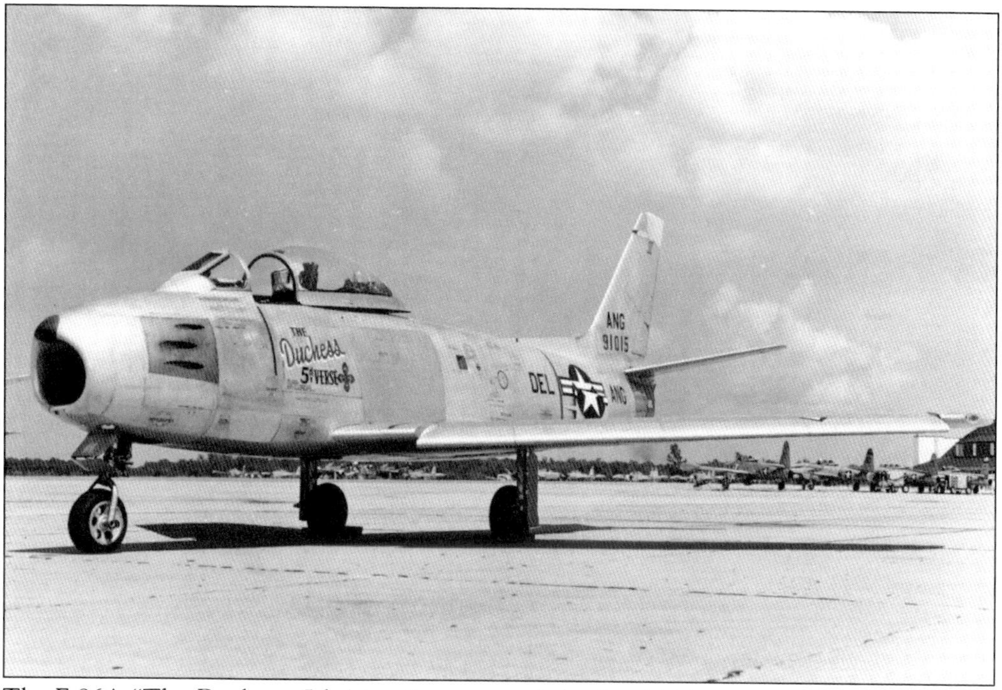

The F-86A "The Duchess, 5th Verse" was one of the first F-86s to arrive in 1954. Notably absent are the usual drop tanks on the wings. (Courtesy of the Delaware Military Heritage and Education Foundation.)

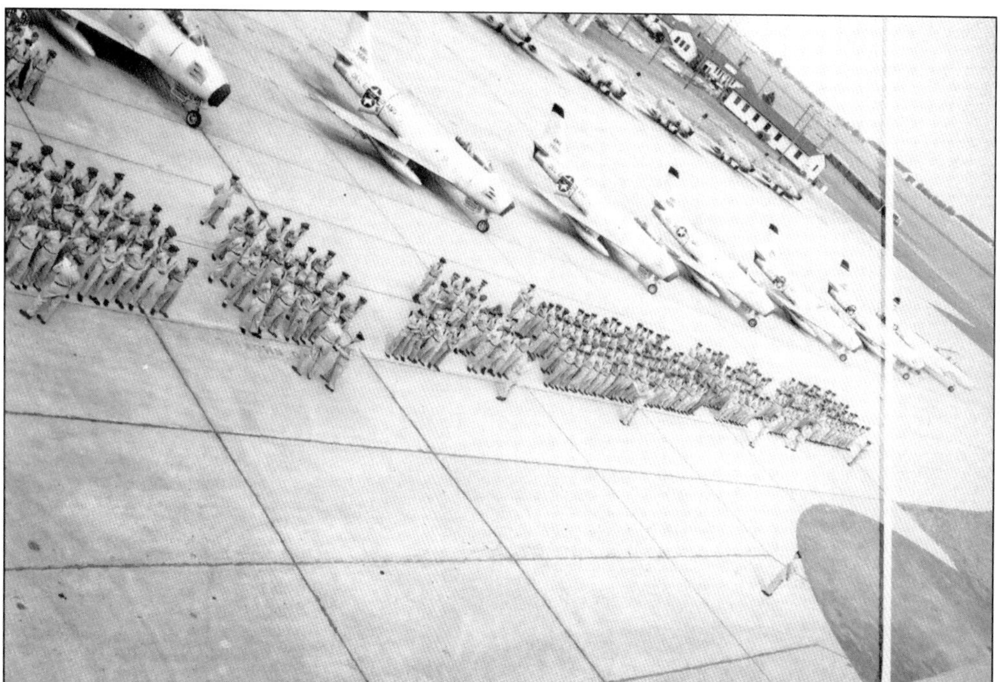

A complementary panoramic view to the opposite page is shown at the unit's 10th anniversary. (Courtesy of the Delaware Military Heritage and Education Foundation.)

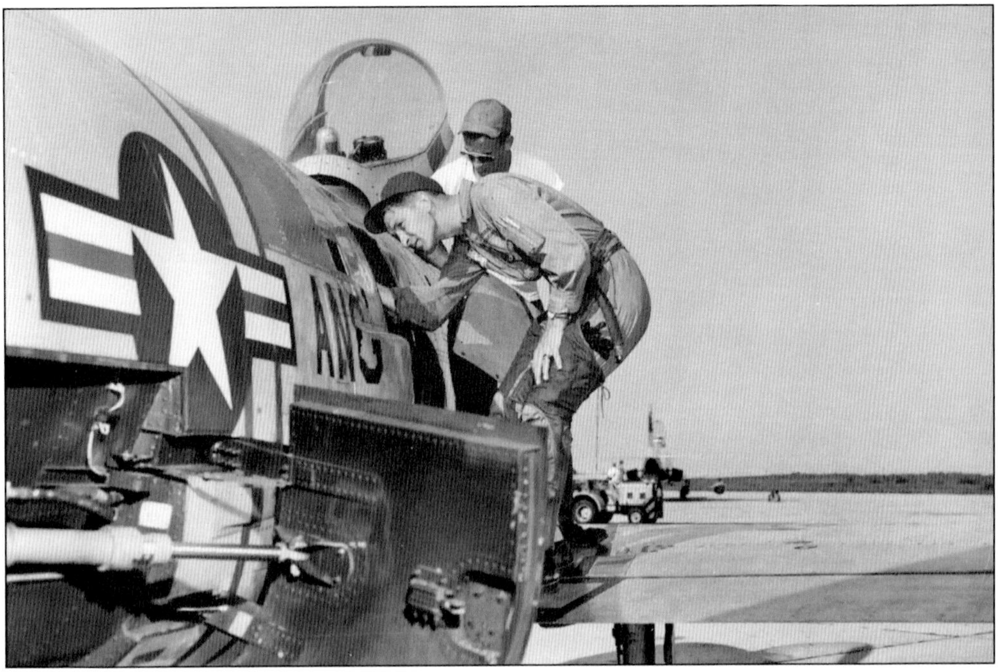

Pilot William F. Hutchison Jr. performs a pre-flight check on his F-86 Sabrejet as maintenance technician Townsend "Muff" Johnson looks on. Hutchison is a University of Delaware graduate and won his commission through ROTC. (Courtesy of the Delaware Military Heritage and Education Foundation.)

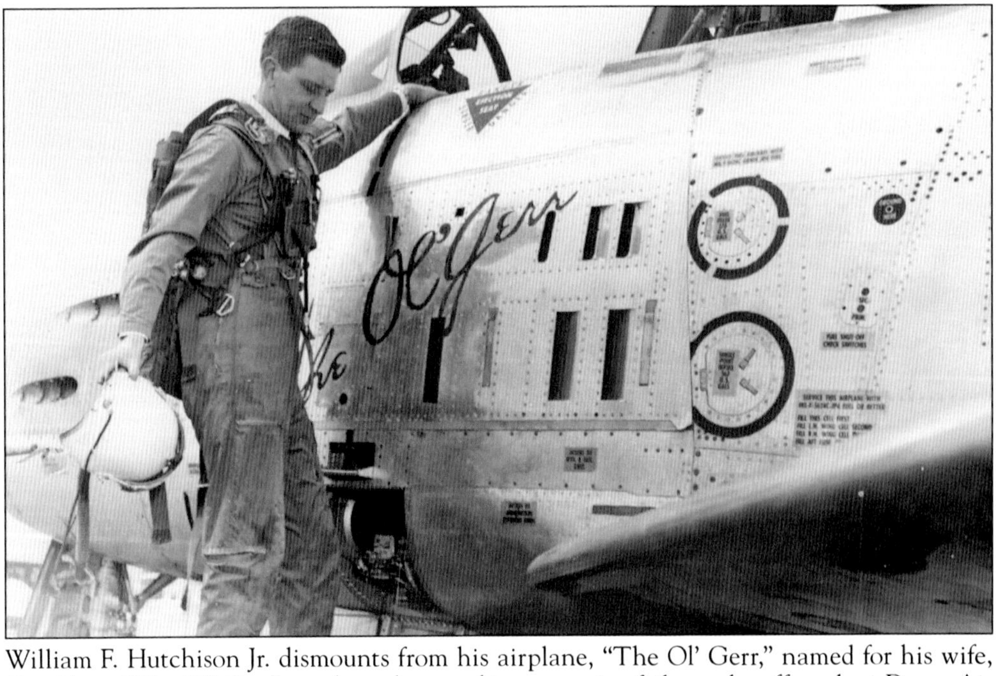

William F. Hutchison Jr. dismounts from his airplane, "The Ol' Gerr," named for his wife, Geraldine. "The Ol' Gerr" was later destroyed in an engine failure take-off crash at Dover Air Force Base, badly burning and injuring its pilot Tom Nale. (Courtesy of the Delaware Military Heritage and Education Foundation.)

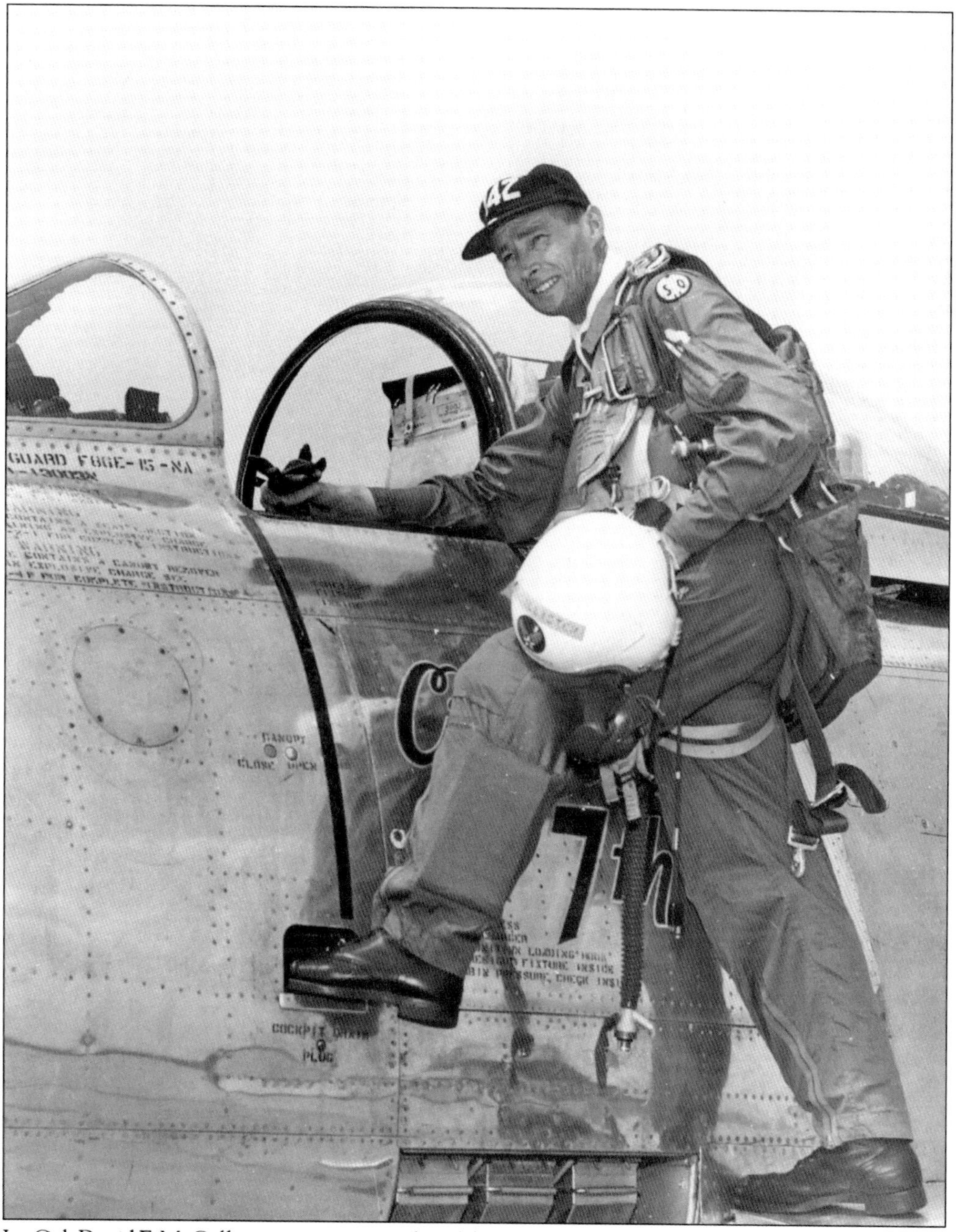

Lt. Col. David F. McCallister, unit commander of the 142nd Fighter Squadron, poses astride his F-86E, "Cindee Lind 7th." (Courtesy of the Delaware Military Heritage and Education Foundation.)

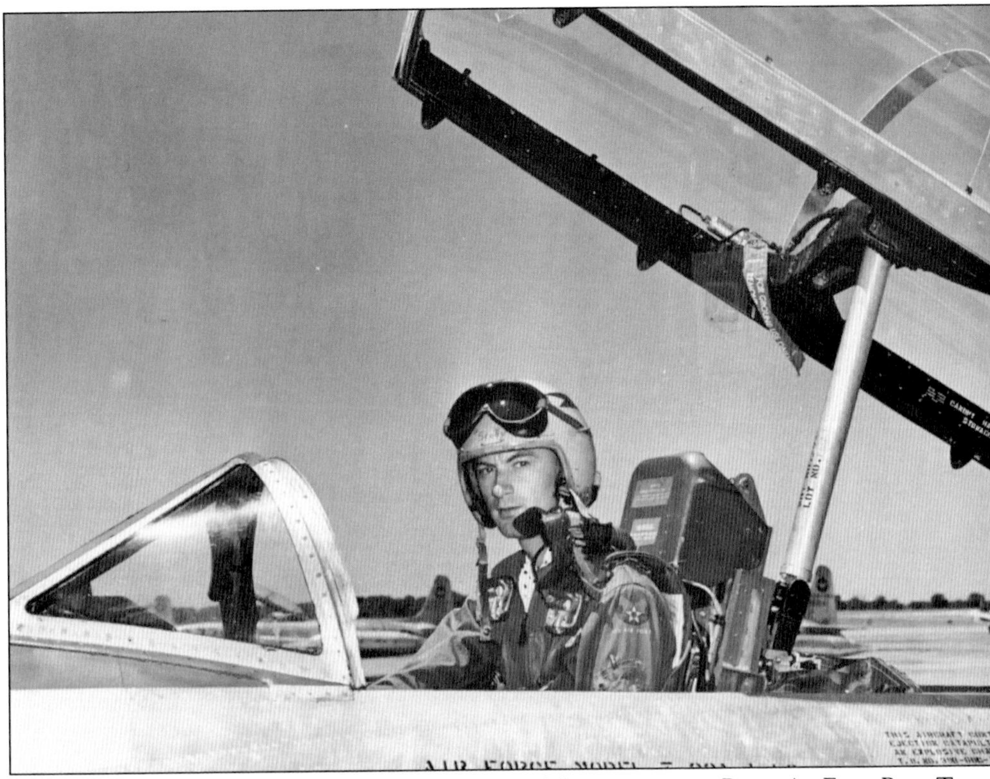

Aviation cadet Lt. James P. Scott II underwent advanced flying training at Bryan Air Force Base, Texas, in a T-33 trainer. (Courtesy of the Delaware Military Heritage and Education Foundation.)

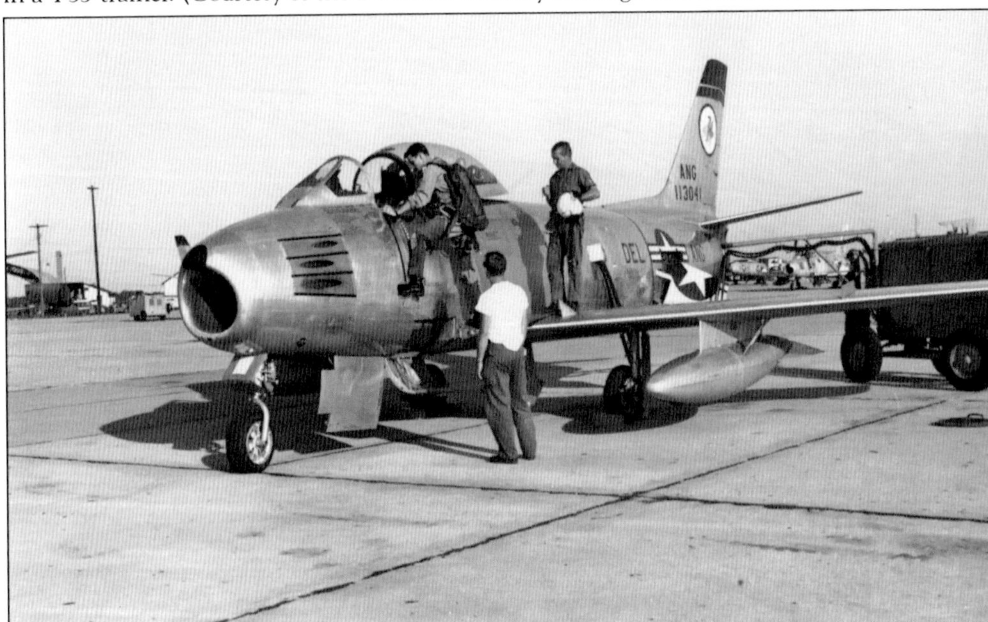

Pilot Ted White enplanes from his F-86E as his crew chief, Bob Quigley, holds his flying helmet and an unidentified maintainer looks on. (Courtesy of the Delaware Military Heritage and Education Foundation.)

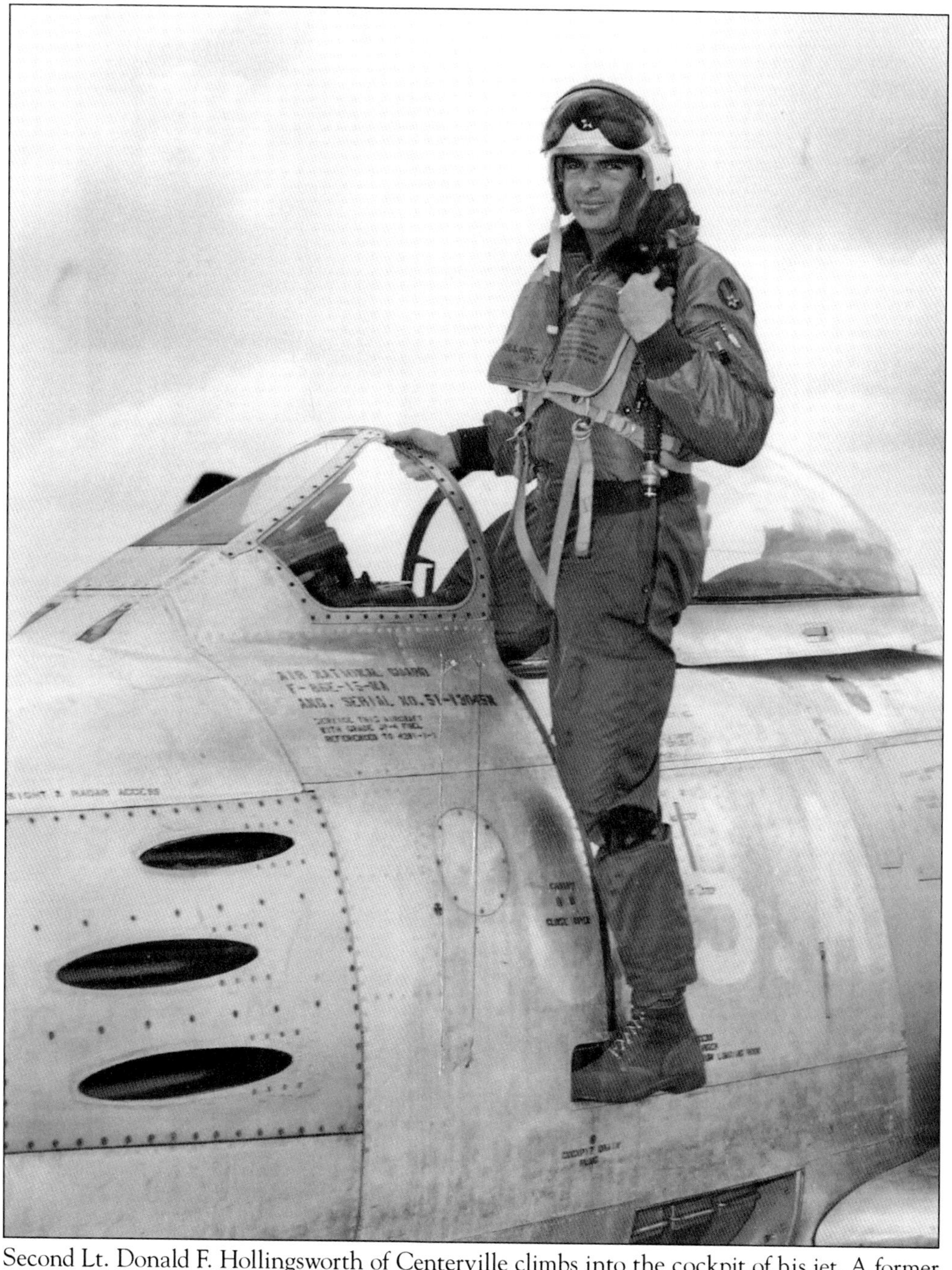

Second Lt. Donald F. Hollingsworth of Centerville climbs into the cockpit of his jet. A former enlisted man, Hollingsworth had recently completed his advanced training as a pilot in the F-86E in April 1956. (Courtesy of the Delaware Military Heritage and Education Foundation.)

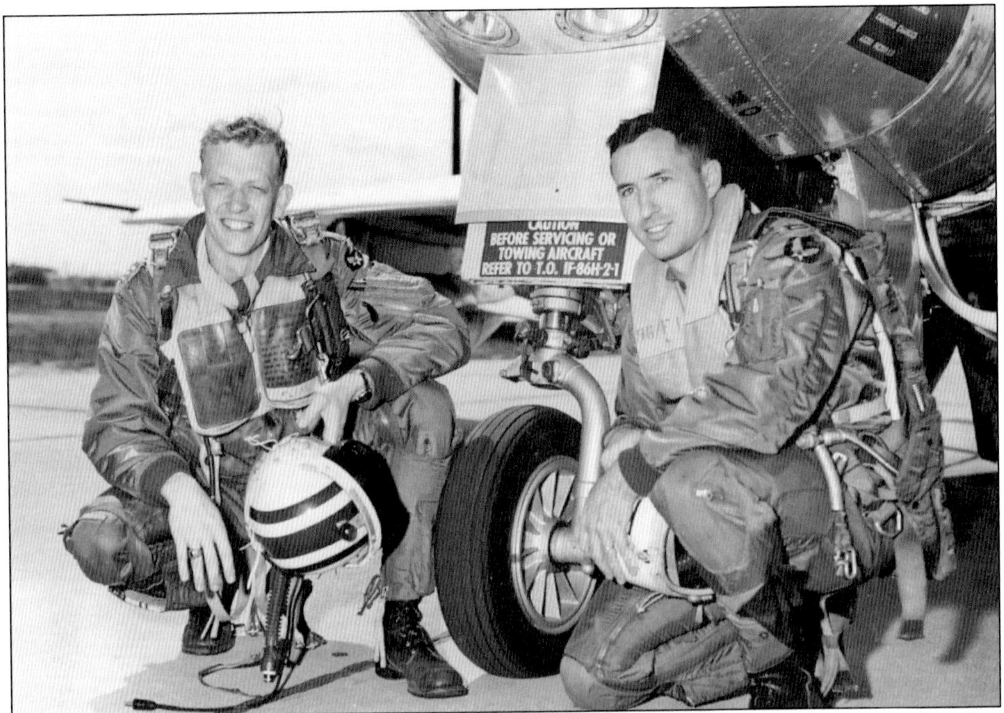

Robert Floyd and Robert Ward pose by the nose gear of an F-86H. Floyd enlisted in the unit in 1948 and was accepted for aviation training after active service during the Korean War, winning his wings in 1953. (Courtesy of the Delaware Military Heritage and Education Foundation.)

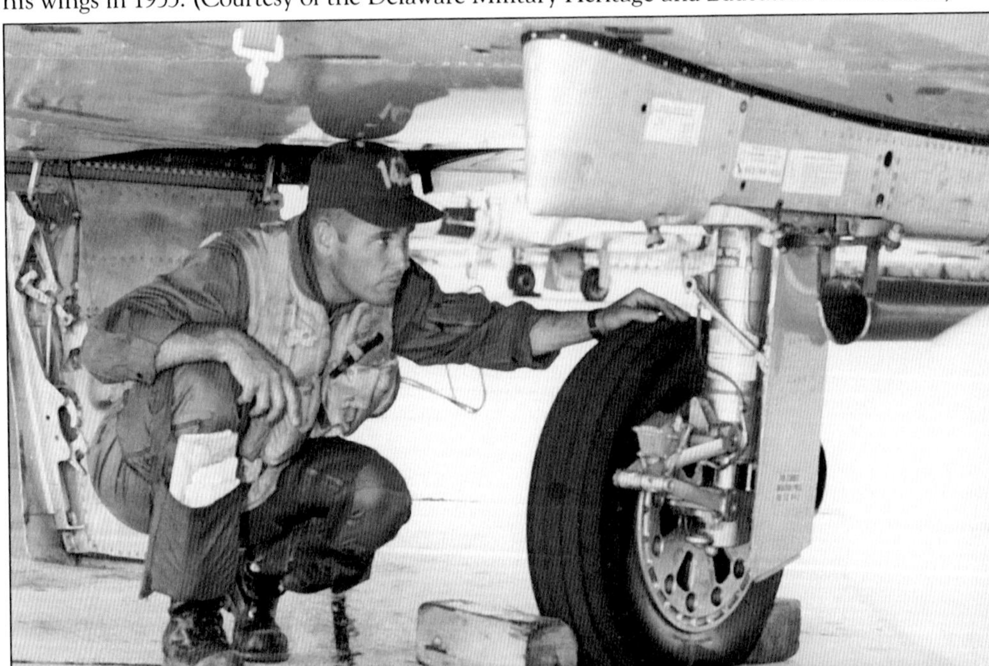

Jack Taylor inspects the main landing gear of his F-86. (Courtesy of the Delaware Military Heritage and Education Foundation.)

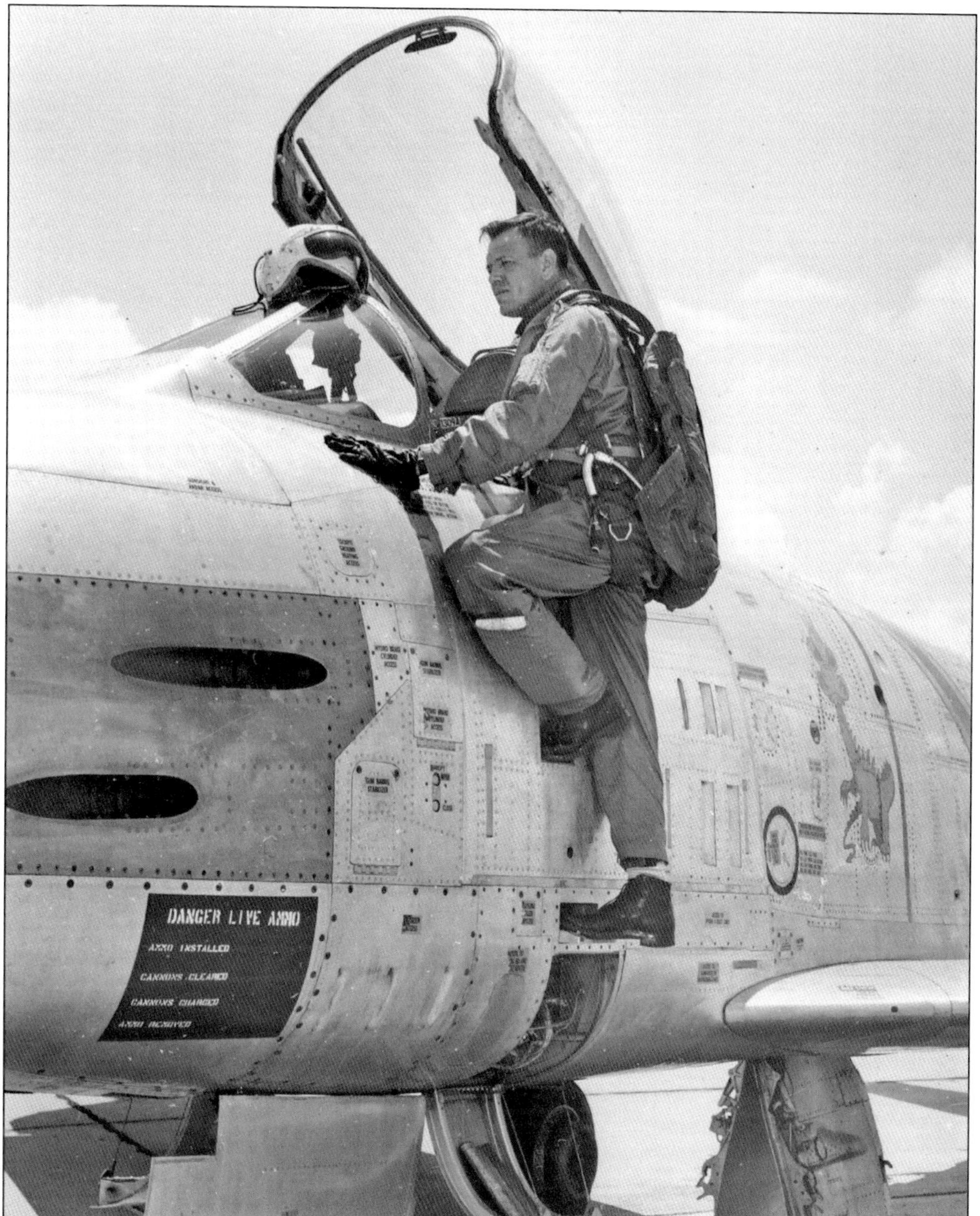

Gordon I. Scott prepares for flight in the "Drexel Dragon," named for his alma mater. (Courtesy of the Delaware Military Heritage and Education Foundation.)

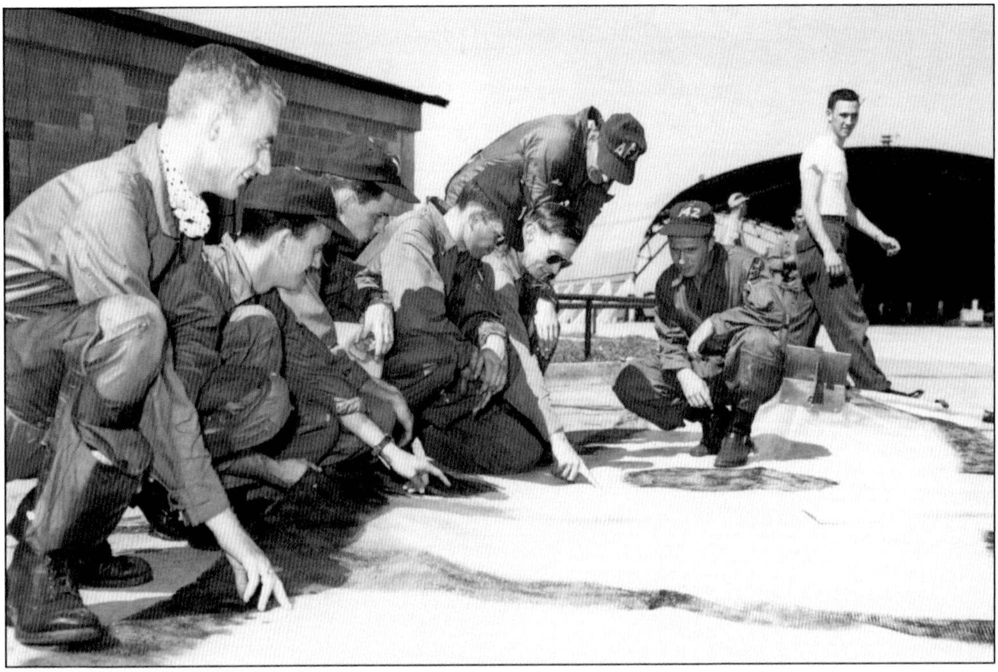

Pilots compare scores on an aerial gunnery target while on deployment to Savannah, Georgia, in 1955. From left to right are James P. Scott II, Nathaniel Hall, Theodore White, William Casey, David "Snapper" McCallister, Raymond Flynt, John Sommerville, and an unidentified passerby. (Courtesy of the Delaware Military Heritage and Education Foundation.)

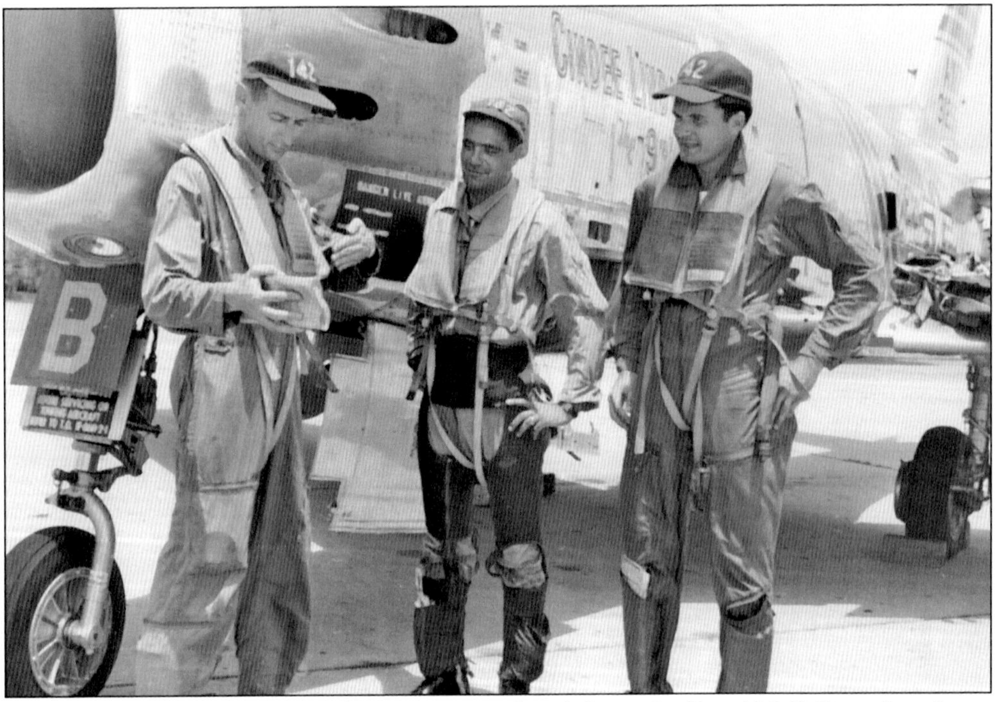

Pilots on the flight line preparing for a mission are, from left to right, David McCallister, Jerry Luce, and Frank Wooten. (Courtesy the Edward W. Blackburn collection.)

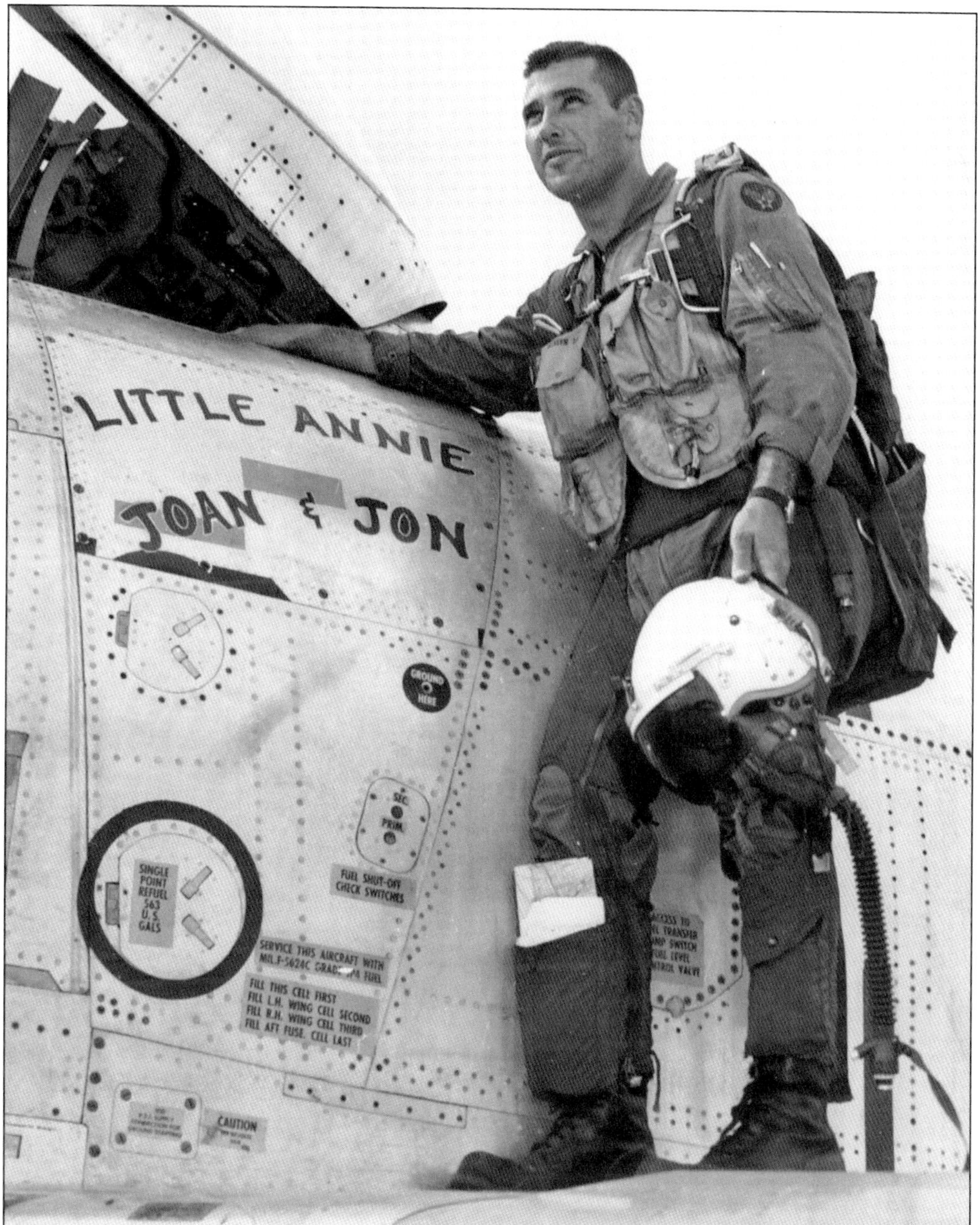

Pilot Jack Taylor embarks upon his jet, "Little Annie, Joan and Jon," an F-86H. (Courtesy of the Delaware Military Heritage and Education Foundation.)

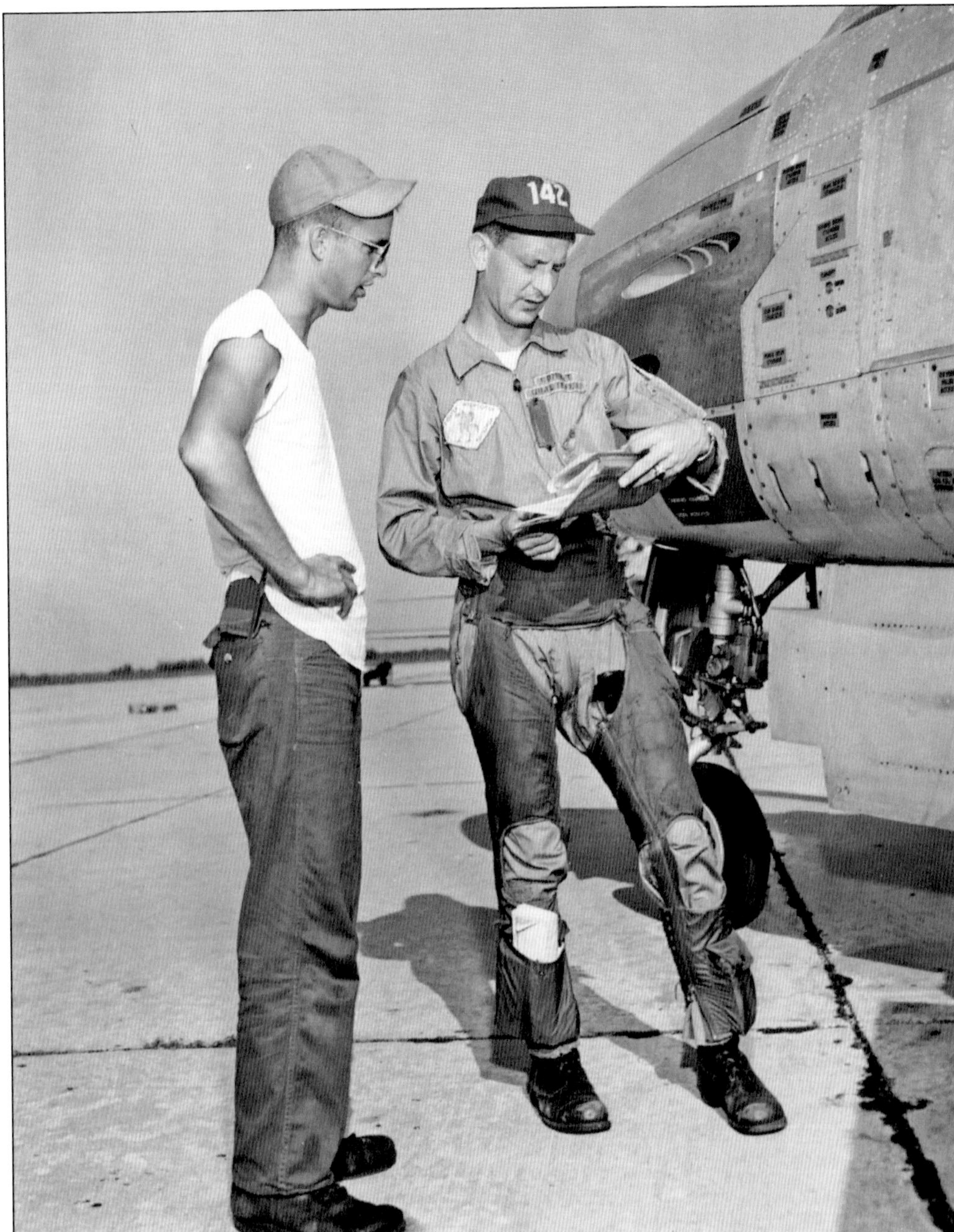

William F. Hutchison Jr. examines the maintenance records on his F-86 with the assistance of crew chief Townsend Johnson. Hutchison was a combat veteran of Korea, holding the Distinguished Flying Cross, and was destined to become a future air commander of the Delaware Air Guard. (Courtesy of the Delaware Military Heritage and Education Foundation.)

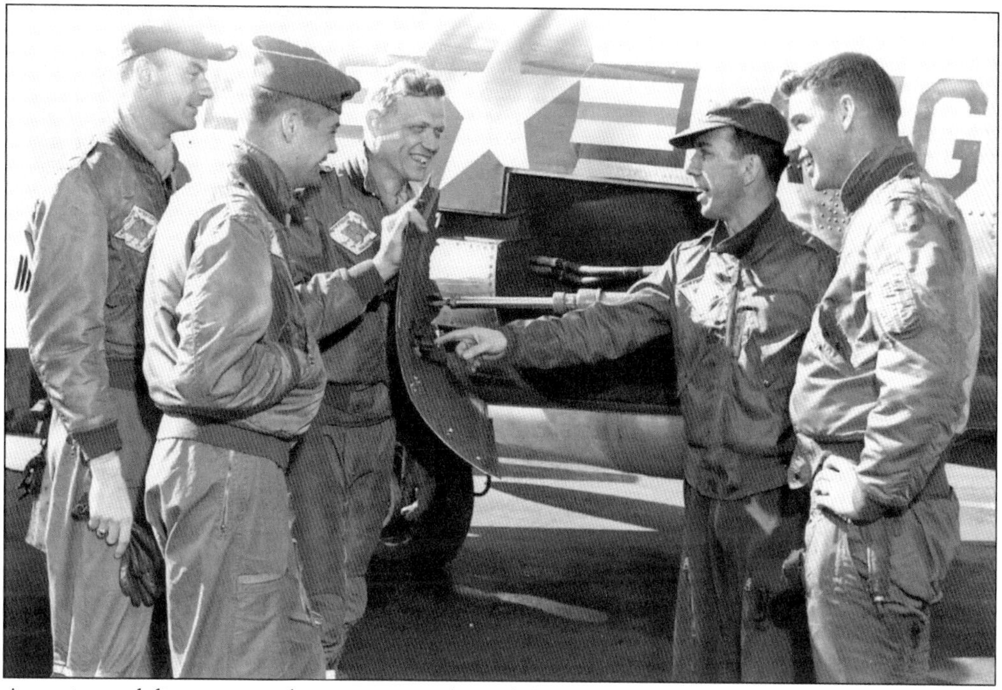

An animated discussion is shown among pilots of the 142nd Fighter Squadron. From left to right are James P. Scott II, Stanley Hopperstead, Robert Floyd, John Schobelock, and Al "Buzz" Hastings. (Courtesy of the Delaware Military Heritage and Education Foundation.)

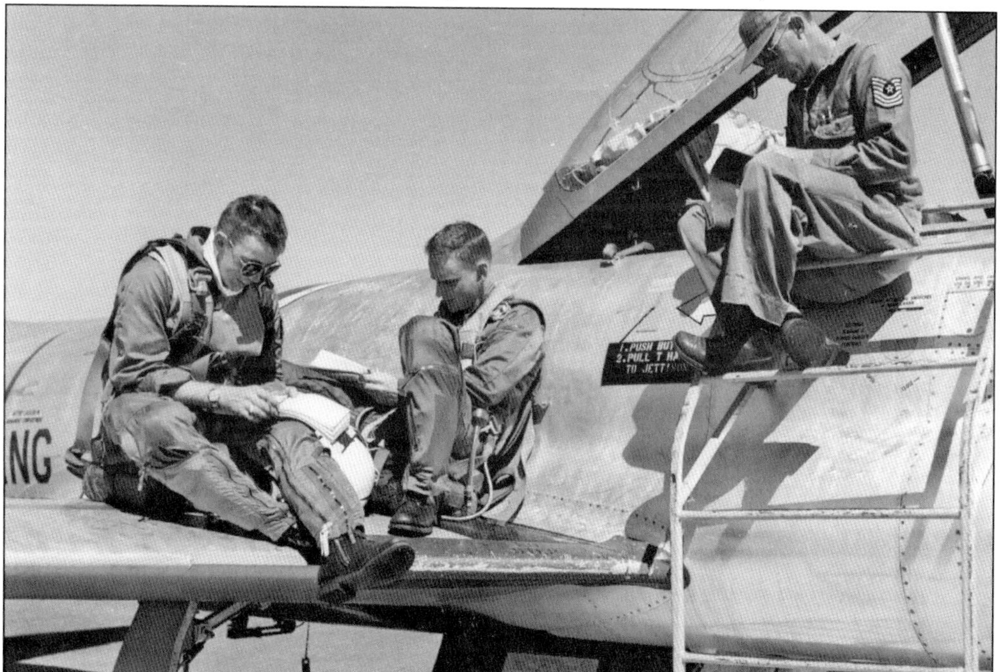

Pilots 2nd Lt. Richard Murphy (left) and 2nd Lt. Paul Flood (right) review paperwork on the wing root of a T-33 trainer as M.Sgt. Vincent "Rex" Riley (a charter member of the unit) researches the technical order. (Courtesy of the Delaware Military Heritage and Education Foundation.)

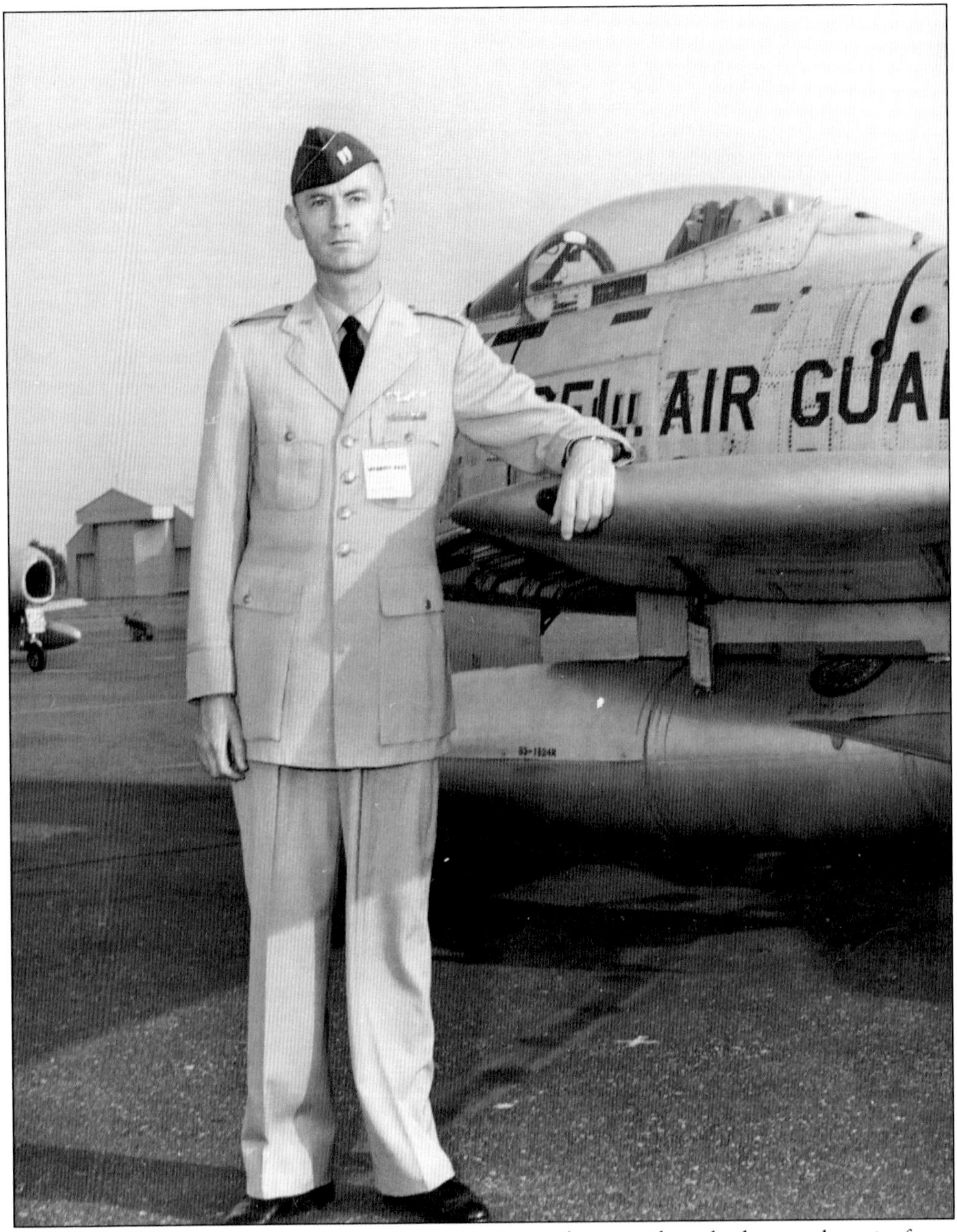

Capt. James P. Scott II poses in his Class A service dress uniform by his airplane in front of the New Castle Air Base "alert hangars." (Courtesy of the Delaware Military Heritage and Education Foundation.)

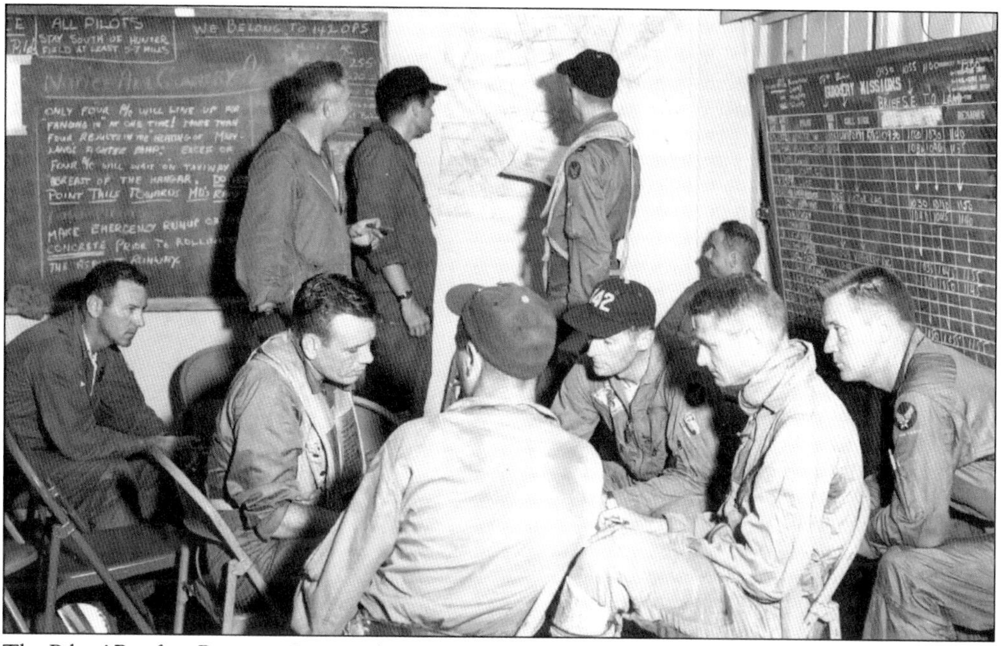

The Pilots' Briefing Room in Savannah, Georgia, is shown in 1958. Here, where missions are planned, are, from left to right, (seated) Robert White, Gordon I. Scott, Jerry Luce, David F. McCallister, Carl Lukens, Rob Railey, and William "Red" White (the U.S. Air Force advisor); (standing) Clav Albright, Stanley Hopperstead, and Britt Lukens. (Courtesy of the Delaware Military Heritage and Education Foundation.)

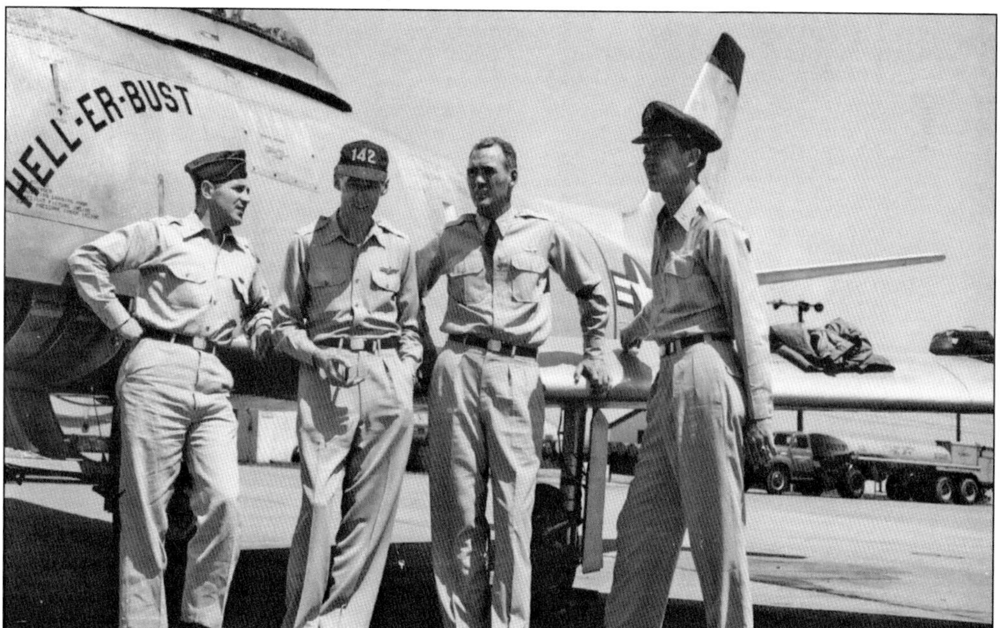

This F-86, "HELL-ER-BUST," is the stage for a flying tactics discussion that includes, from left to right, Clarence E. "Ed" Atkinson, David F. "Snapper" McCallister, U.S. Air Force instructor Edwin C. Heller, and William F. Hutchison Jr. (Courtesy of the Delaware Military Heritage and Education Foundation.)

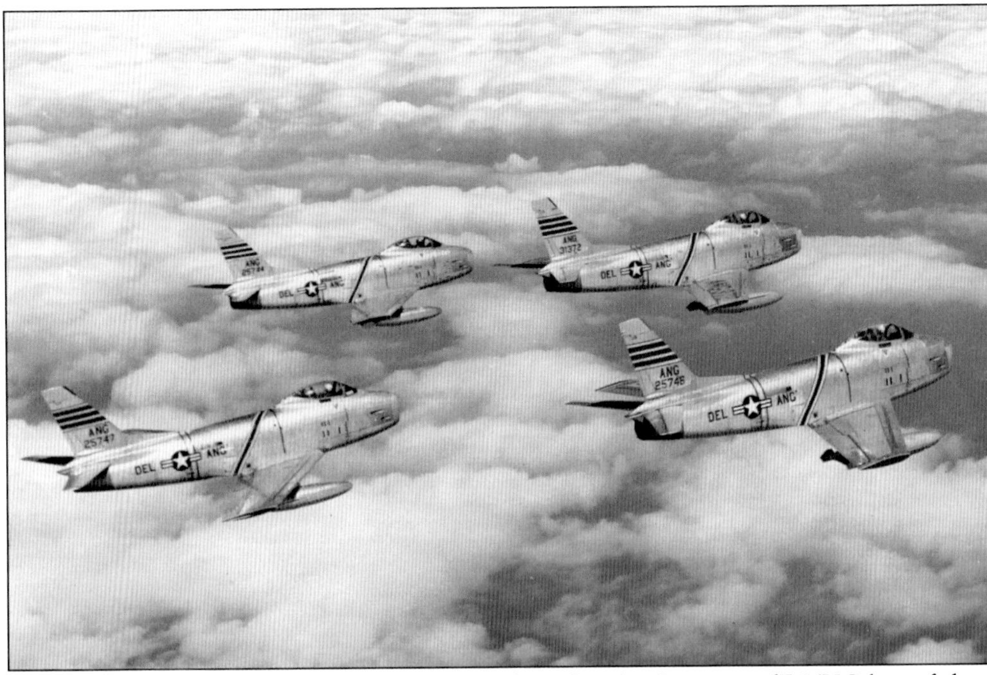

A March 1958 photograph of the "Delaware Diamond"—a four-ship formation of F-86H Sabrejet fighter/bombers—is led by Maj. John Schobelock and includes left wing, flown by Lt. Stanley Hopperstead; right wing, Capt. Robert Floyd; and slot position, Capt. James P. Scott II. (Delaware is known as the "Diamond State.") These Sabrejets were a common sight in the skies of northern Delaware in the 1950s. (Courtesy of the Delaware Military Heritage and Education Foundation.)

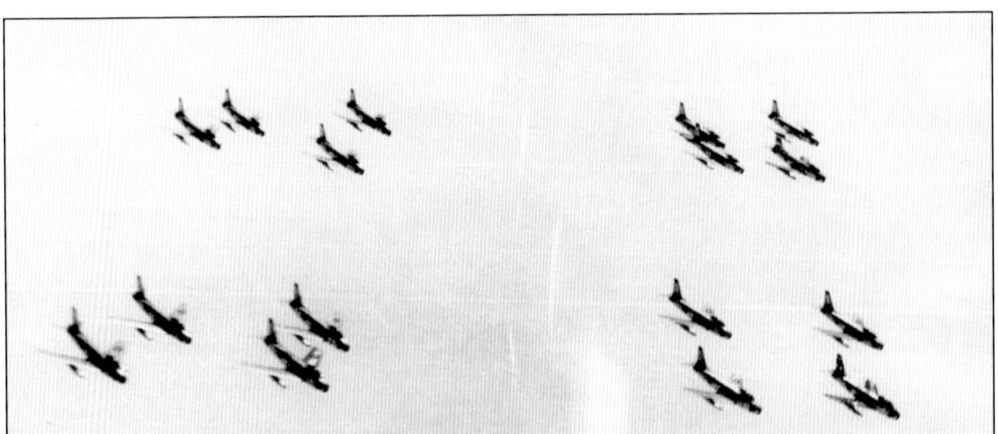

A rare assembly of the "Diamond of Diamonds," a 16-ship flying formation, is led by Lieutenant Colonel McCallister about 1960. (Courtesy of the Delaware Military Heritage and Education Foundation.)

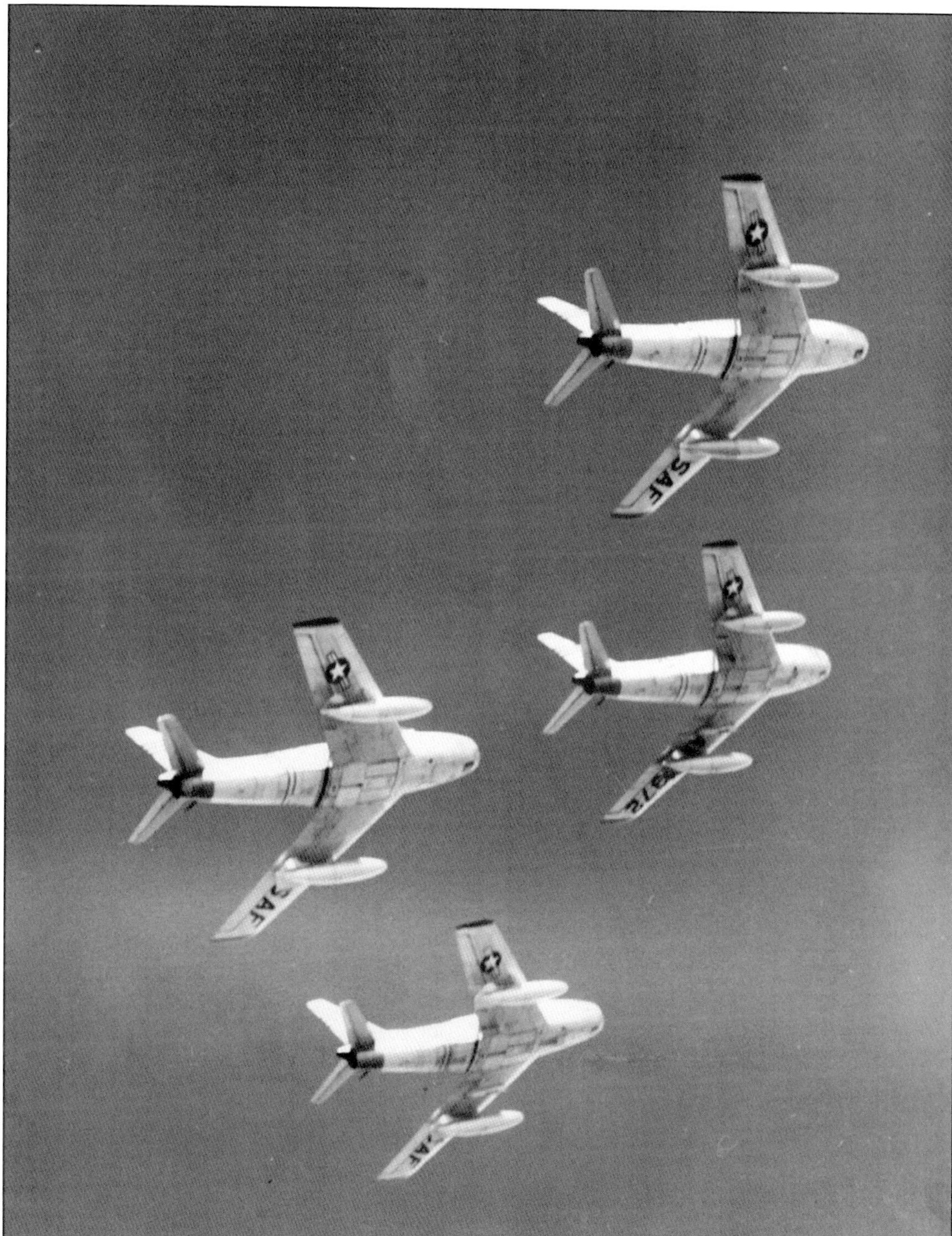

Ceiling and visibility are unlimited ("CAVU") for a sunlit four-ship formation of Delaware Air National Guard F-86Hs. (Courtesy of the Delaware Military Heritage and Education Foundation.)

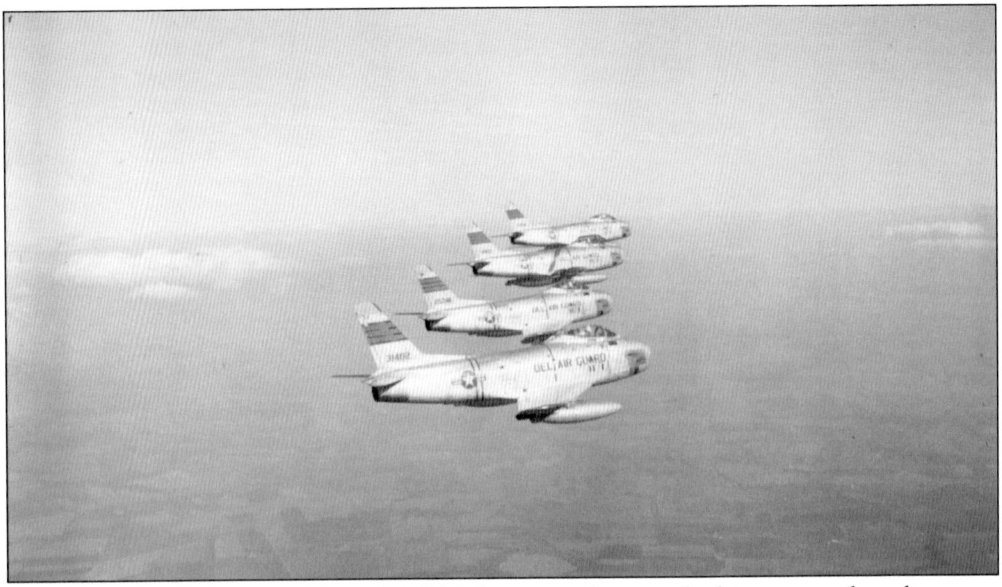

An echelon formation of Delaware F-86H Sabrejets is photographed in near-perfect alignment from a T-33 trainer. (Courtesy of the Delaware Military Heritage and Education Foundation.)

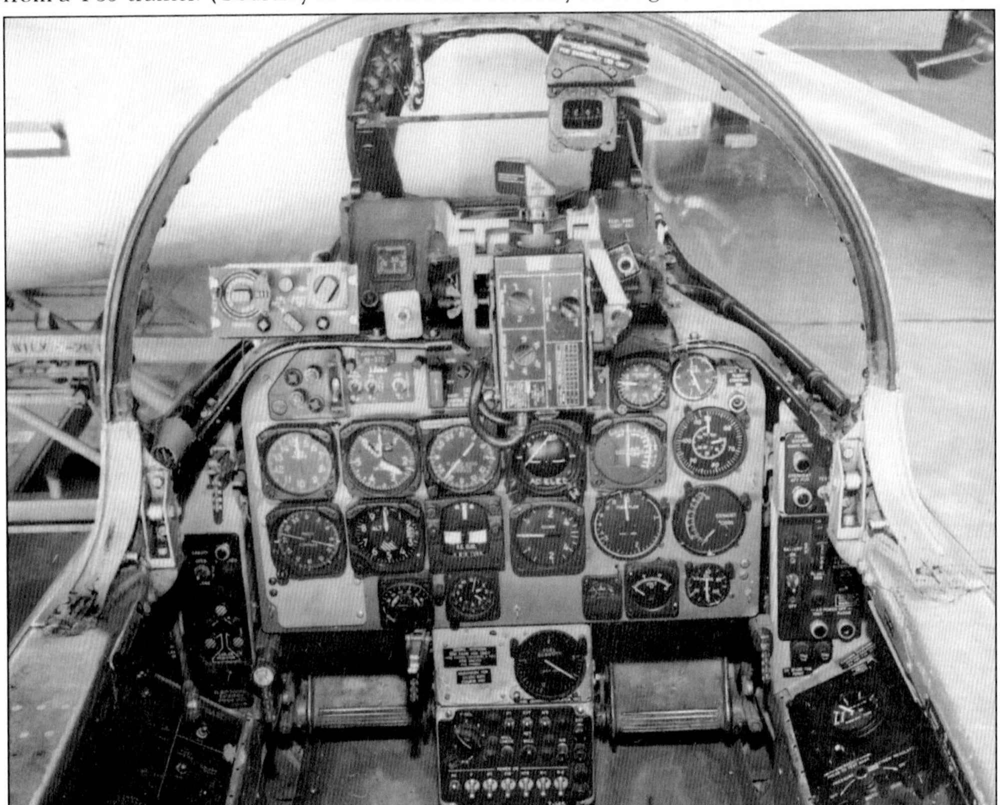

The cockpit of the F-86H Sabrejet was a tight fit and a complex workplace that kept pilots at their highest situational awareness. (Courtesy of the Delaware Military Heritage and Education Foundation.)

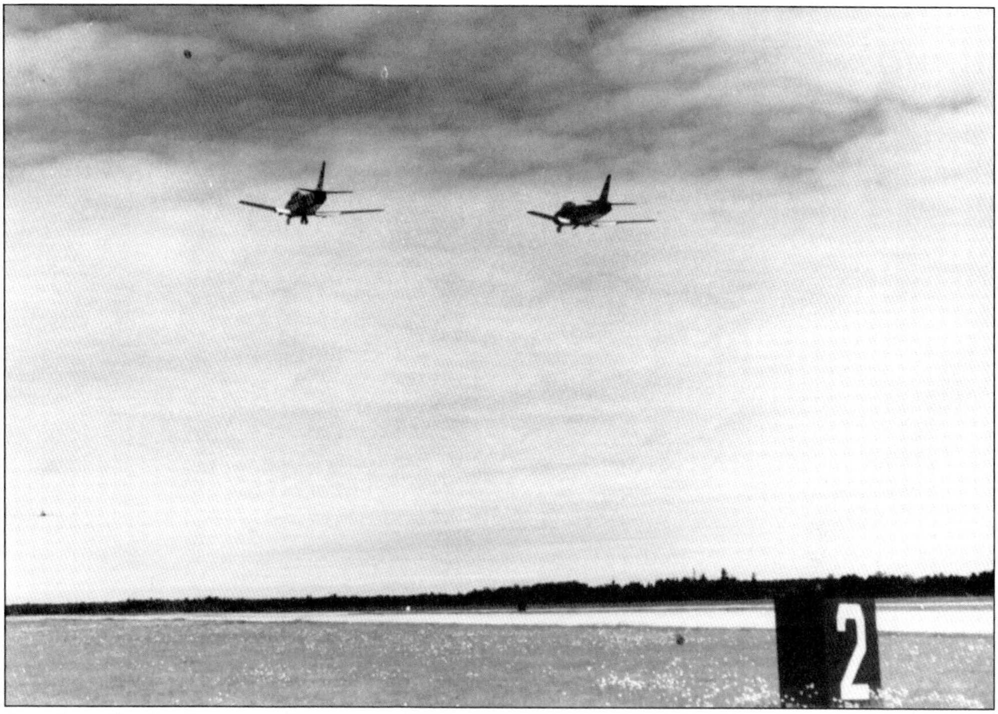

At take-off, wheels are up for a pair of F-86s on a training mission. (Courtesy of the Delaware Military Heritage and Education Foundation.)

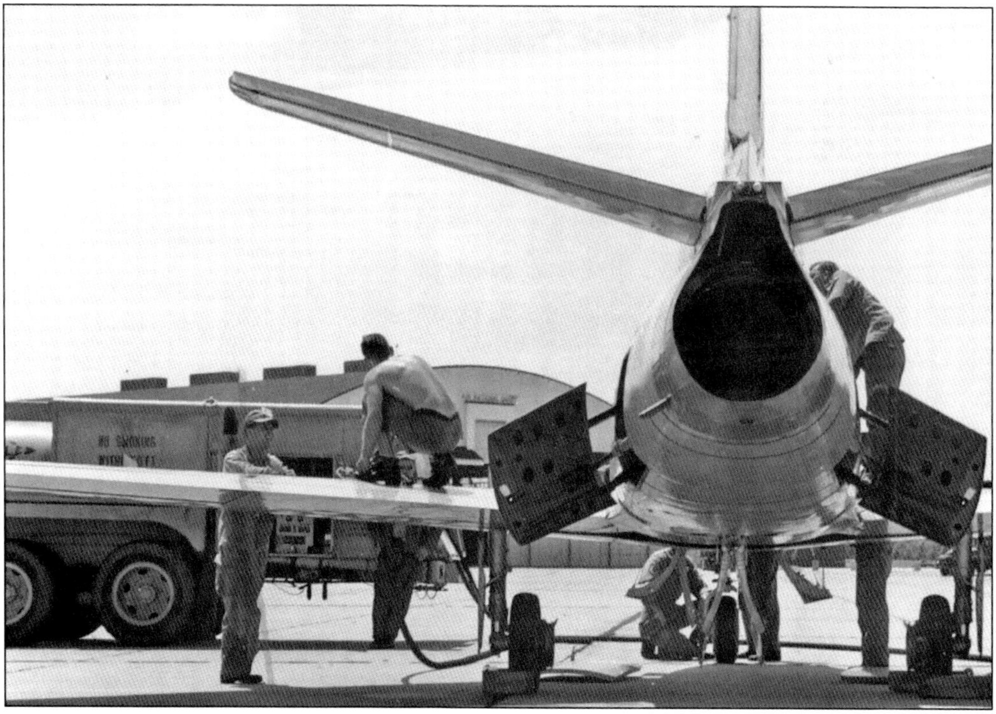

An F-86 is refueled on the New Castle flight line. (Courtesy of the Delaware Military Heritage and Education Foundation.)

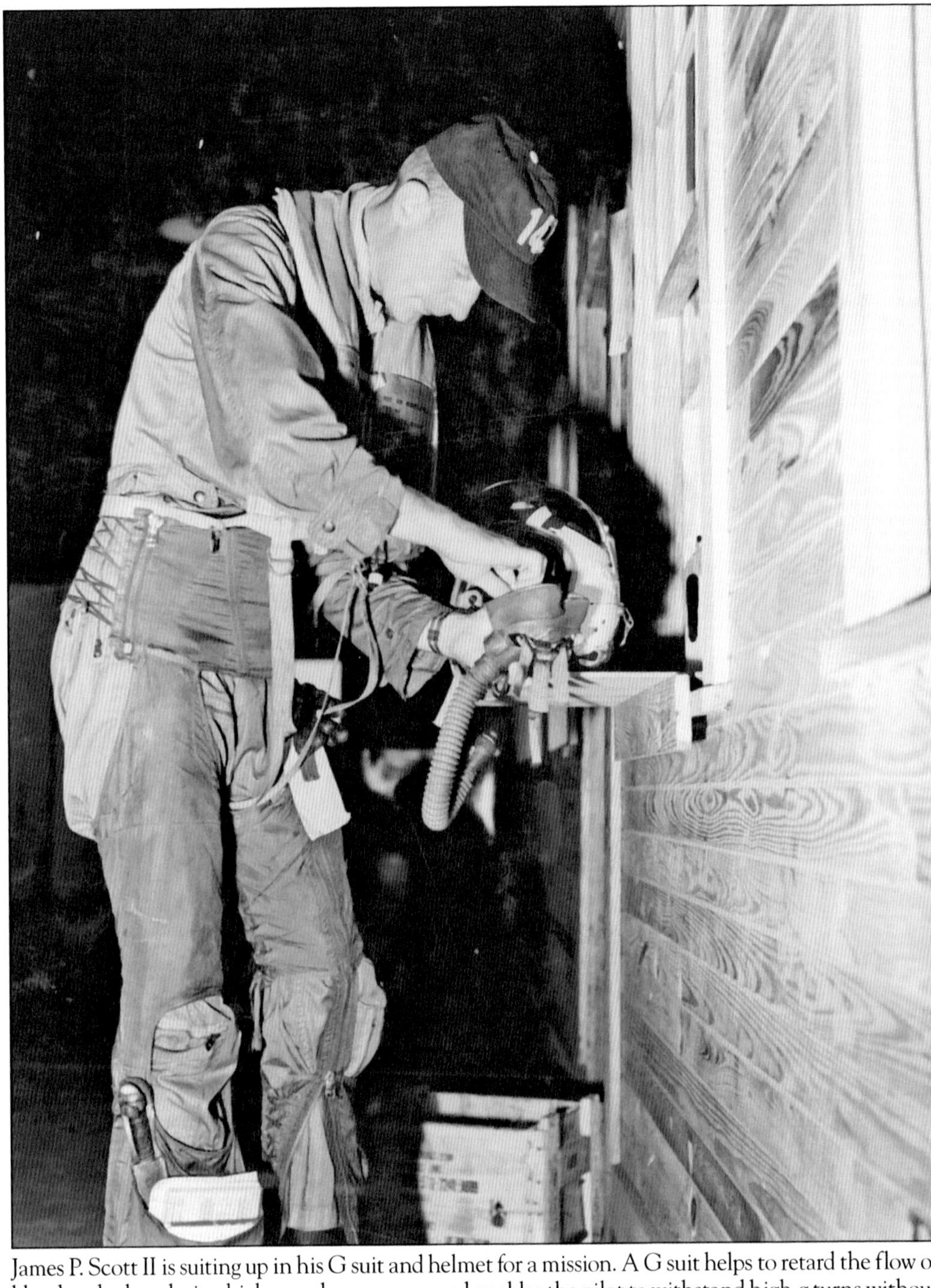

James P. Scott II is suiting up in his G suit and helmet for a mission. A G suit helps to retard the flow of blood to the legs during high-speed maneuvers and enables the pilot to withstand high-g turns without blacking out. (Courtesy of the Delaware Military Heritage and Education Foundation.)

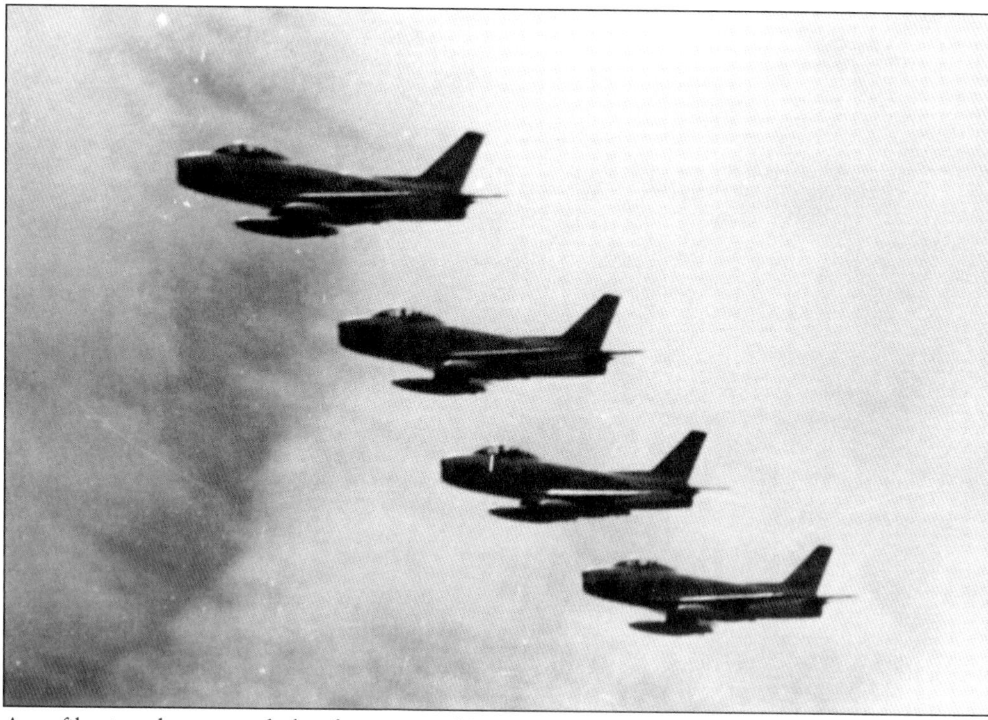

A profile view shows an echelon formation of F-86Hs. (Courtesy of the Delaware Military Heritage and Education Foundation.)

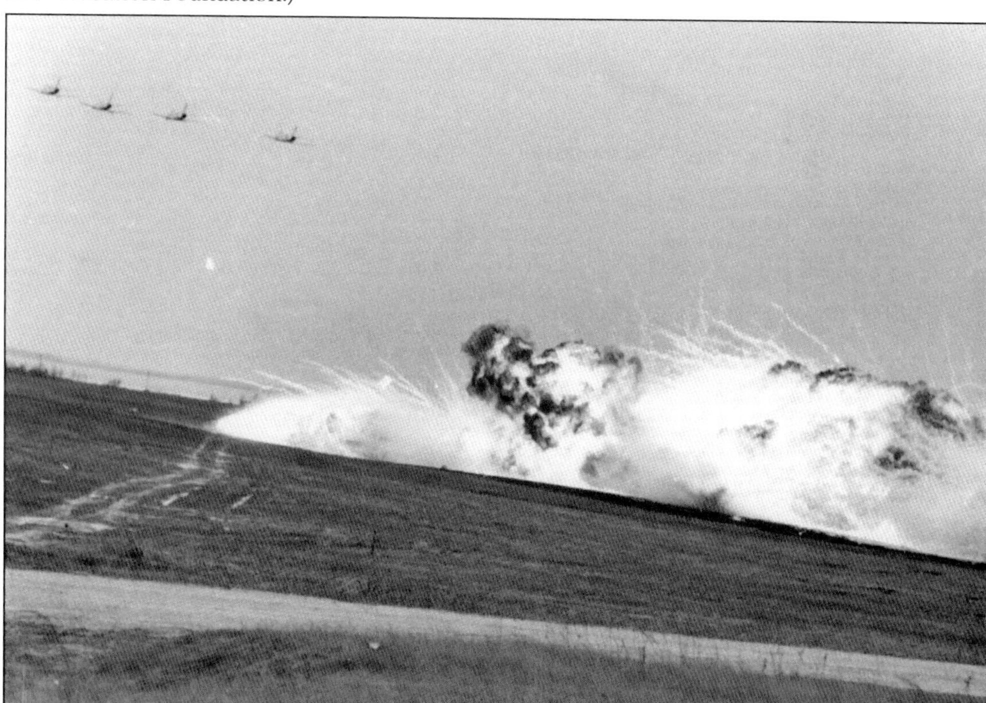

Demonstrations of firepower at Aberdeen Proving Ground, Maryland, include F-86s dropping napalm in 1959. (Courtesy of the Delaware Military Heritage and Education Foundation.)

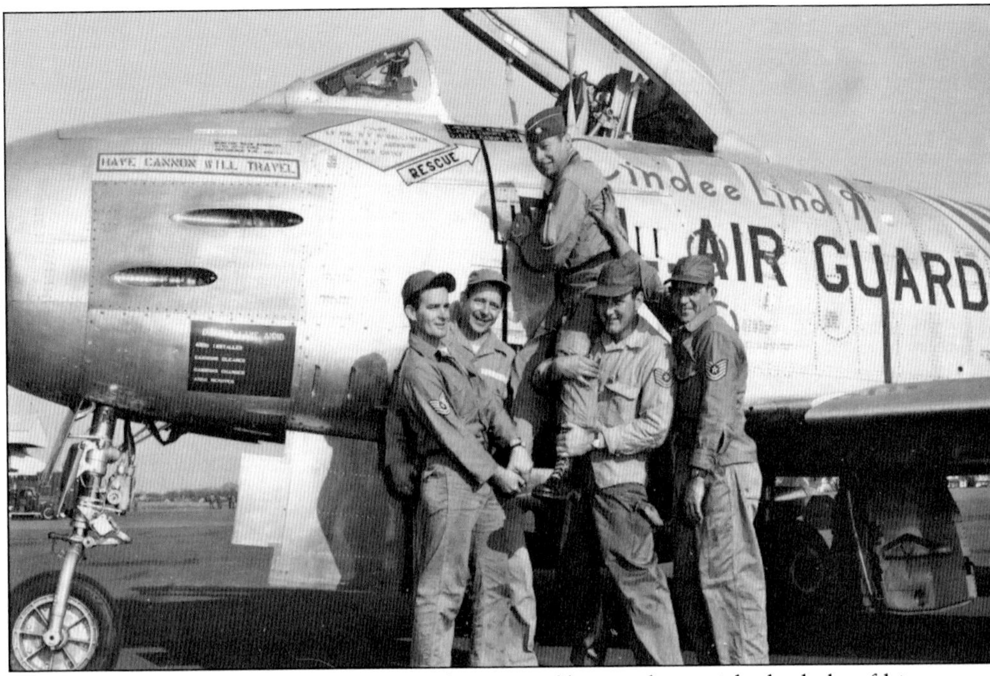

Lt. Col. David McCallister is mounting the steps of his airplane with the help of his present and former crew chiefs: from left to right, Ed Blackburn ("Cindee Lind 7th"), Everett Whitten ("Cindee Lind 6th"), Bill Jackson ("Cindee Lind 9th"), and C. T. Lee ("Cindee Lind 8th"). (Courtesy of the Delaware Military Heritage and Education Foundation.)

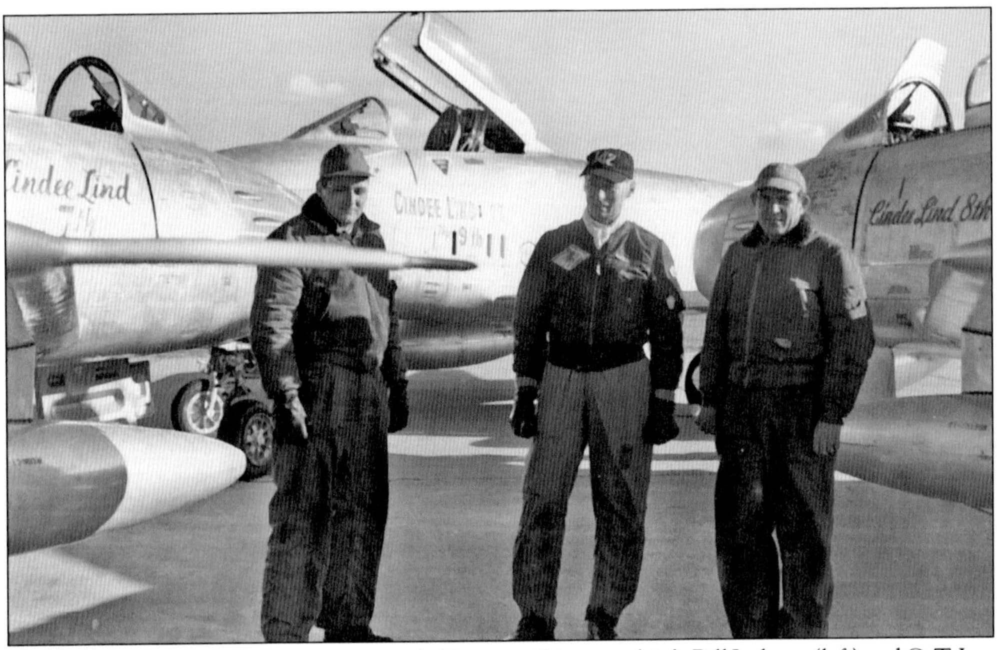

Lieutenant Colonel McCallister is surrounded by two of his crew chiefs, Bill Jackson (left) and C. T. Lee (right), and three of his airplanes: from left to right are "Cindee Lind 7th," "Cindee Lind 9th," and "Cindee Lind 8th." (Courtesy of the Delaware Military Heritage and Education Foundation.)

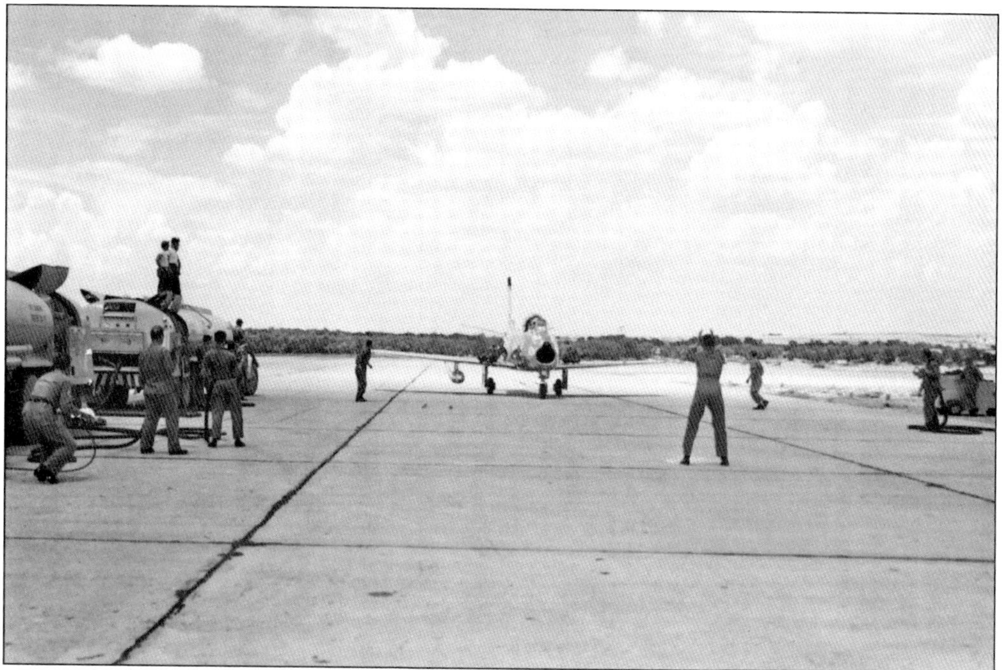

"Cindee Lind 7th," piloted by Lt. Col. David McCallister, is taxiing into position during the annual Ricks Trophy cross-country race. His crew chief for the race was Bill Roberts, assisted by Ed Blackburn, Jack Ellingsworth, and others. (Courtesy of the Delaware Military Heritage and Education Foundation.)

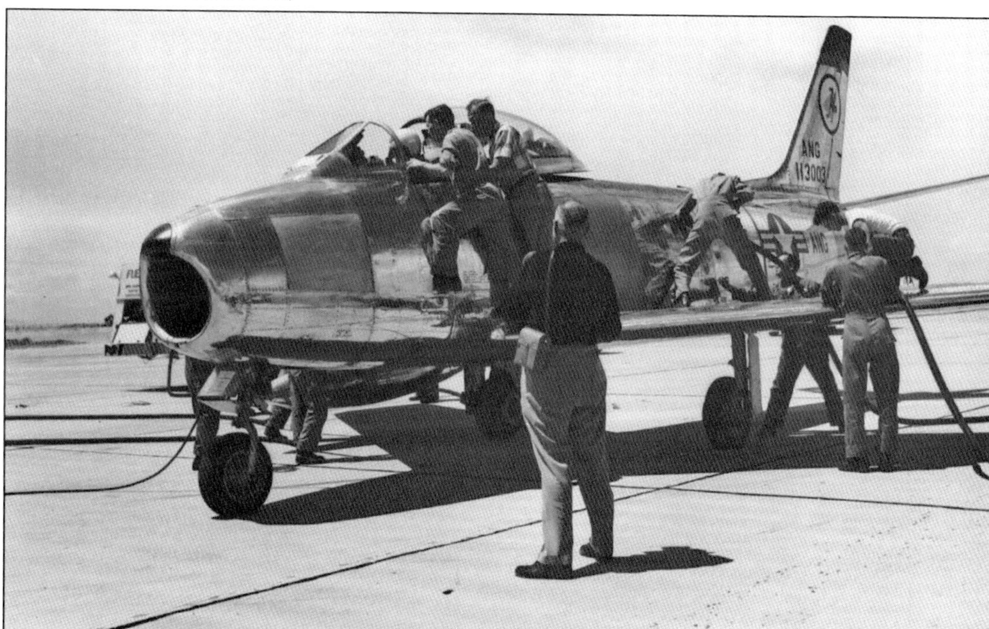

"Cindee Lind 7th" is refueled, with engine running, during a pit stop at the Ricks Trophy Race in 1956. Note the high polish, a single drop tank, and the faired-over gun ports to reduce aerodynamic drag and increase air speed. Pilot David McCallister took first place in the 1956 race across the United States. (Courtesy of the Delaware Military Heritage and Education Foundation.)

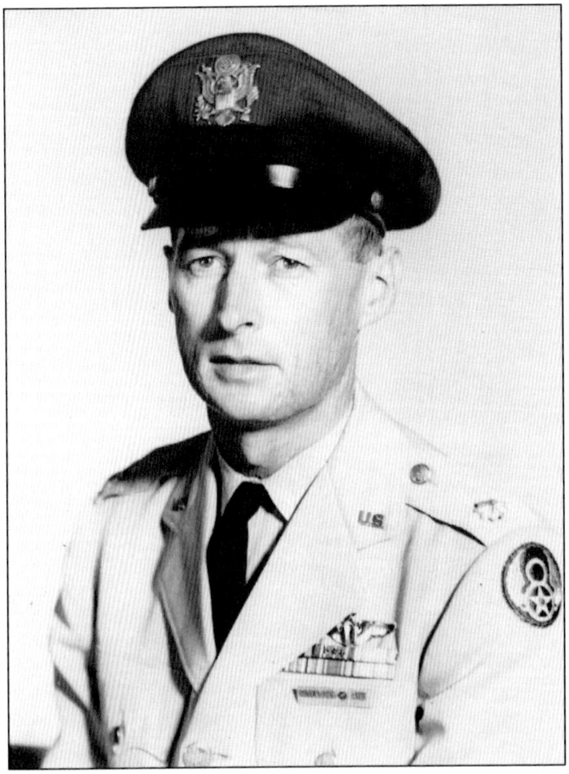

Lt. Col. David "Snapper" McCallister was the commander of the 142nd Fighter Squadron. He flew with the 8th Air Force in Europe. His nickname was related to his family's catering business, which presumably offered snapper soup, a local delicacy made from the notoriously aggressive and dangerous snapping turtle. A test pilot for All-American Engineering, he was also the author of a novel entitled *Sabres over the Brandywine*. (Courtesy of the Delaware Military Heritage and Education Foundation.)

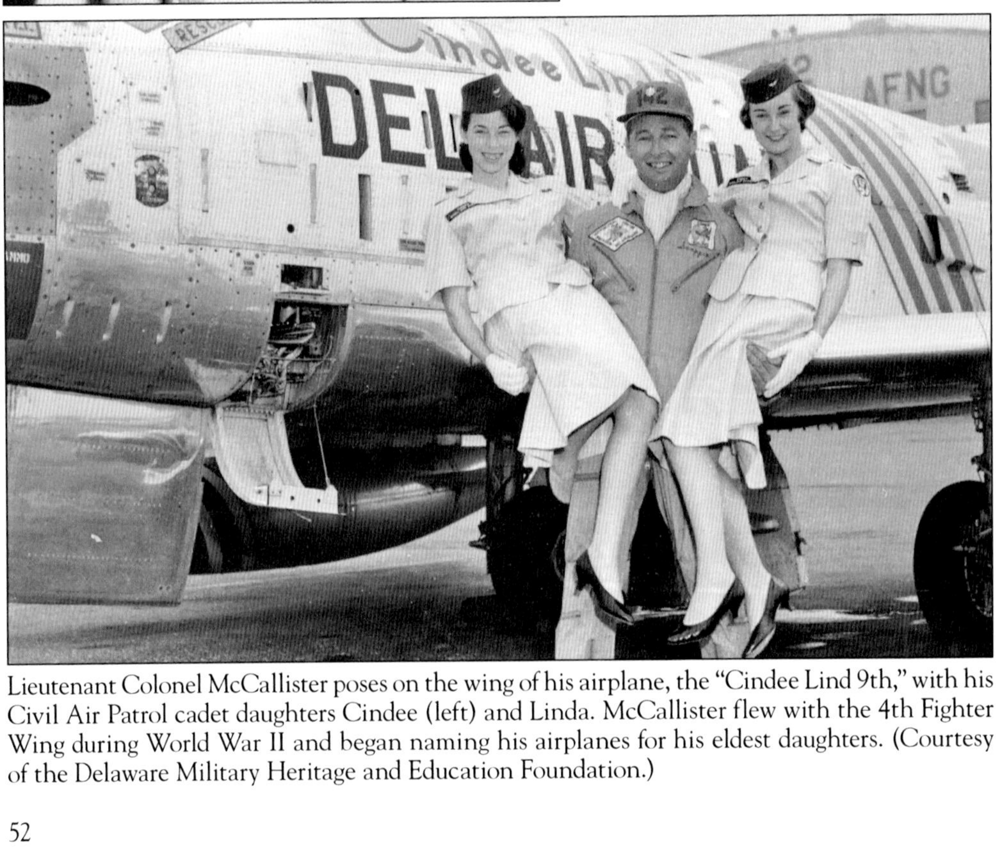

Lieutenant Colonel McCallister poses on the wing of his airplane, the "Cindee Lind 9th," with his Civil Air Patrol cadet daughters Cindee (left) and Linda. McCallister flew with the 4th Fighter Wing during World War II and began naming his airplanes for his eldest daughters. (Courtesy of the Delaware Military Heritage and Education Foundation.)

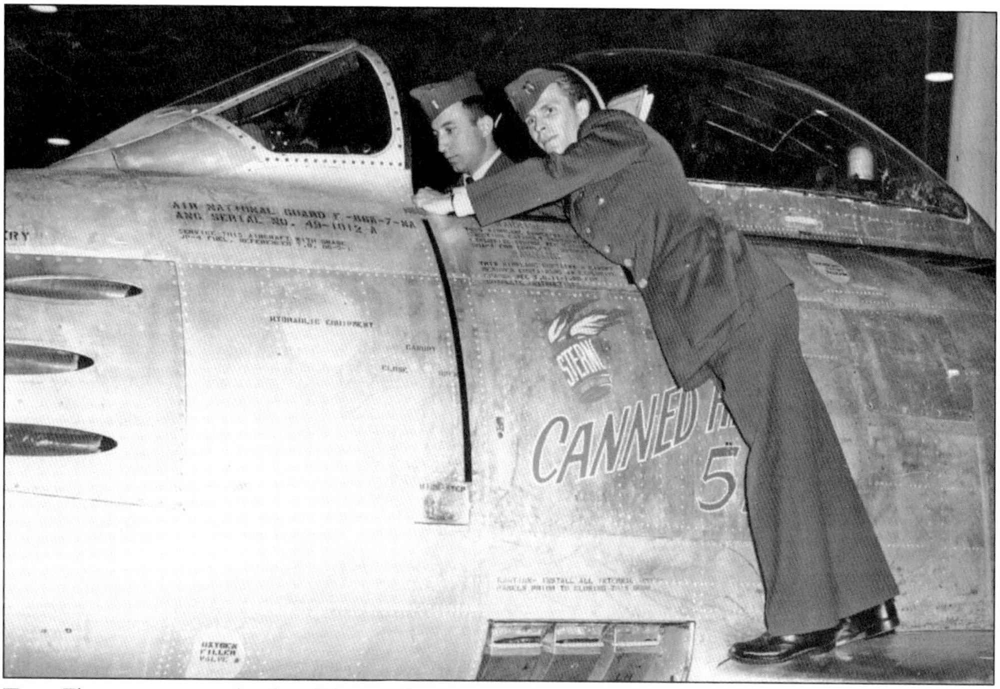

Tony Florio tries out the fit of the cockpit as Capt. John Sommerville assists from the wing in 1954. The airplane is "Canned Heat 5th," piloted by Frank Stern. (Courtesy of the Delaware Military Heritage and Education Foundation.)

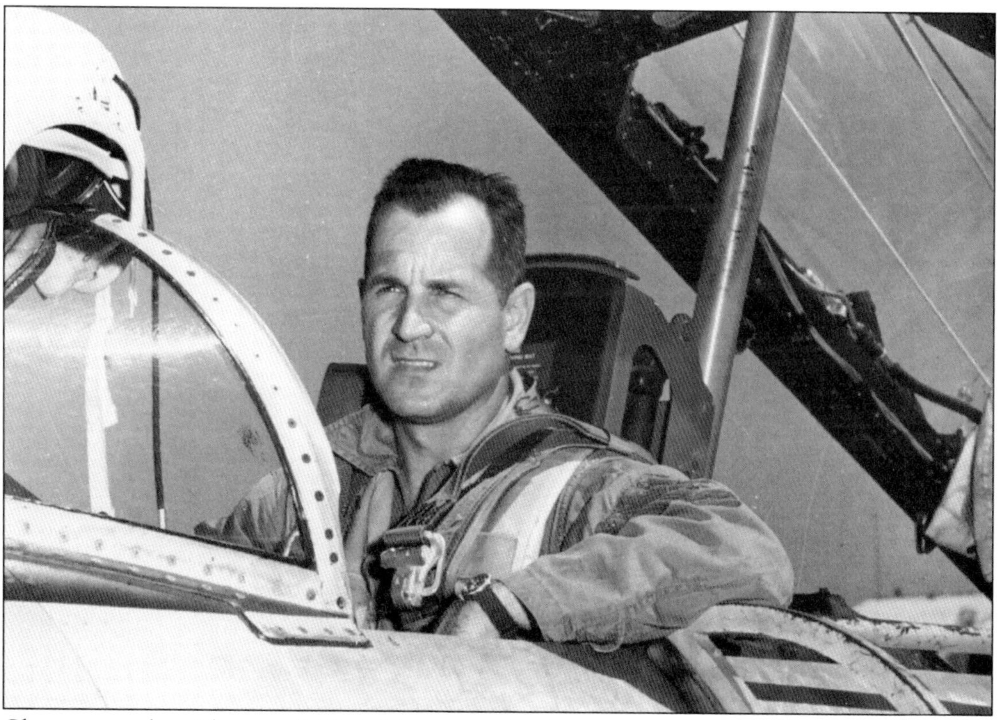

Charter member Clarence "Ed" Atkinson sits in the cockpit of the unit's T-33A jet trainer. (Courtesy of the Delaware Military Heritage and Education Foundation.)

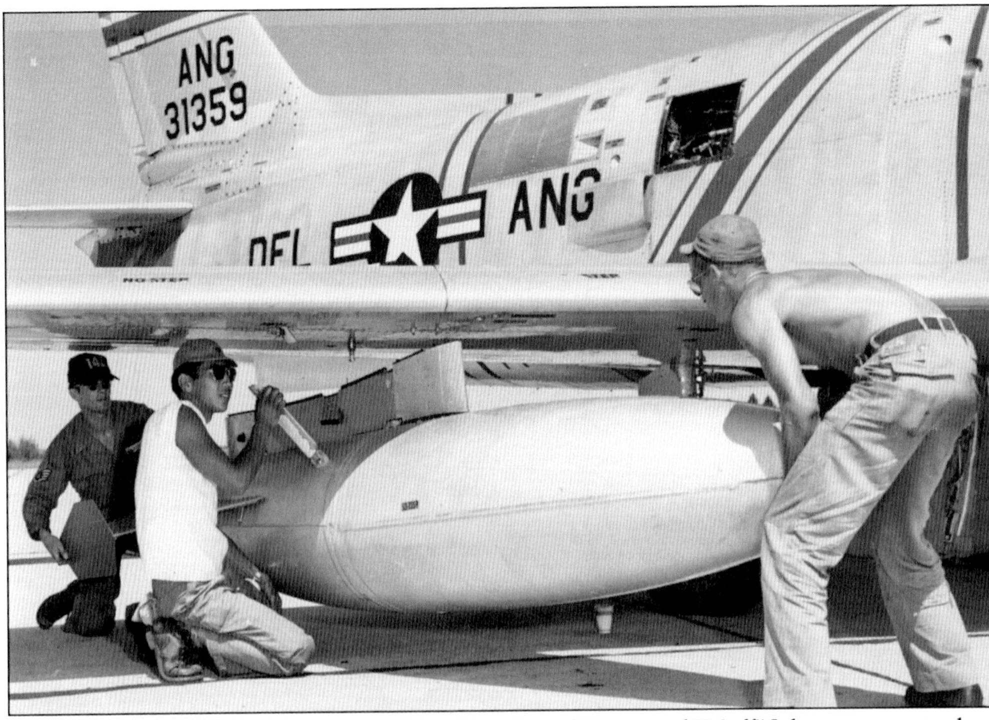

From left to right, Ed Blackburn assists Dick Harada and Townsend "Muff" Johnson mount a drop tank on an F-86H. (Courtesy of the Delaware Military Heritage and Education Foundation.)

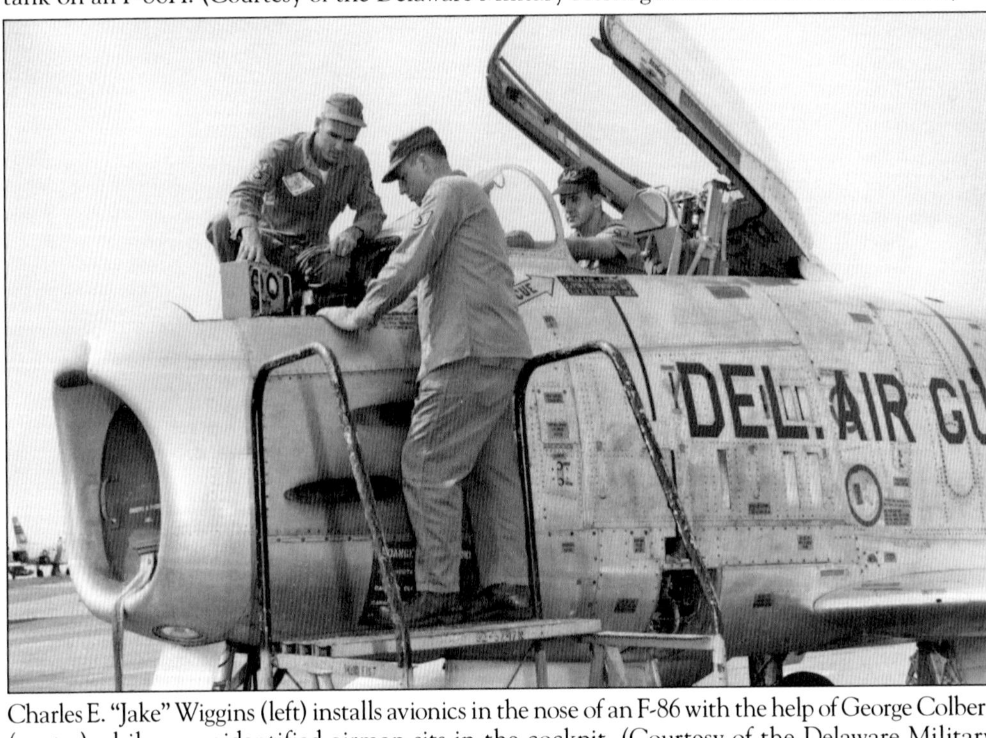

Charles E. "Jake" Wiggins (left) installs avionics in the nose of an F-86 with the help of George Colbert (center) while an unidentified airman sits in the cockpit. (Courtesy of the Delaware Military Heritage and Education Foundation.)

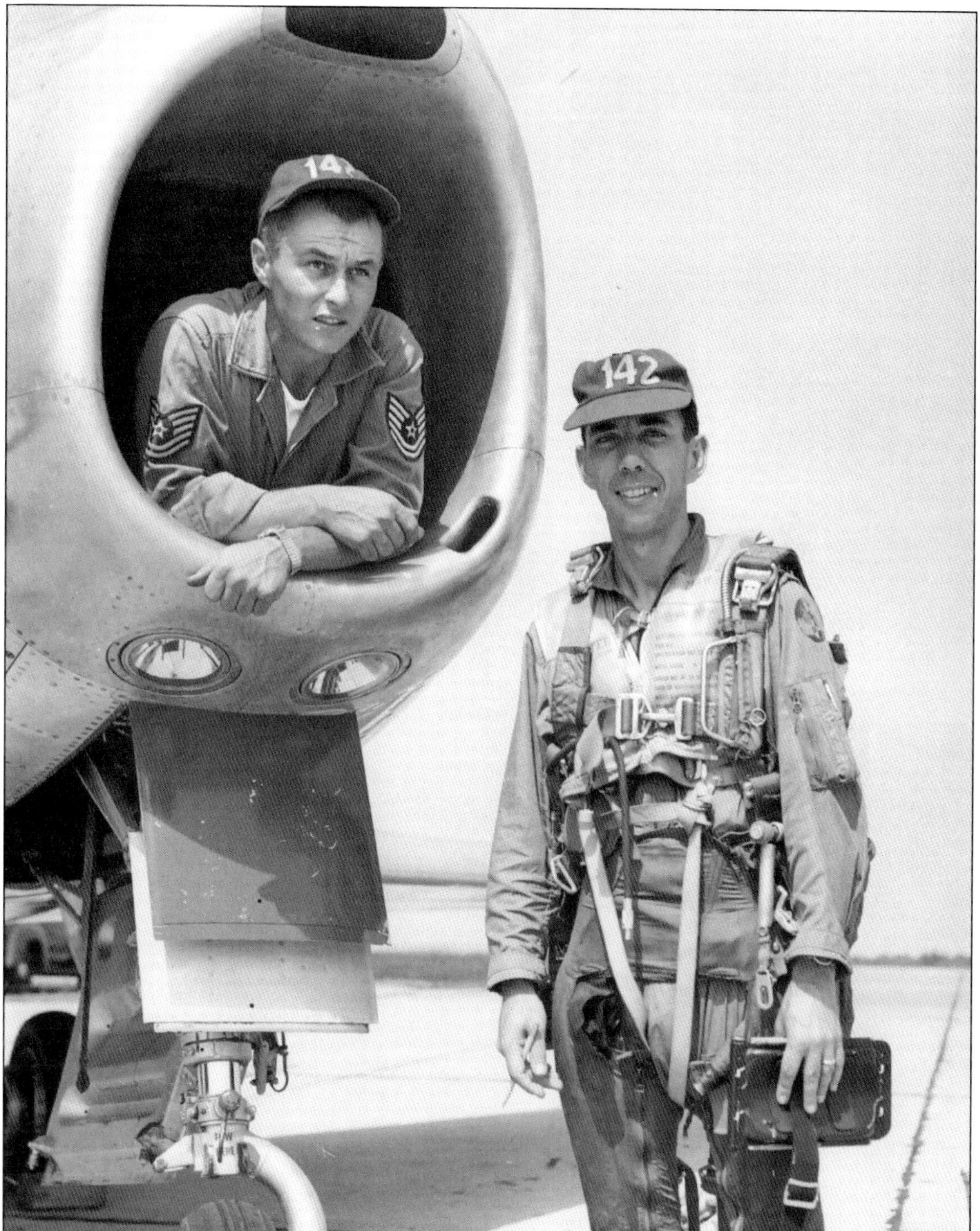

Crew chief T.Sgt. John Quigley poses in the air scoop of his F-86H with his pilot, John Schobelock. (Courtesy of the Delaware Military Heritage and Education Foundation.)

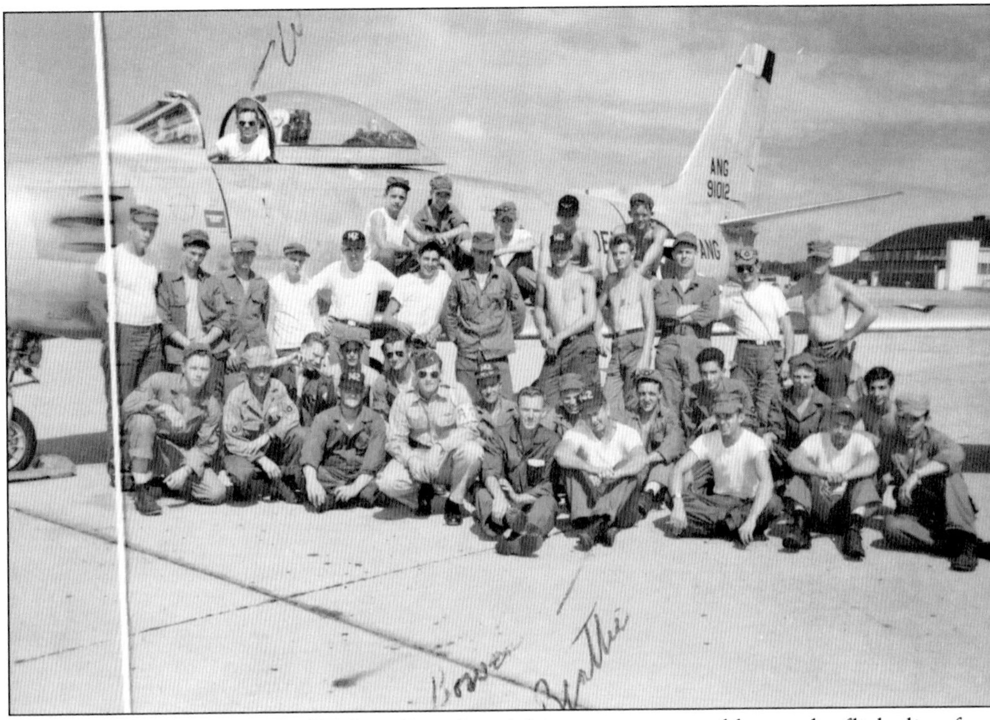

The Armorers Section, 142nd Fighter Squadron Maintenance, assembles on the flight line for a group picture. (Courtesy of the Delaware Military Heritage and Education Foundation.)

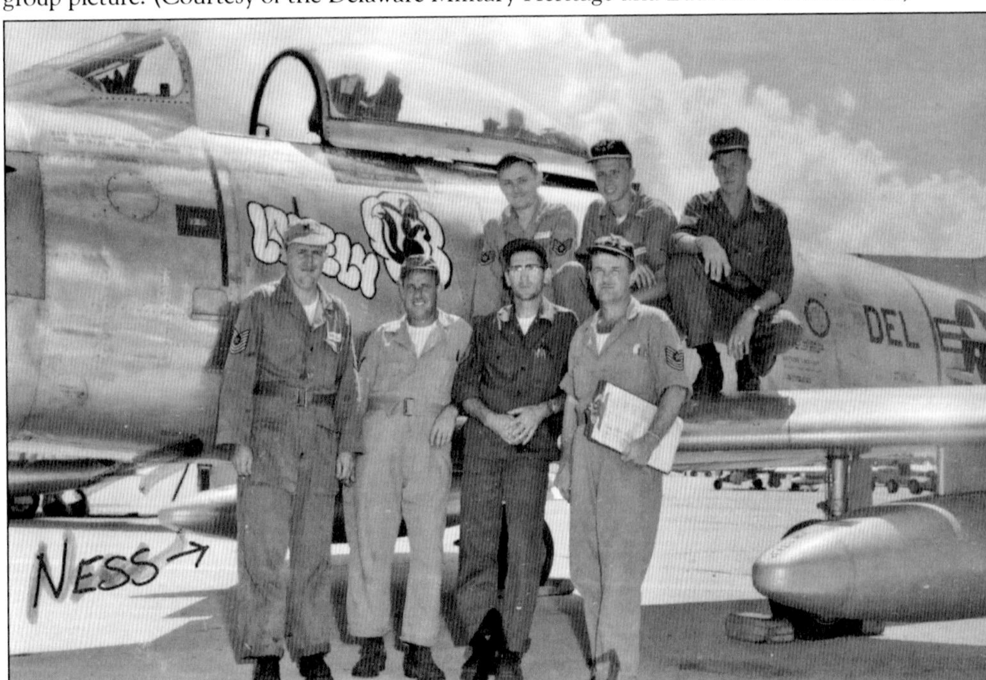

Inspectors assembled in front of F-86 "Lonely" (with skunk) are, from left to right, (standing) "Pop" Ness, Jake Swan, Robert Loeffel, and Larry Vieth; (on wing) Staff Sergeant Strett and two unidentified airmen. (Courtesy of the Delaware Military Heritage and Education Foundation.)

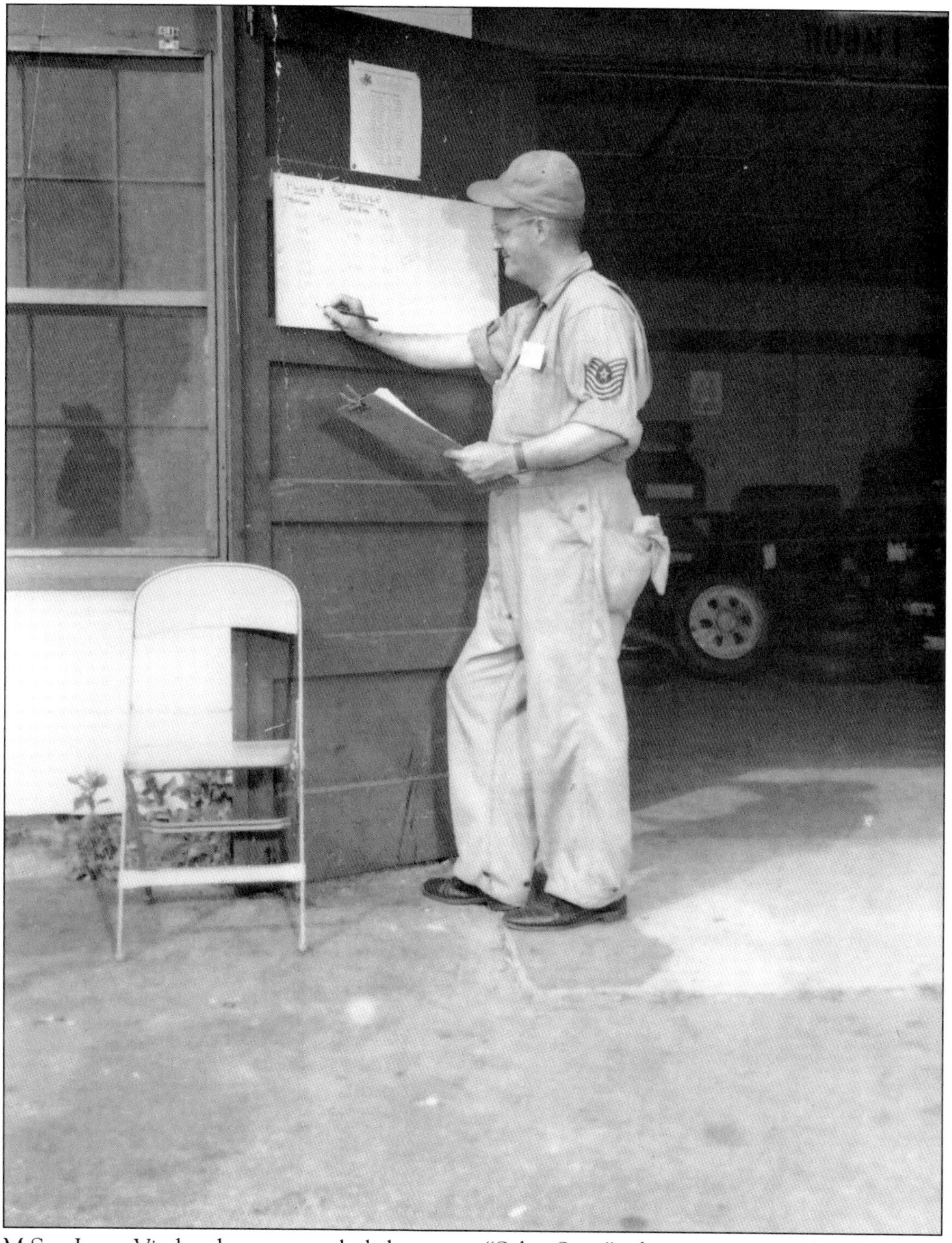

M.Sgt. Larry Vieth, who was popularly known as "Sabre Sam," takes a grease pencil to the flying schedule. (Courtesy of the Delaware Military Heritage and Education Foundation.)

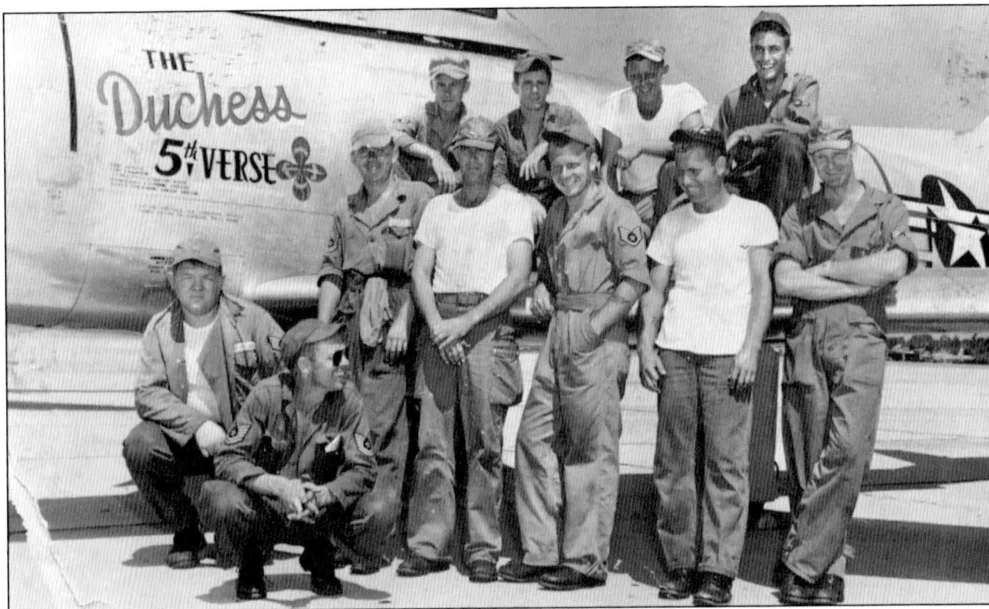

From left to right are (kneeling) ? Schiocki and Paul Smith; (standing) Joe Jenecke, Charles Thomas Lee, Paul "Bronco" Lane, Bill Roberts, and Jake Powell; (on the wing) Ed Eicholz, Ed Blackburn, Bob Hill, and Townsend Johnson. (Courtesy of the Ed Blackburn collection.)

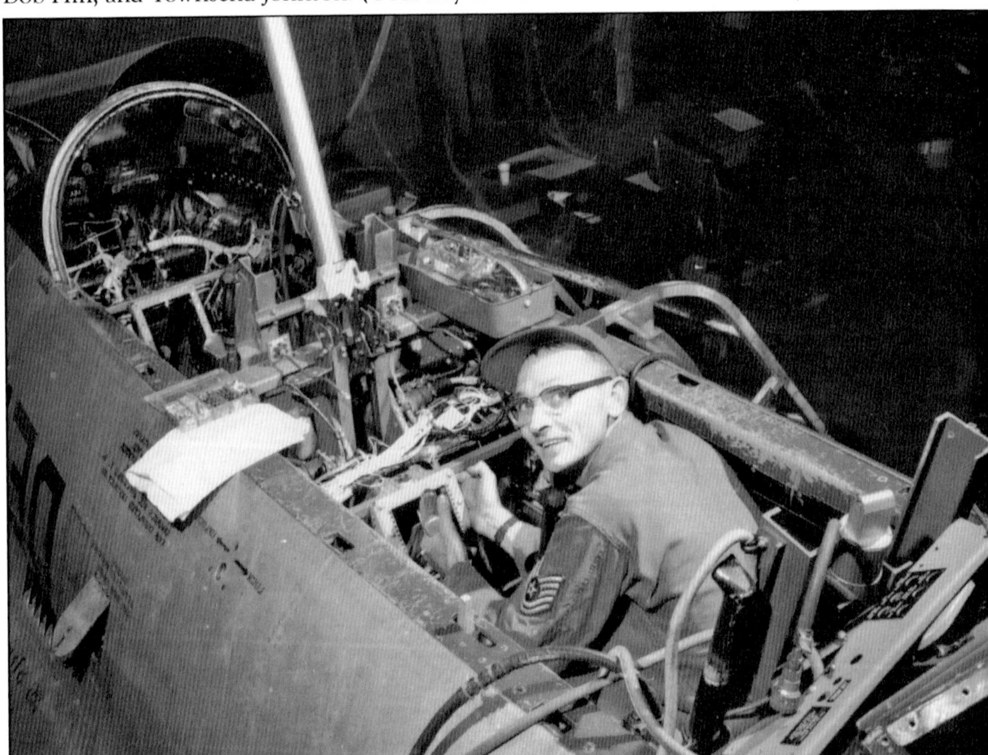

T.Sgt. Lawrence Wiggins Sr. performs a maintenance check in the backseat of a T-33. (Courtesy of the Delaware Military Heritage and Education Foundation.)

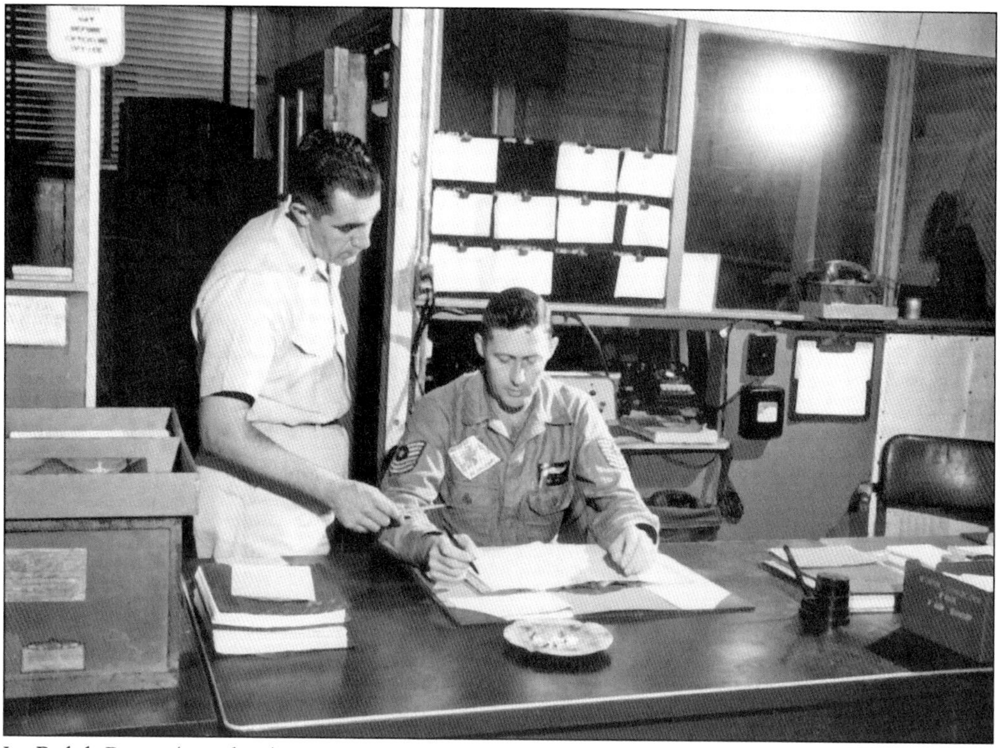

Lt. Ralph Piazza (standing) supervises M.Sgt. Vincent Riley in the maintenance office/back shop of the main hangar. (Courtesy of the Delaware Military Heritage and Education Foundation.)

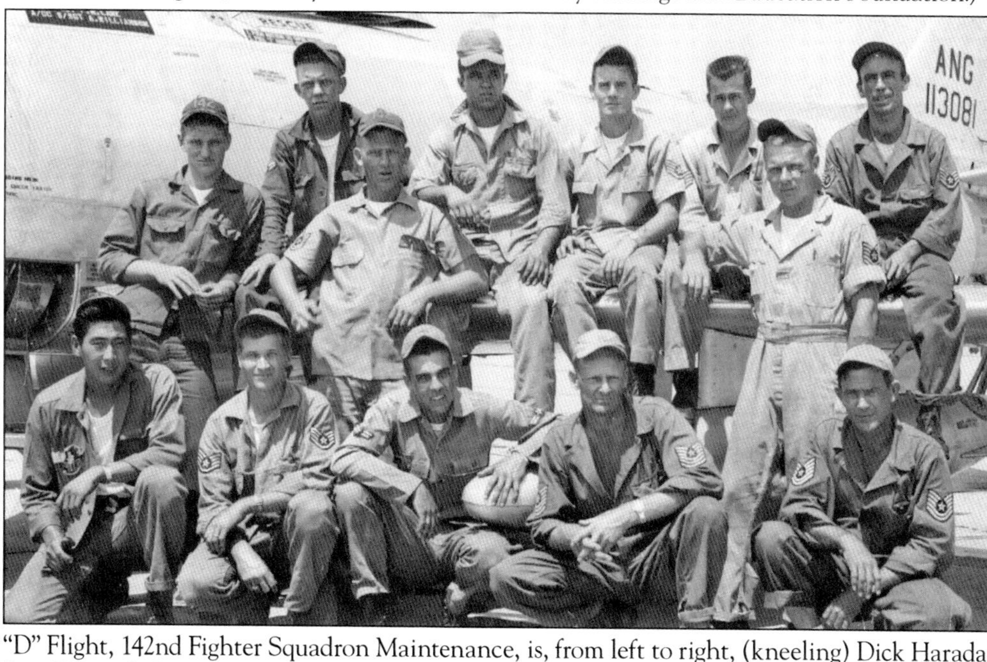

"D" Flight, 142nd Fighter Squadron Maintenance, is, from left to right, (kneeling) Dick Harada, Ray Whitzel, Ernie Antes, Jake Powell, and C. T. Lee; (standing) unidentified, Bob Gravatt, Bob Hill, Tony Moretti, Ed Blackburn, Ed Eicholz, Paul Lane, and Al Williamson. (Courtesy the Ed Blackburn collection.)

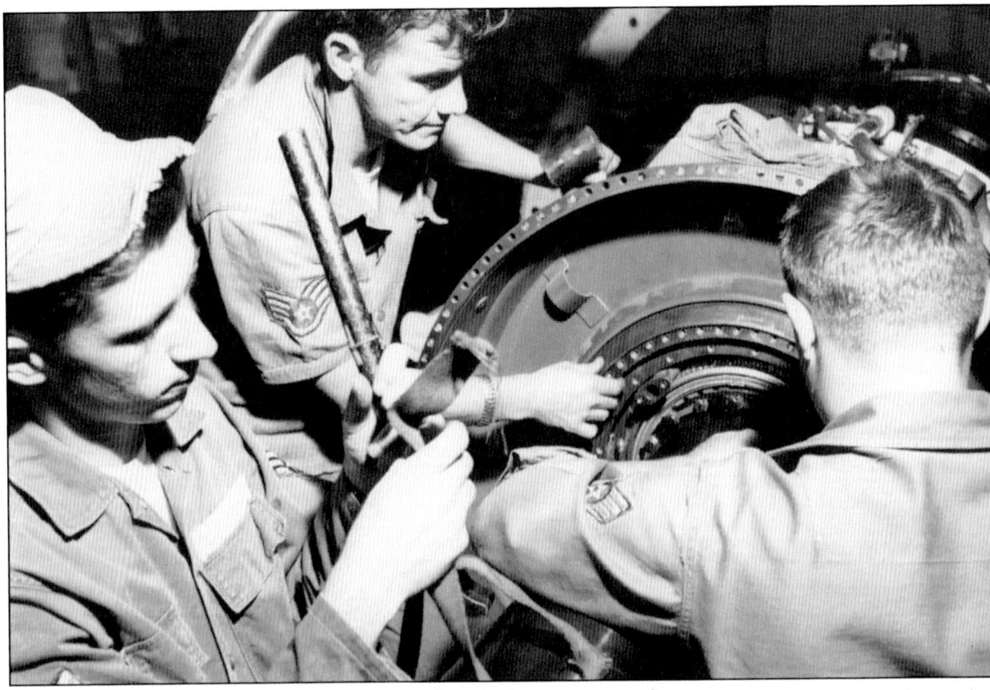

S.Sgt. Victor Macey (top) is aided by two unidentified assistants performing maintenance on a jet engine in the engine shop. (Courtesy of the Delaware Military Heritage and Education Foundation.)

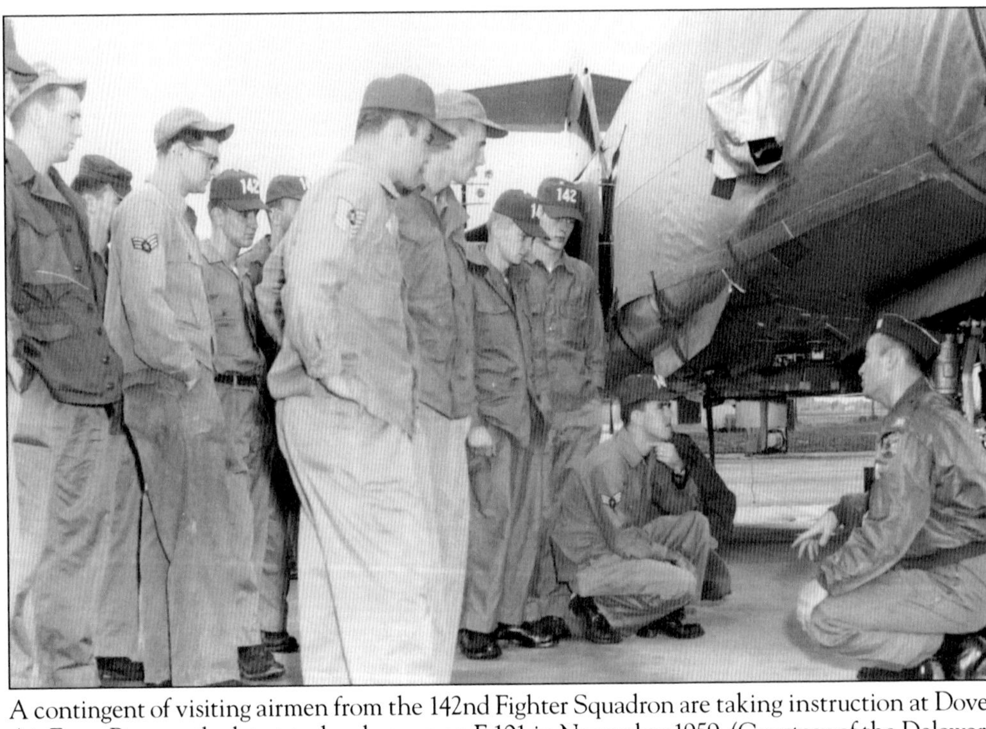

A contingent of visiting airmen from the 142nd Fighter Squadron are taking instruction at Dover Air Force Base on the latest technology on an F-101 in November 1959. (Courtesy of the Delaware Military Heritage and Education Foundation.)

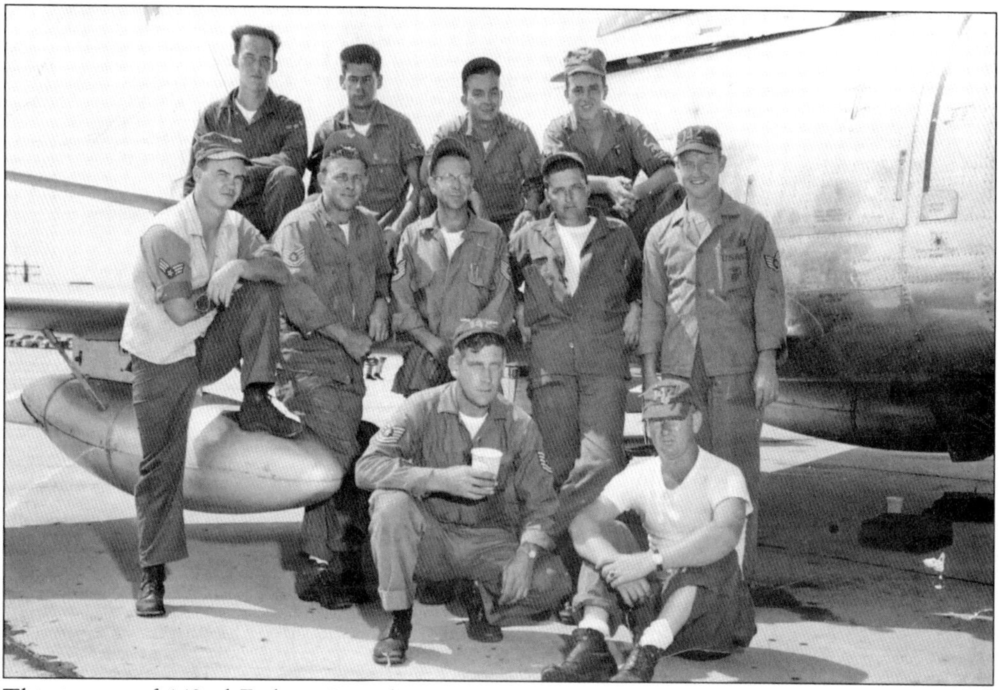

This image of 142nd Fighter Squadron Maintenance shows, from left to right, (first row) Ron Hill and Paul Shotwell; (second row) ? Smith, Jack Weber, Lou Godwin, Bill Jackson, and Tucker Pierce; (third row) unidentified, Clayton Stafford, Bill Craig, and unidentified. (Courtesy of the Ed Blackburn collection.)

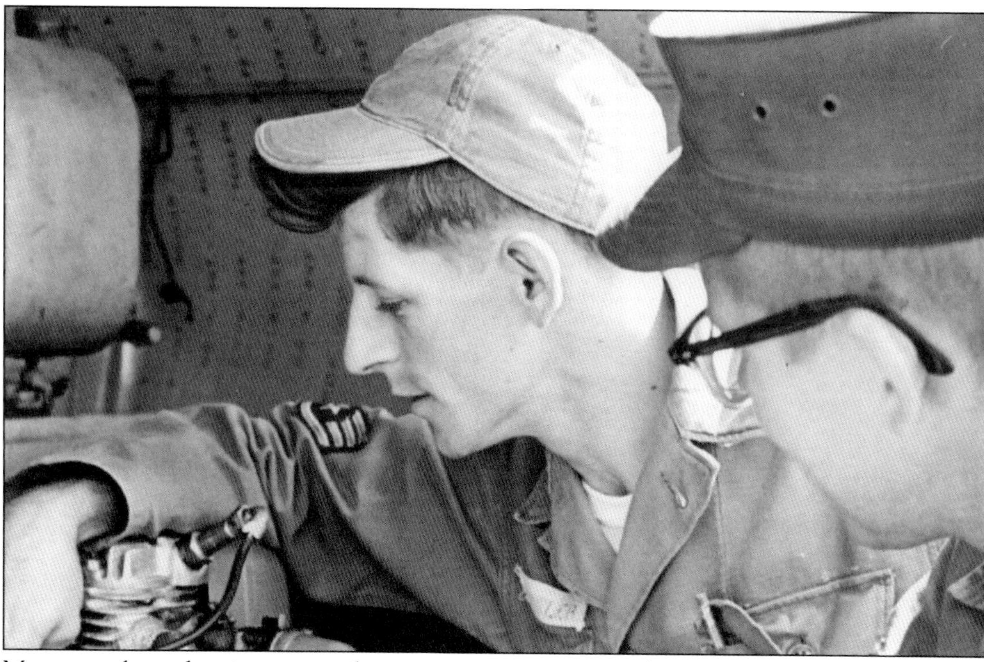

Motor pool mechanics are working on a pump motor. Shown are S.Sgt. Allan Bowers (left) and A1c. Marvin Sterling (right). (Courtesy of the Delaware Military Heritage and Education Foundation.)

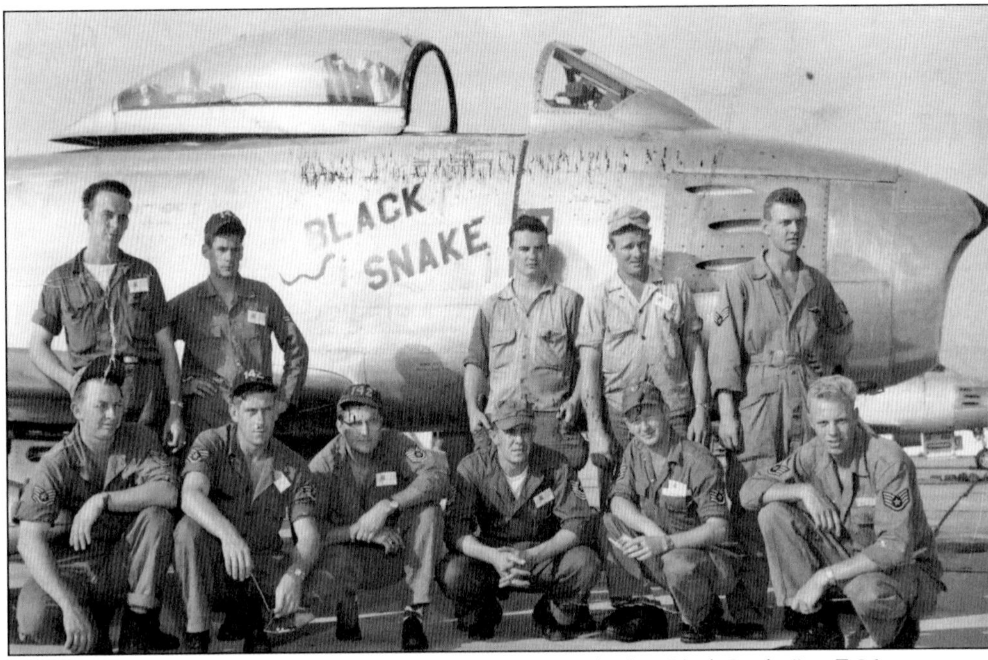

In this official 142nd Fighter-Interceptor Squadron photograph, the "Black Snake," an F-86 interceptor, serves as a backdrop for, from left to right, (kneeling) Newt Brackin, Ron Hill, Bill Jackson, Ralph Piazza, Paul Shotwell, and Bob Garvey; (standing) unidentified, Clayton Stafford, P. Smith, Jack Weber, and Ben Phillips. (Courtesy of the Ed Blackburn collection.)

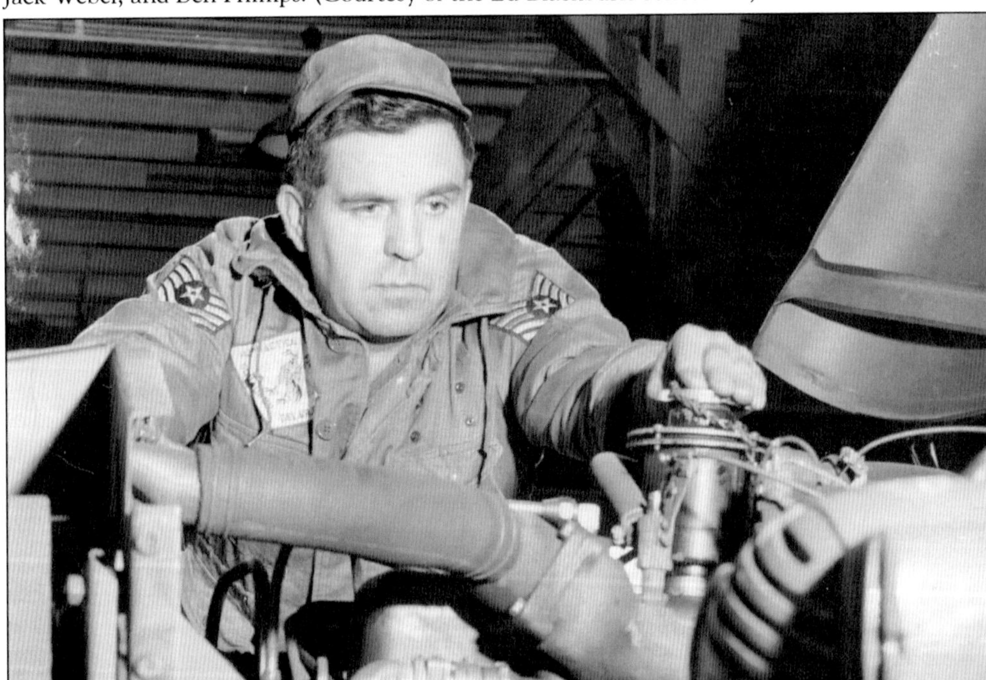

T.Sgt. Joseph Manion, who was a charter member of the unit, performs a test on an auxiliary component. (Courtesy of the Delaware Military Heritage and Education Foundation.)

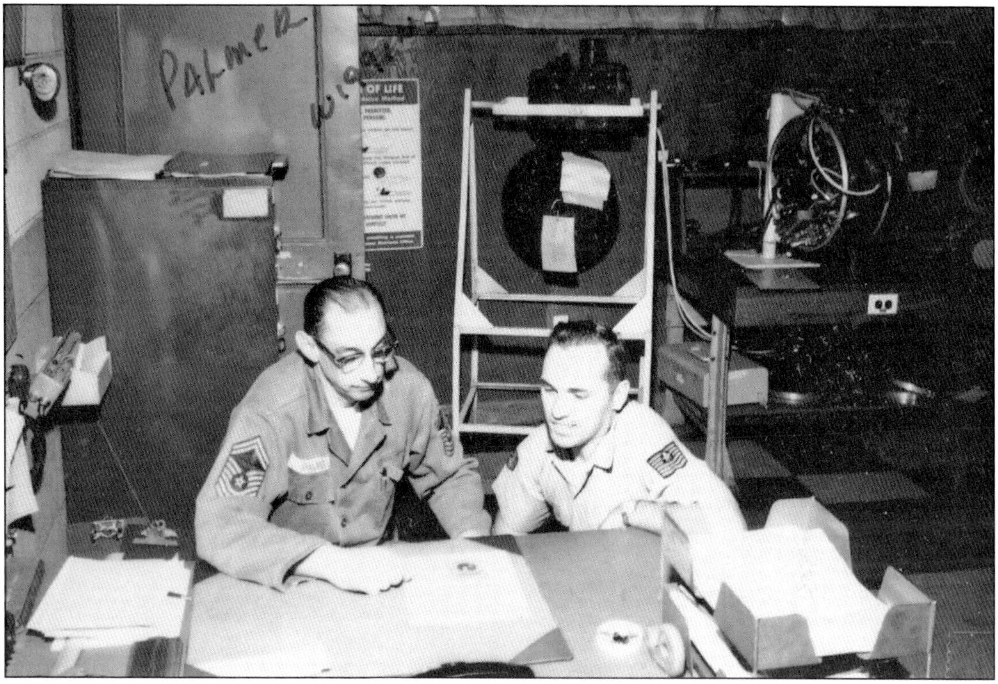

C.M.Sgt. Charlie Palmer (left), avionics supervisor, and M.Sgt. Charles E. Wiggins review avionics maintenance paperwork. (Courtesy of the Delaware Military Heritage and Education Foundation.)

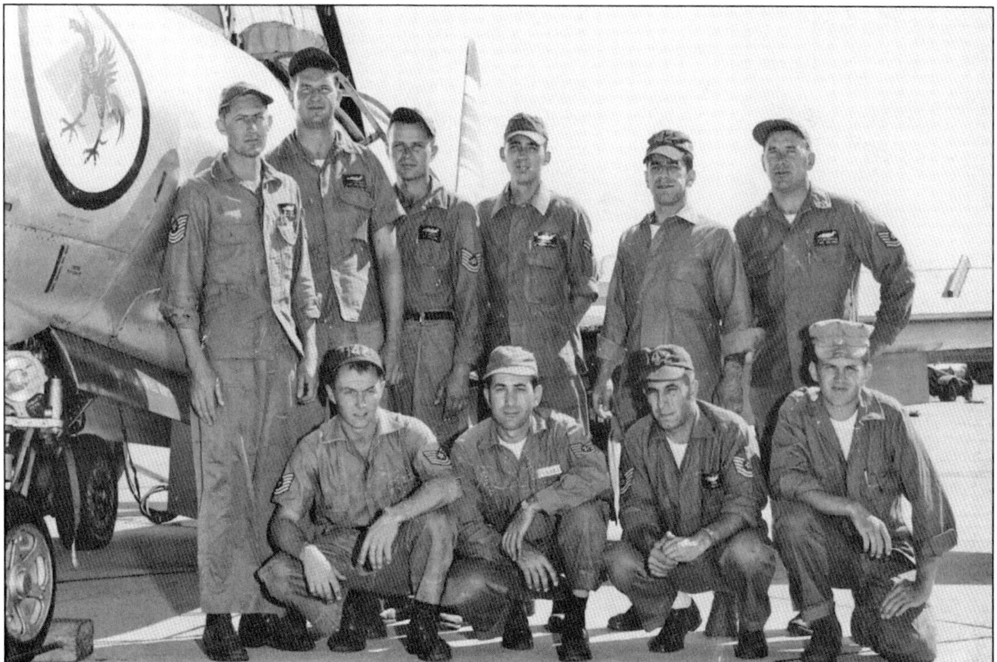

Next to a T-33 trainer are, from left to right, (kneeling) Bob Quigley, Al DiSabatino, Armand Piazza, and ? Eastburn; (standing) Vincent Riley, Jim Thompson, Ed Betley, unidentified, Ernie Piazza, and Don McGowan. (Courtesy of the Ed Blackburn collection.)

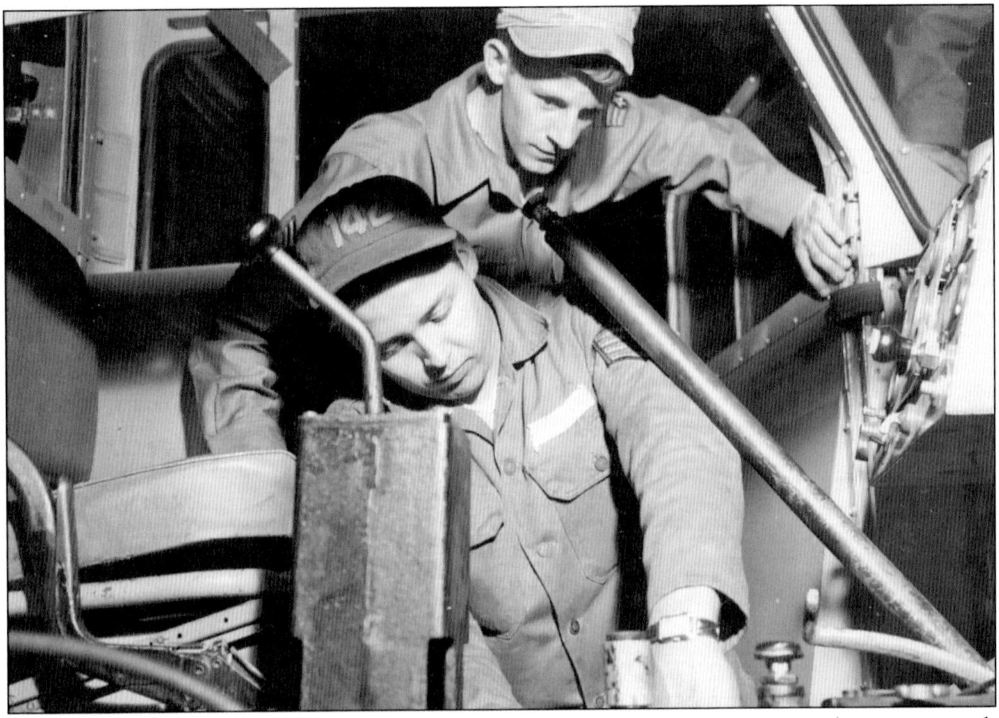

A1c. Allan Bowers (top) and an unidentified mechanic from the motor pool repair a truck transmission at New Castle County Airport around 1958. (Courtesy of the Delaware Military Heritage and Education Foundation.)

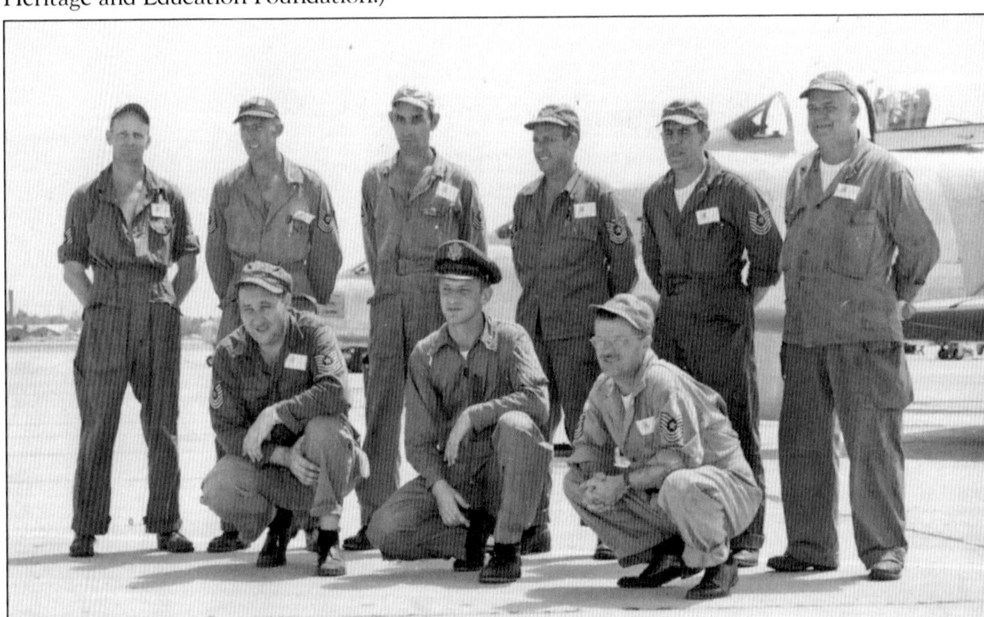

Included here in an official 142nd Fighter-Interceptor Squadron photograph, from left to right, are (kneeling) Albert Seidel, maintenance officer Bill Hutchison, and Larry Vieth; (standing) Jake Powell, Vince Riley, Bill Kelley, Jake Swan, Ralph Piazza, and Zeke Cooper. (Courtesy of the Ed Blackburn collection.)

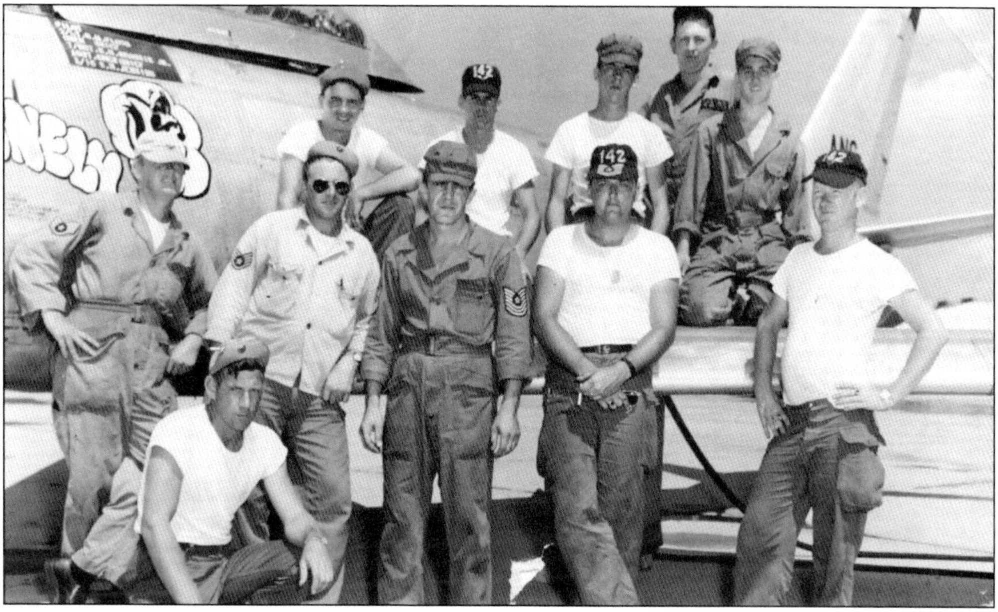

This official 142nd Fighter-Interceptor Squadron Maintenance Team photograph from the 1950s features, from left to right, (kneeling on the ground) Ron ?; (standing on the ground) unidentified, Jake Weber, Ralph Piazza, Bill Jackson, and Paul Shotwell; (kneeling on the wing) all unidentified; (standing on the wing) Newt Brackin. (Courtesy of the Ed Blackburn collection.)

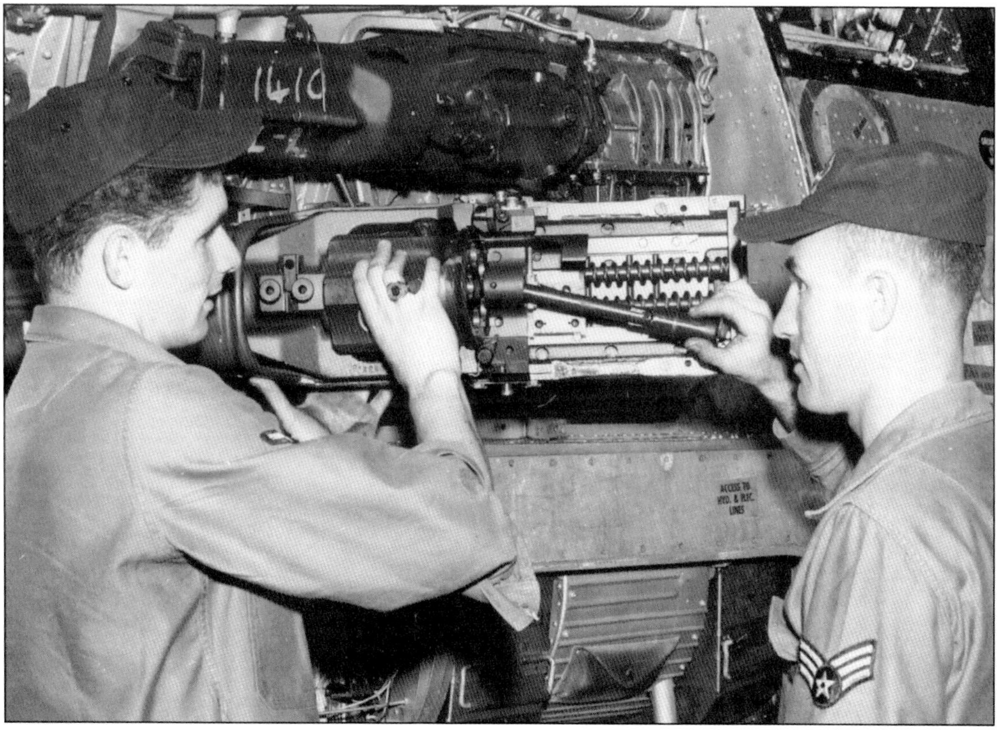

Armorers maintain the 20-mm cannon on an F-86H around 1958. An unidentified airman is on the left, and A1c. Joe Young is on the right. (Courtesy of the Delaware Military Heritage and Education Foundation.)

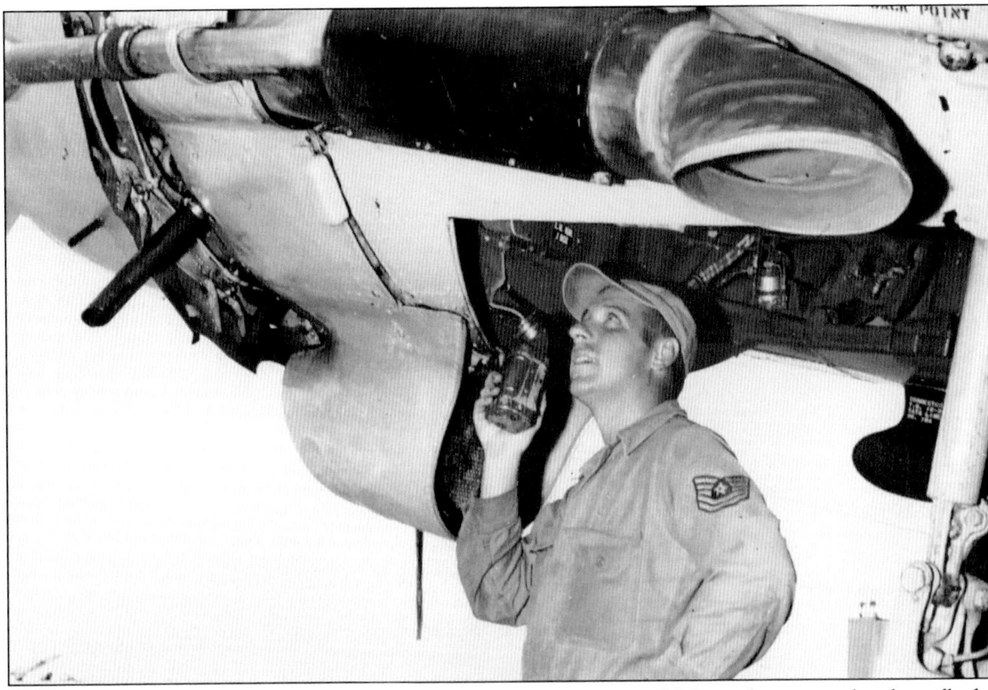

T.Sgt. Al Cucco inspects the engine of a C-47. Cucco would later become the first flight engineer on the unit's C-97 transports in 1961. (Courtesy of the Delaware Military Heritage and Education Foundation.)

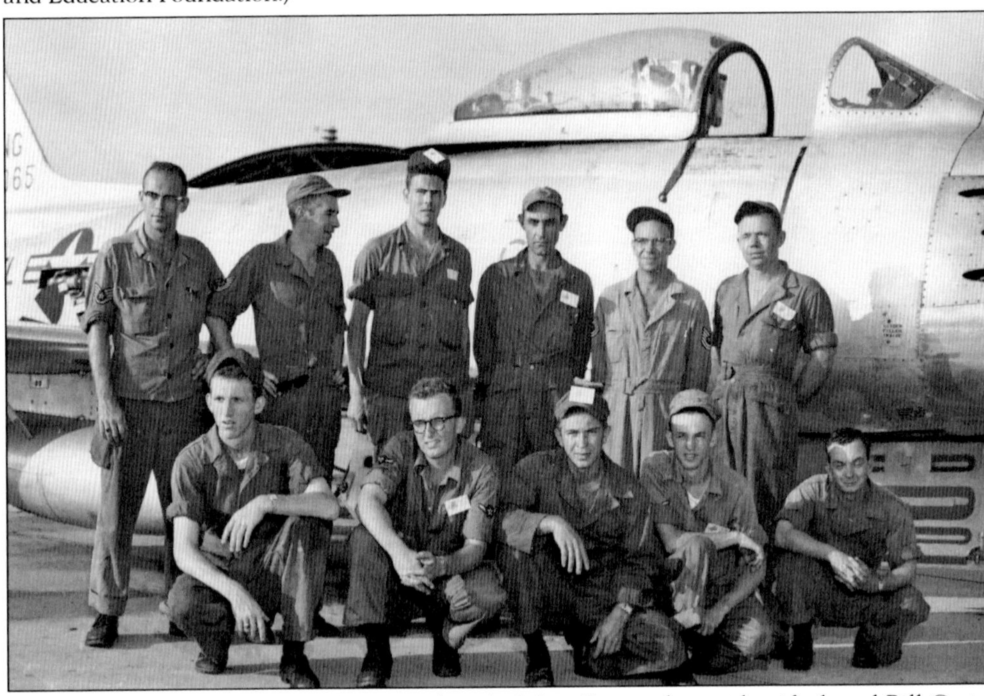

From left to right are (kneeling) two unidentified, Jim Gestwicki, unidentified, and Bill Craig; (standing) unidentified, Sid Powers, unidentified, Bill Kelley, Lou Godwin, and Joe Jenecke. (Courtesy of the Ed Blackburn collection.)

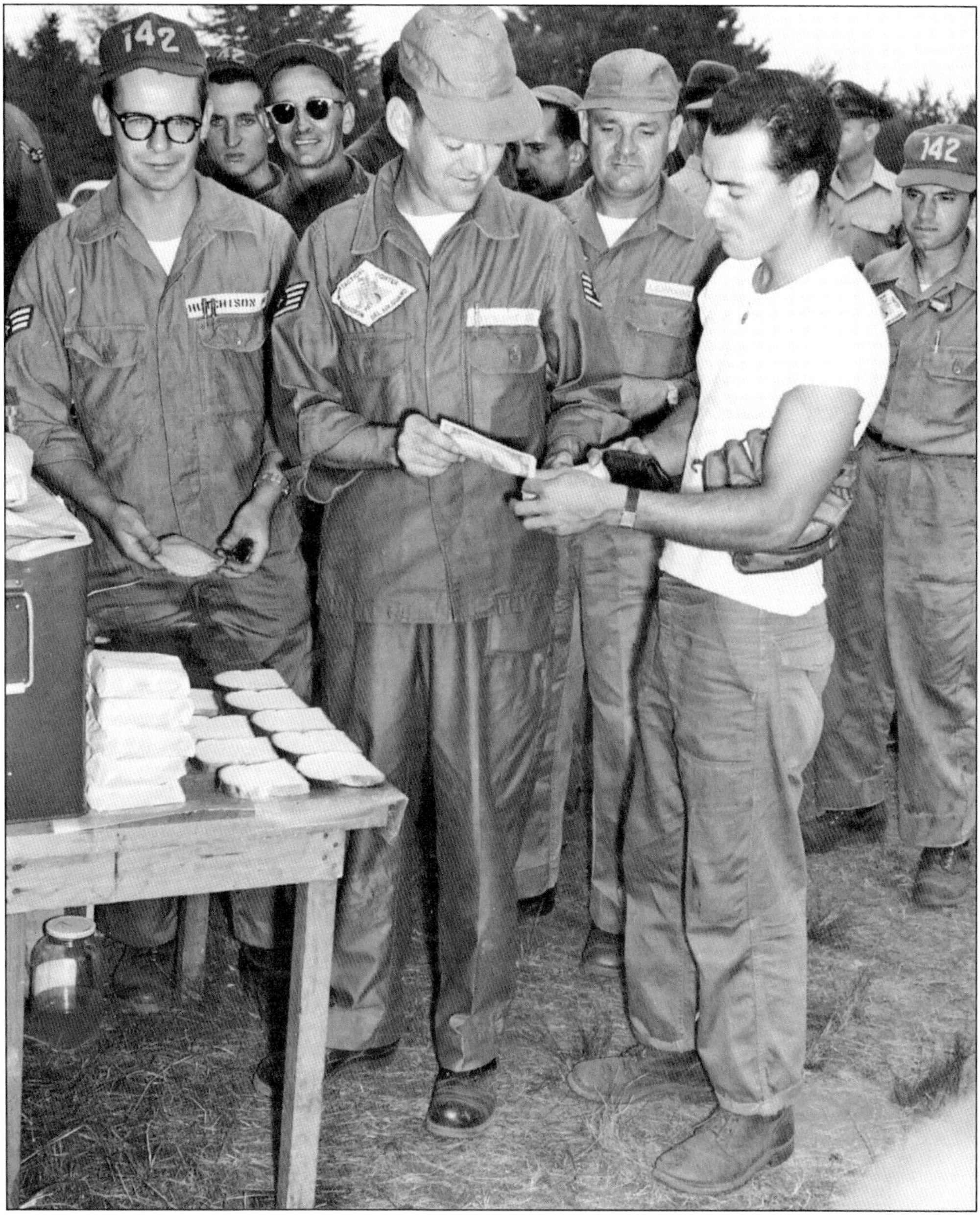

Queuing for lunch are, from left to right, Bob Hutchison, Larry Wiggins (in sunglasses), Glen Stewart, Bill Lenhart, and Tony Lepore. (Courtesy of the Delaware Military Heritage and Education Foundation.)

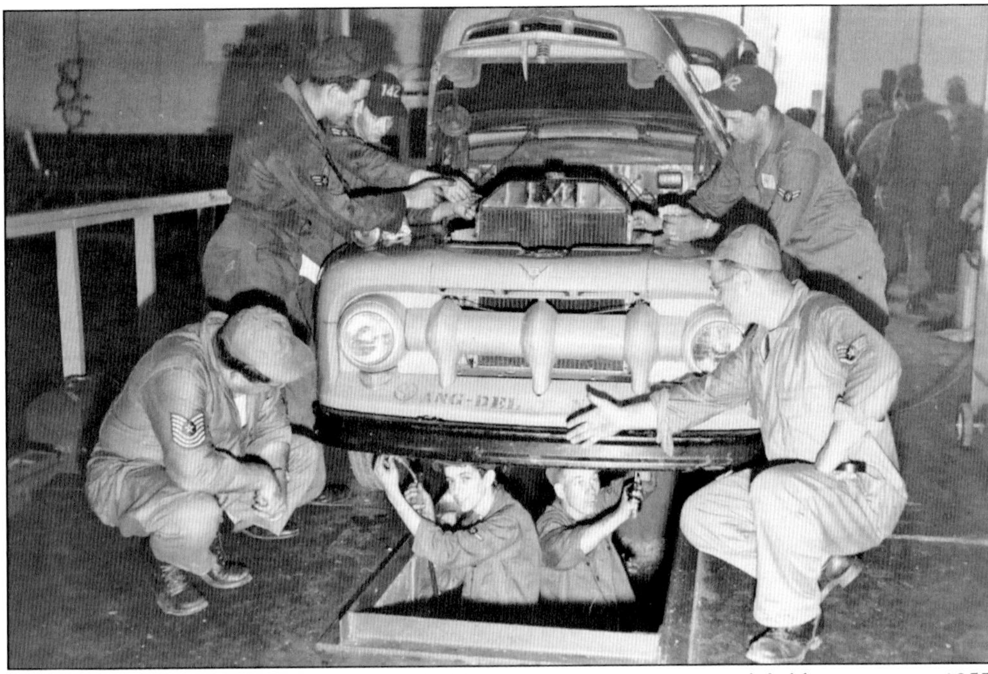

These motor pool mechanics pose at the Savannah, Georgia, annual field training in 1955. From left to right are William Baker, William "Andy" Andreavich, Peter Gorgi, Joe Manion, David Goddall, and two unidentified airmen in the pit. (Courtesy of the Delaware Military Heritage and Education Foundation.)

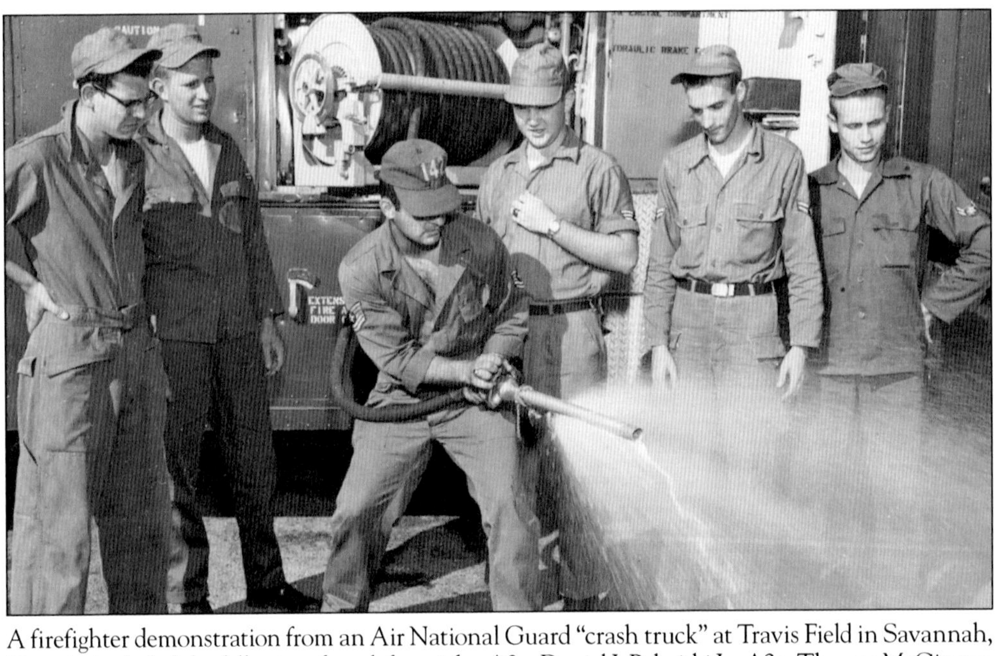

A firefighter demonstration from an Air National Guard "crash truck" at Travis Field in Savannah, Georgia, included the following: from left to right, A2c. Daniel J. Pokoiski Jr., A2c. Thomas McGinnes, A1c. Samuel Newell, T.Sgt. Paul Perrone (holding hose), A2c. William N. Carroll, and A1c. Richard McDaniel. (Courtesy of the Delaware Military Heritage and Education Foundation.)

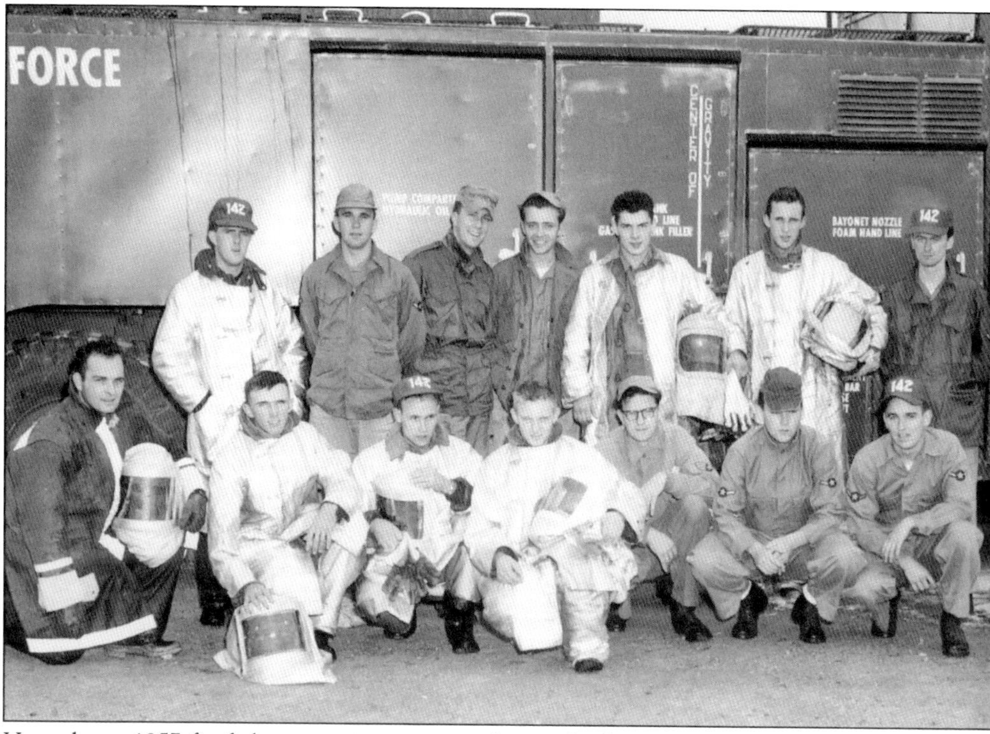

Here the *c.* 1957 firefighters section poses in front of a fire truck. (Courtesy of the Delaware Military Heritage and Education Foundation.)

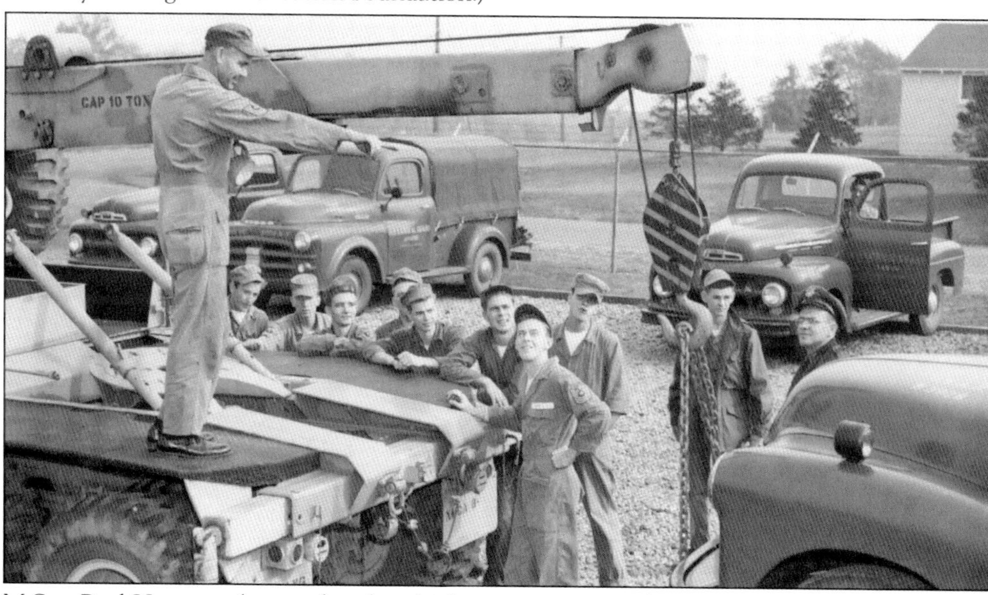

M.Sgt. Paul Henretty (center, hand on hip) supervises a wrecker among members of the motor pool. Henretty was later to become support squadron commander, retiring at the grade of lieutenant colonel. From left to right are Doug Sheldon (on wrecker), Dick DuVaul, Bob Shumate, Edwin Pickhaver, Wayne Henretty, Richard Garvey, Jim Blake, Richard Rutter, Paul Henretty, Raymond Thompson, John Carroll, and Don Williams. (Courtesy of the Delaware Military Heritage and Education Foundation.)

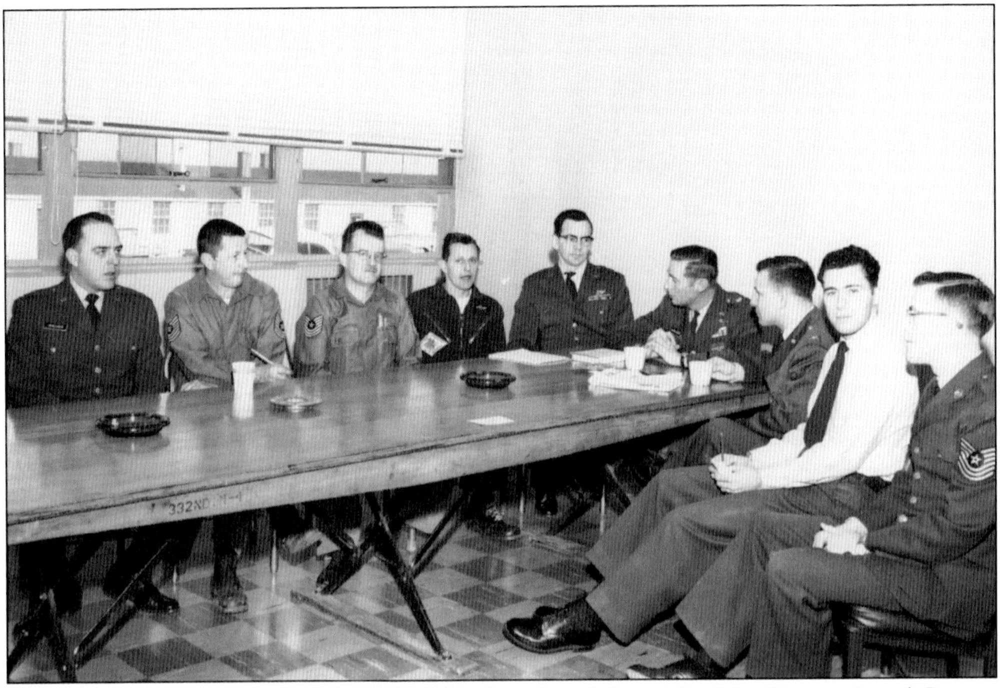

The staff of the base newspaper, the *DANG Truth*, is, from left to right, John Shearer, Joseph Beatty, Lawrence Vieth, Walt Hannum, John Carroll, David McCallister, Thomas Morelli, Gary Tatman, and Paul Henretty. (Courtesy of the Delaware Military Heritage and Education Foundation.)

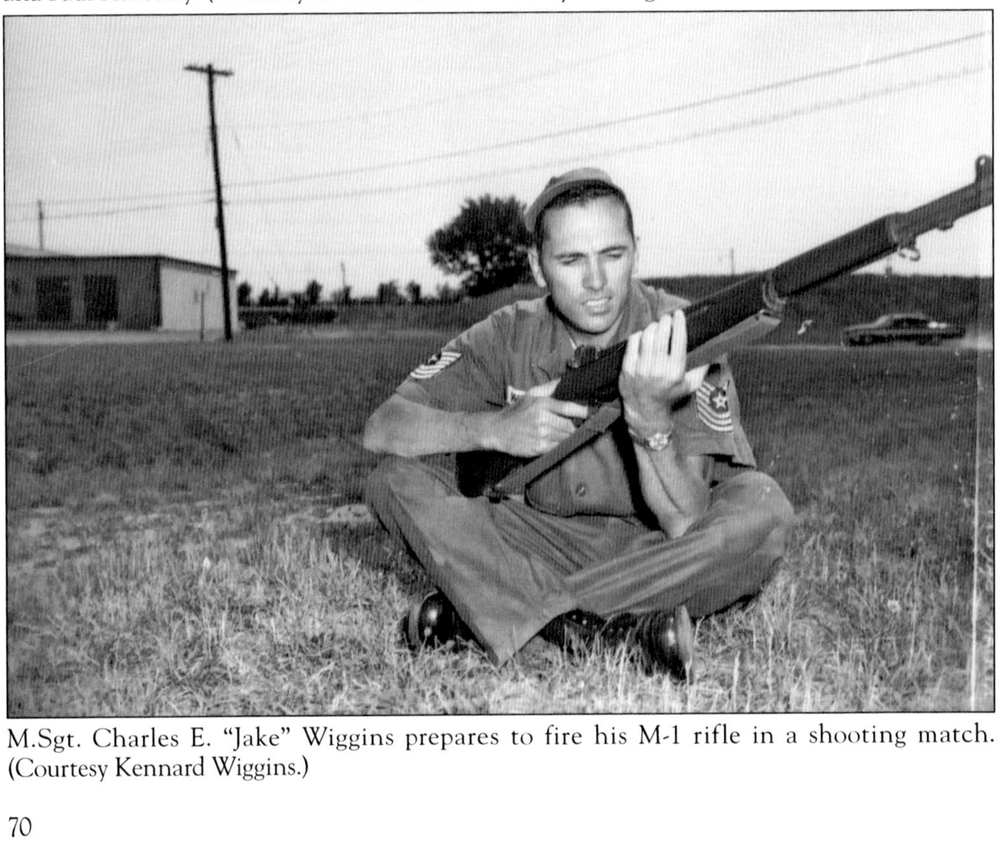

M.Sgt. Charles E. "Jake" Wiggins prepares to fire his M-1 rifle in a shooting match. (Courtesy Kennard Wiggins.)

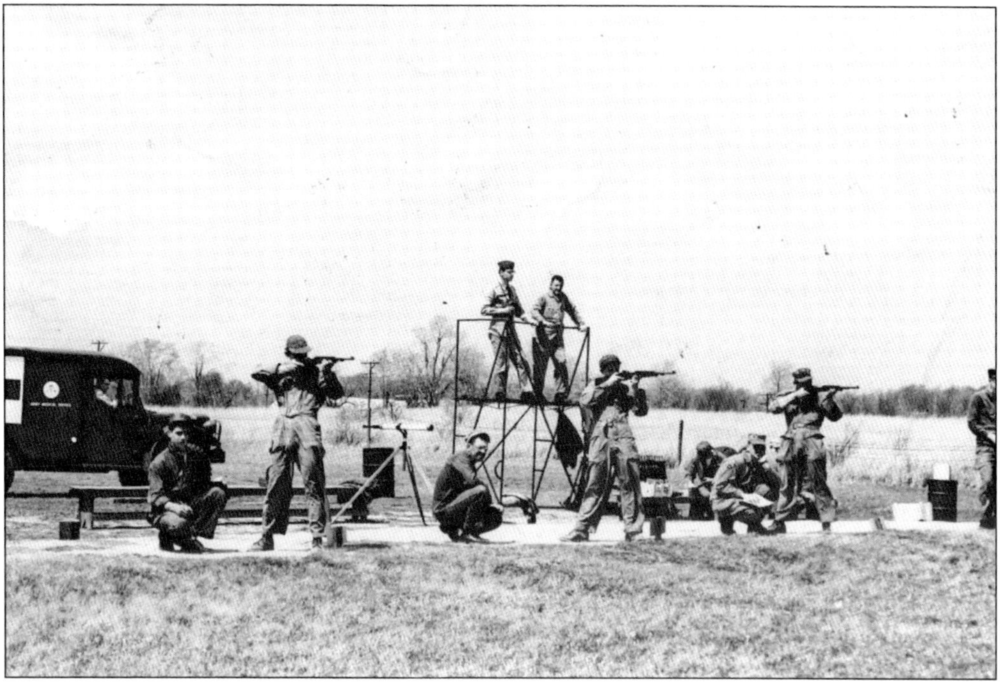

"The Great Turkey Shoot of 1956" is written on this photograph of the rifle range on River Road south of New Castle, where Delaware Air Guardsmen qualified on weapons. (Courtesy of the Delaware Military Heritage and Education Foundation.)

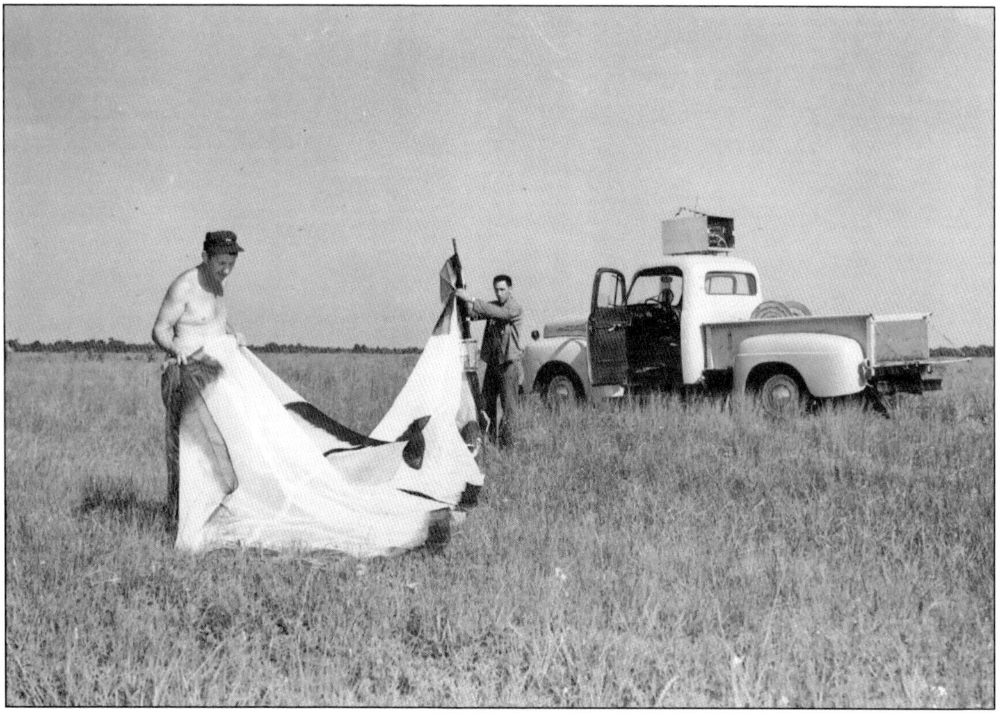

A shirtless Joe Beatty and his unidentified helper retrieve a towed target used in aerial gunnery practice. (Courtesy of the Delaware Military Heritage and Education Foundation.)

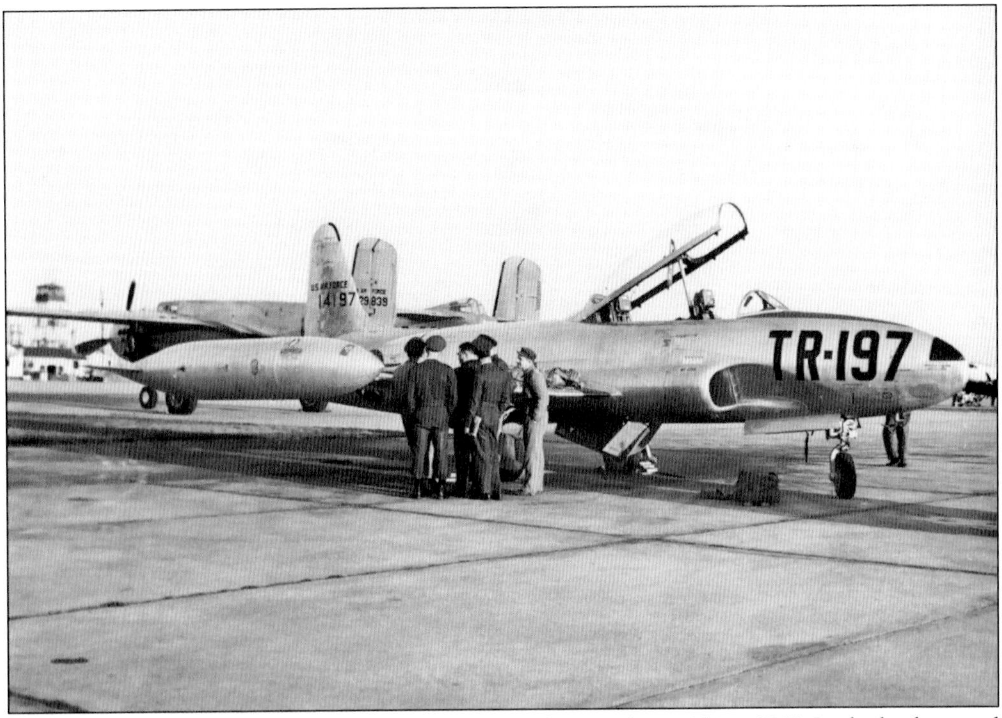

This T-33A jet trainer was used to maintain flying proficiency from 1954 to 1962. In the background is a B-25 bomber. (Courtesy of the Delaware Military Heritage and Education Foundation.)

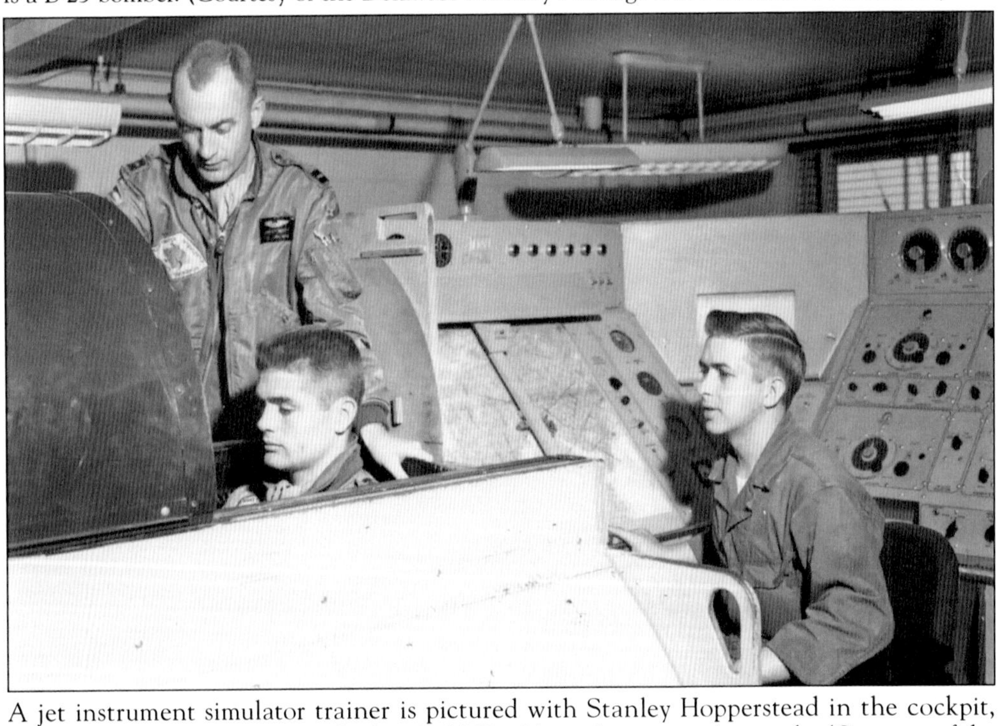

A jet instrument simulator trainer is pictured with Stanley Hopperstead in the cockpit, James P. Scott II looking on, and John "Jack" Kunkle at the operator's console. (Courtesy of the Delaware Military Heritage and Education Foundation.)

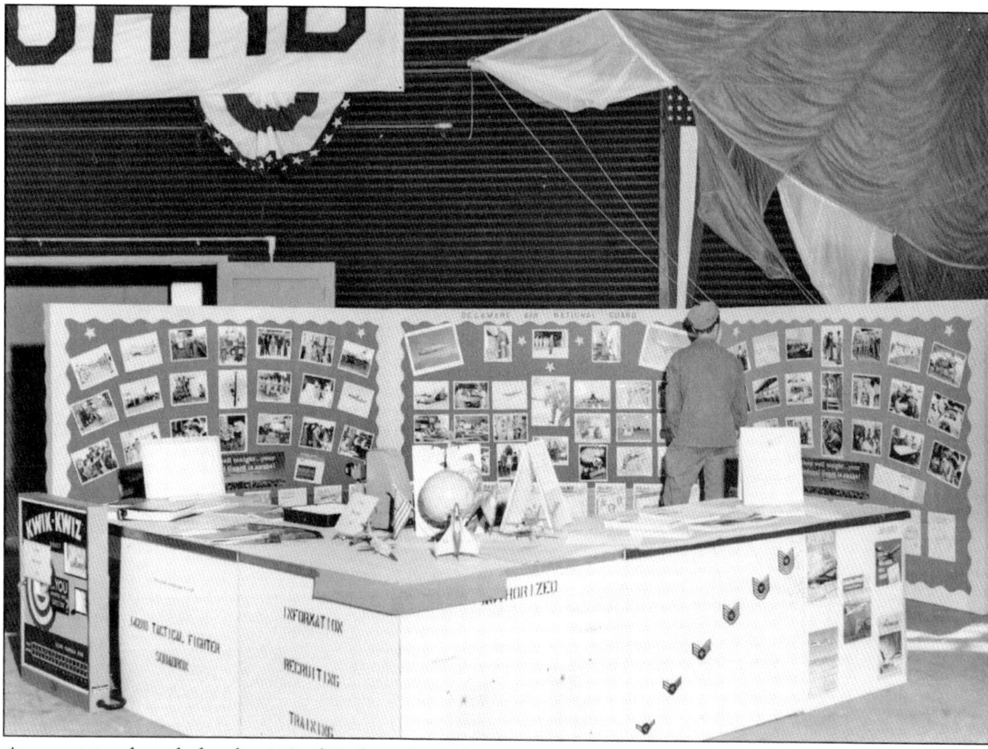

A recruiting booth for the 142nd Fighter Squadron from the late 1950s was set up in the main hangar during an open house event. One can just make out an old popular slogan, "Sleep well tonight . . . Your Air National Guard is Awake!" Recruiting was critical, as the unit had to rebuild itself after the Korean War. This recruiting display provided information to prospects for the 142nd Tactical Fighter Squadron. (Courtesy of the Delaware Military Heritage and Education Foundation.)

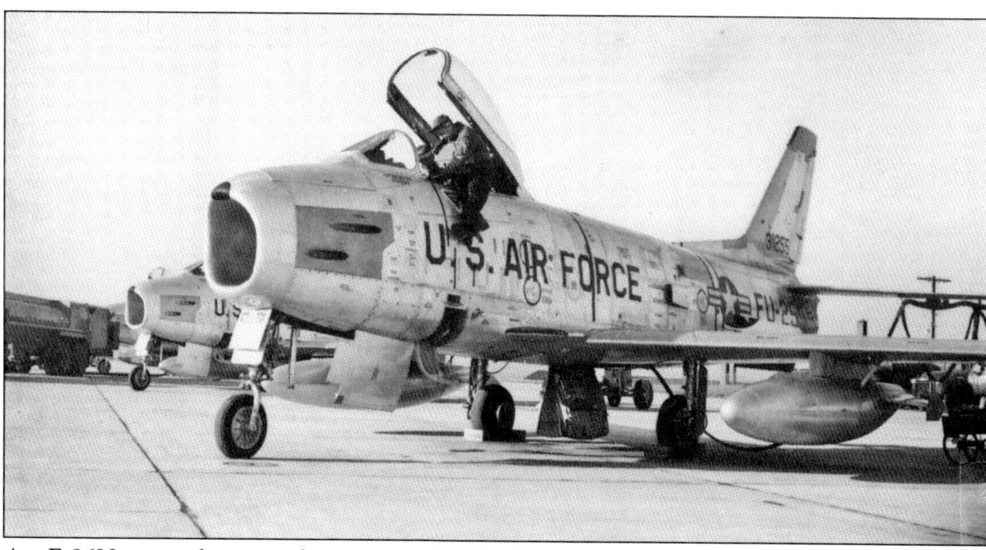

An F-86H is newly arrived in U.S. Air Force (compared to Air Guard) markings. This airplane was the mount of pilot Walt Hannum. (Courtesy of the Delaware Military Heritage and Education Foundation.)

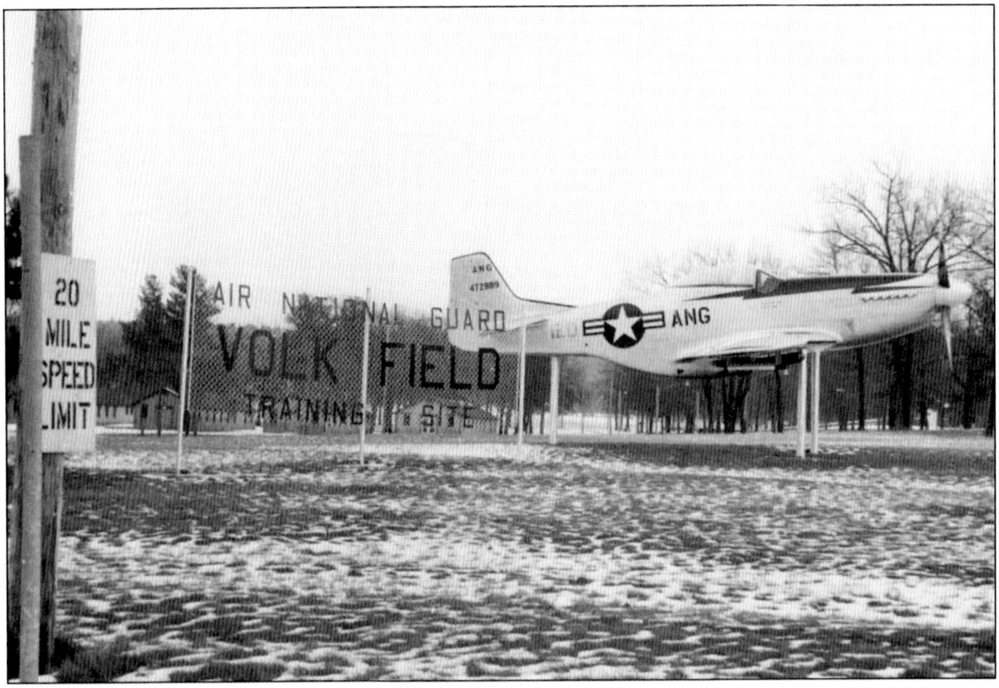

Volk Field, Wisconsin, an Air National Guard training site for encampments, has a P-51 Mustang mounted on a pylon as "gate guard." The Delaware Air Guard deployed here for annual field training. (Courtesy of the Delaware Military Heritage and Education Foundation.)

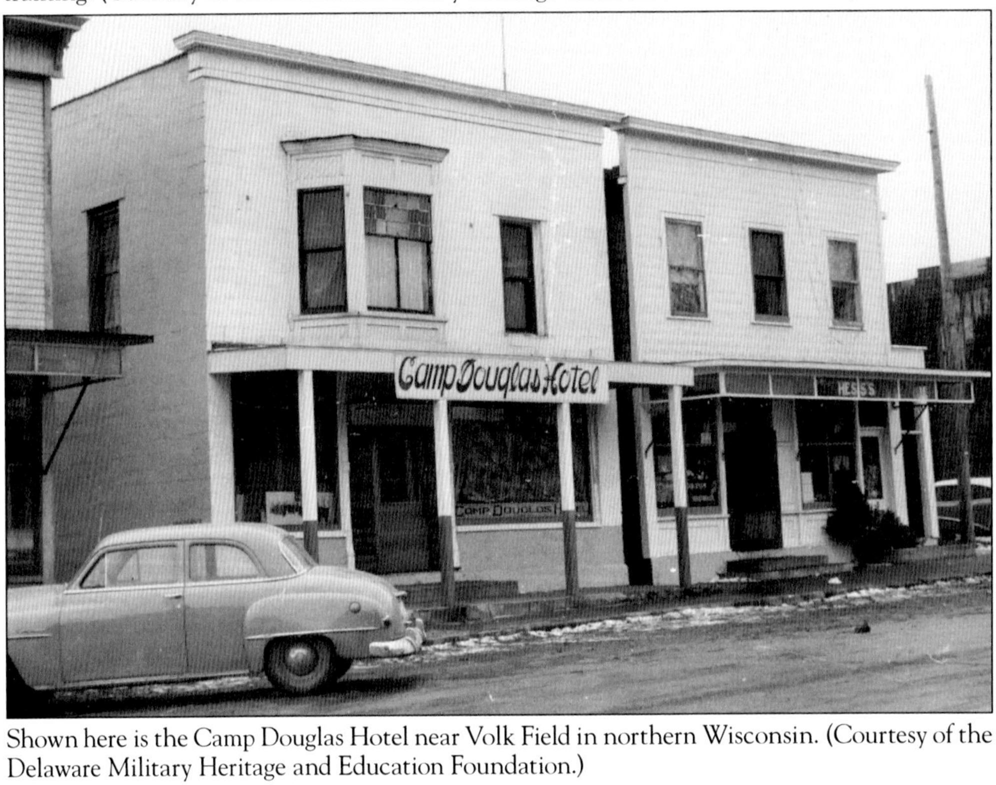

Shown here is the Camp Douglas Hotel near Volk Field in northern Wisconsin. (Courtesy of the Delaware Military Heritage and Education Foundation.)

A tongue-in-cheek descriptive sign is shown for the 142nd Air Police Section. (Courtesy of the Delaware Military Heritage and Education Foundation.)

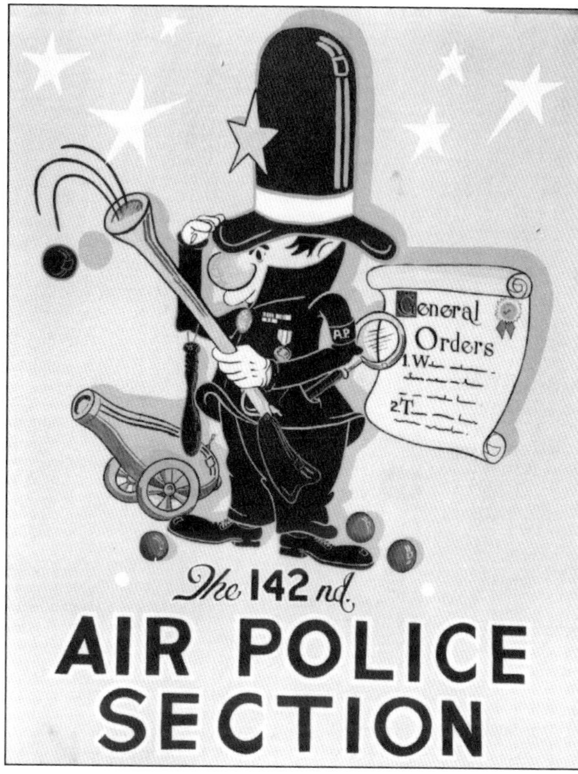

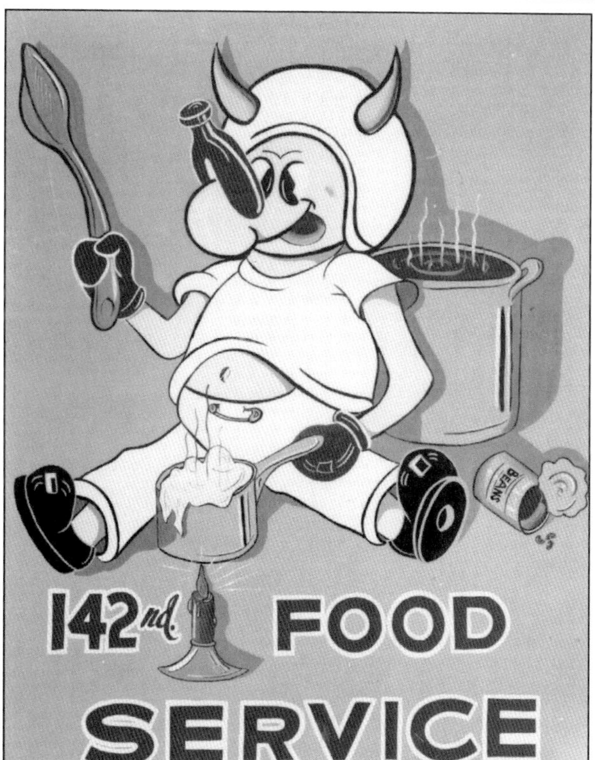

The sign for the dining hall was emblematic of the GI food and service available around 1958. (Courtesy of the Delaware Military Heritage and Education Foundation.)

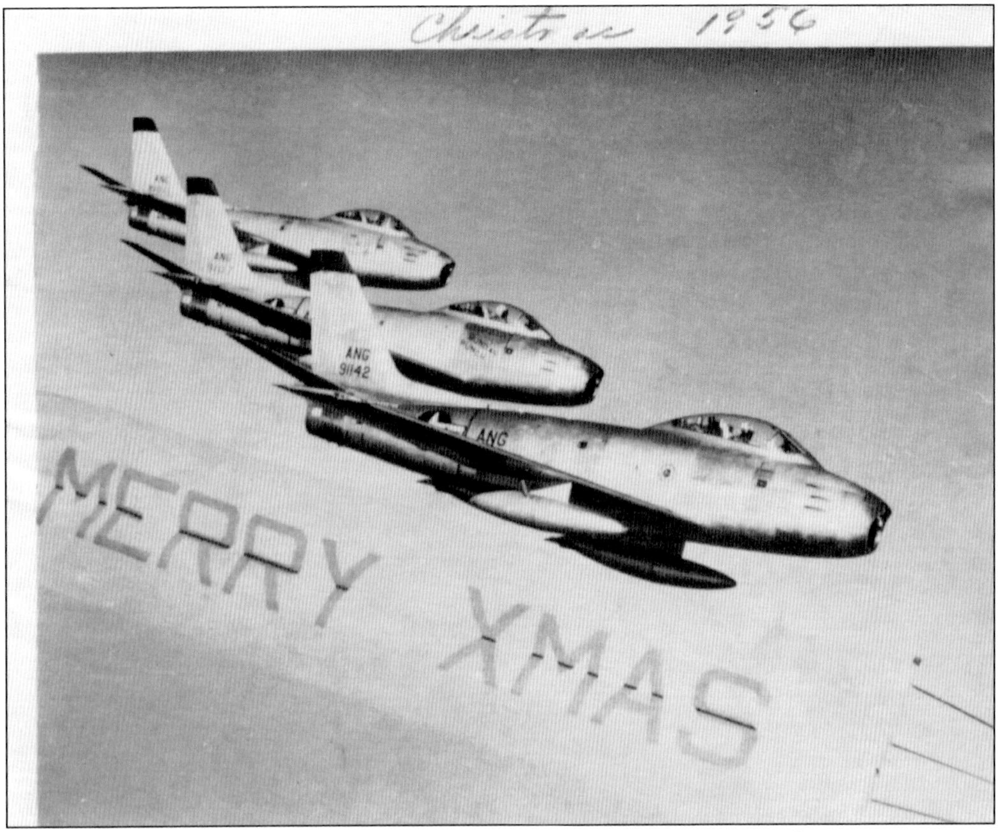

The inside of a unit Christmas card in 1956 reads, "Merry Christmas and Happy New Year, Personnel of the 142nd Fighter Interceptor Squadron, Delaware Air National Guard." (Courtesy of the Delaware Military Heritage and Education Foundation.)

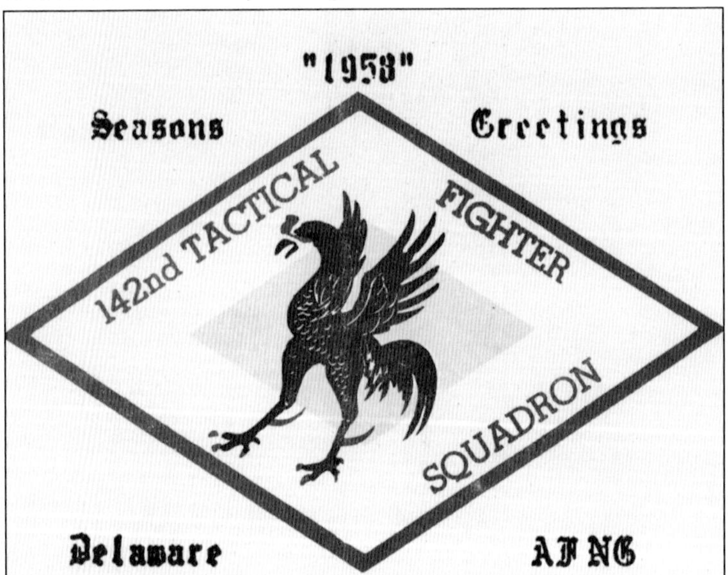

"Seasons Greetings" from the 142nd Tactical Fighter Squadron. This 1958 card is signed inside by squadron commander David McCallister on behalf of the squadron. (Courtesy of the Delaware Military Heritage and Education Foundation.)

A Merry Christmas postcard features Lieutenant Colonel McCallister's F-86H. (Courtesy of the Delaware Military Heritage and Education Foundation.)

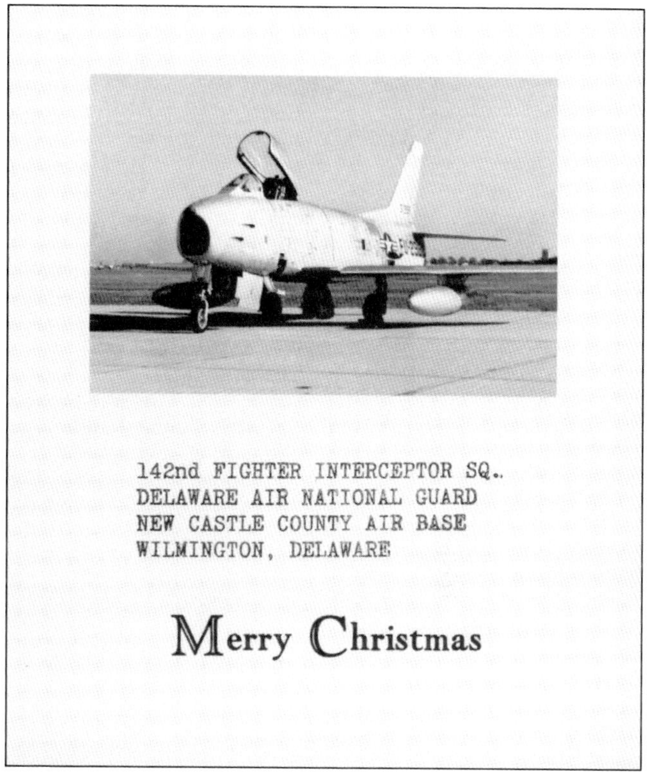

This is a Christmas 1955 card. The inside reads, "Seasons Greetings from the 142nd Fighter Interceptor Squadron." (Courtesy of the Delaware Military Heritage and Education Foundation.)

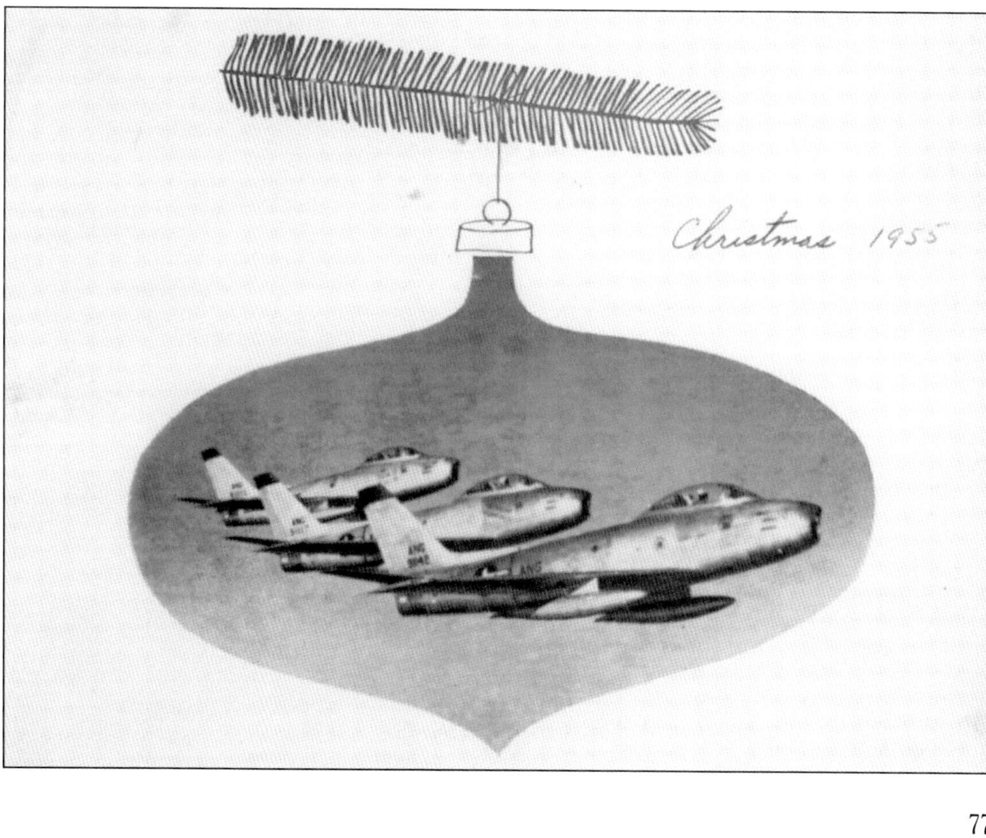

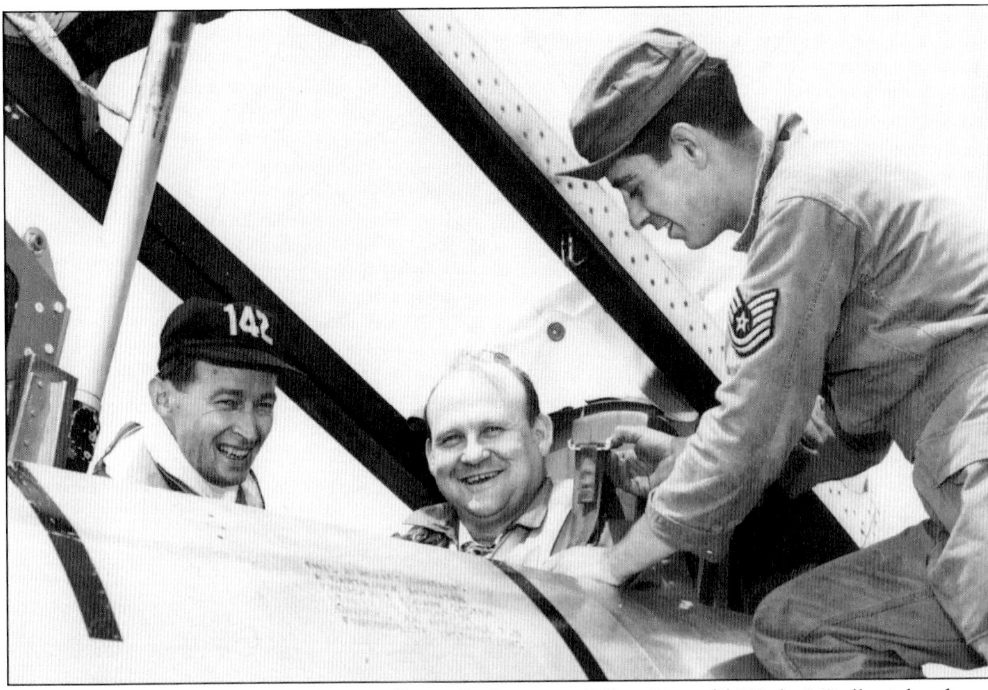

A smiling pilot, Lt. Col. David McCallister, looks on as T.Sgt. Donald "Gabe" Galbraith adjusts safety straps on Lt. Gov. John Rollins for an orientation in the T-33 cockpit around 1960. (Courtesy of the Delaware Military Heritage and Education Foundation.)

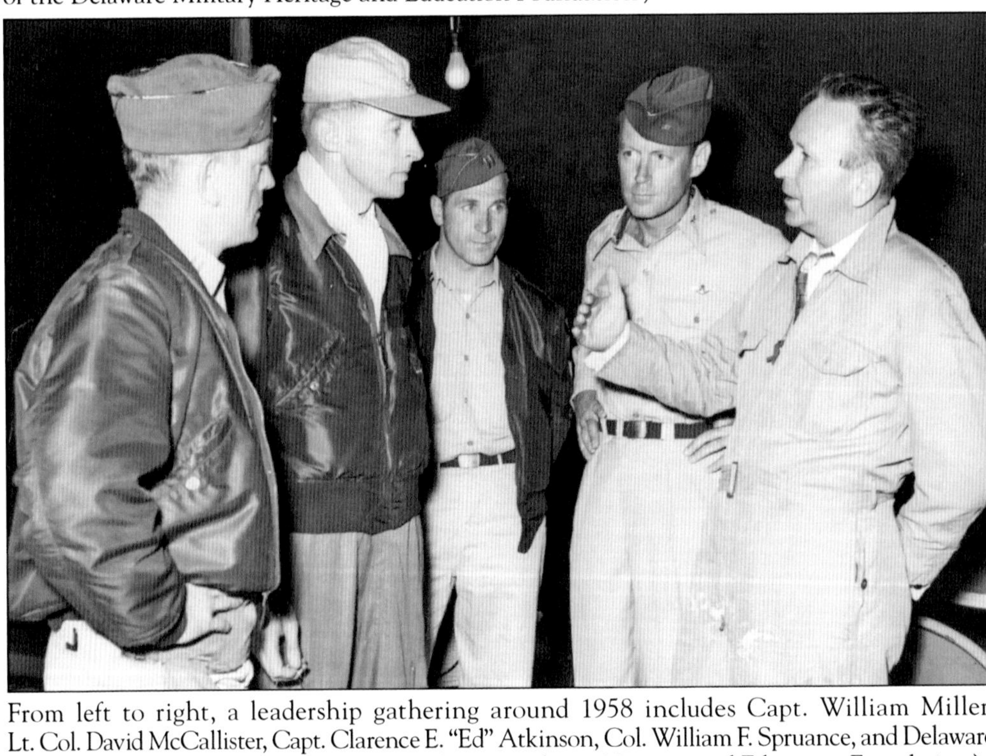

From left to right, a leadership gathering around 1958 includes Capt. William Miller, Lt. Col. David McCallister, Capt. Clarence E. "Ed" Atkinson, Col. William F. Spruance, and Delaware governor Caleb Boggs. (Courtesy of the Delaware Military Heritage and Education Foundation.)

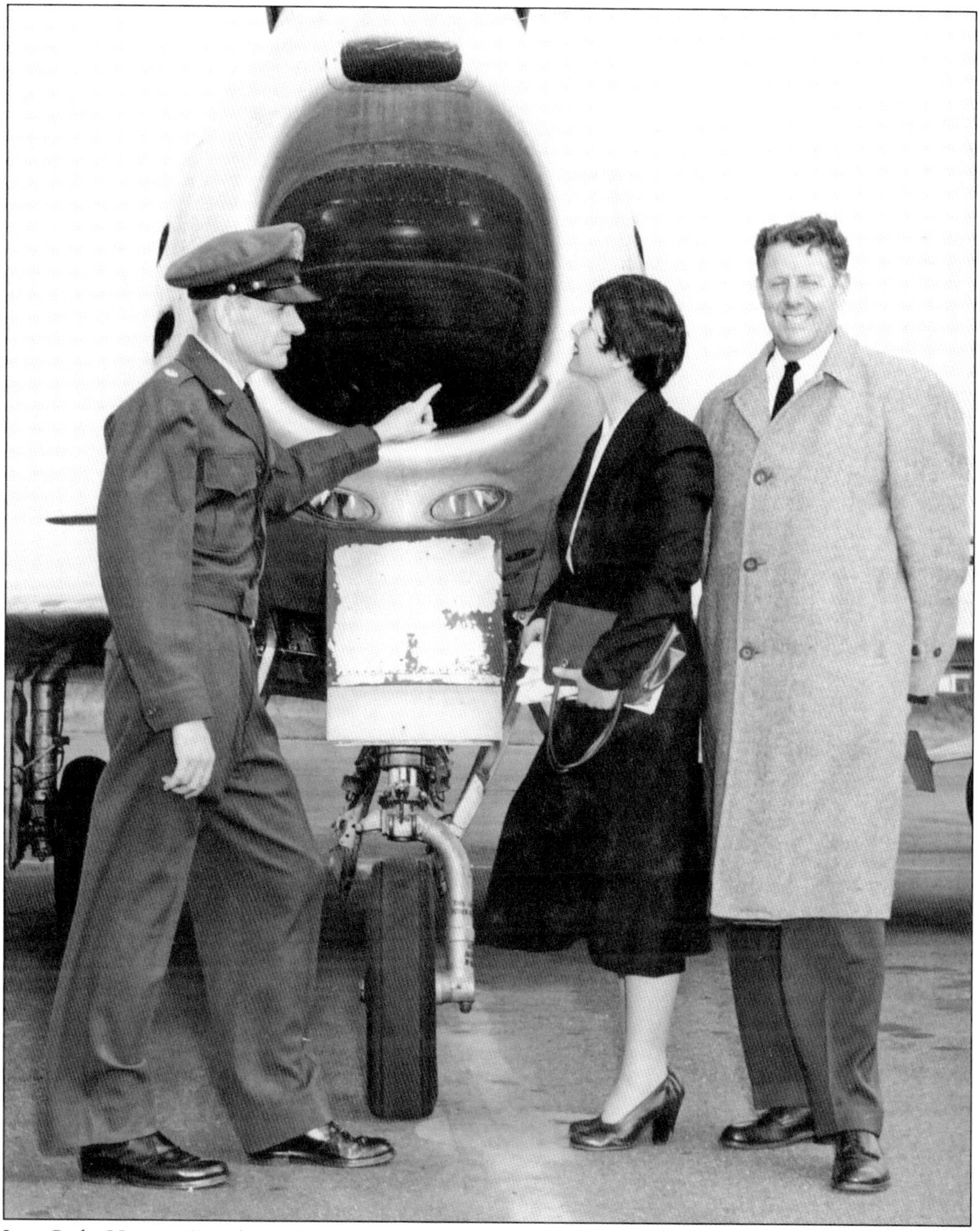

Lt. Col. Harry Staulcup demonstrates features of the F-86H around 1960 for state legislators Meg Manning and Rudy Williams. (Courtesy of the Delaware Military Heritage and Education Foundation.)

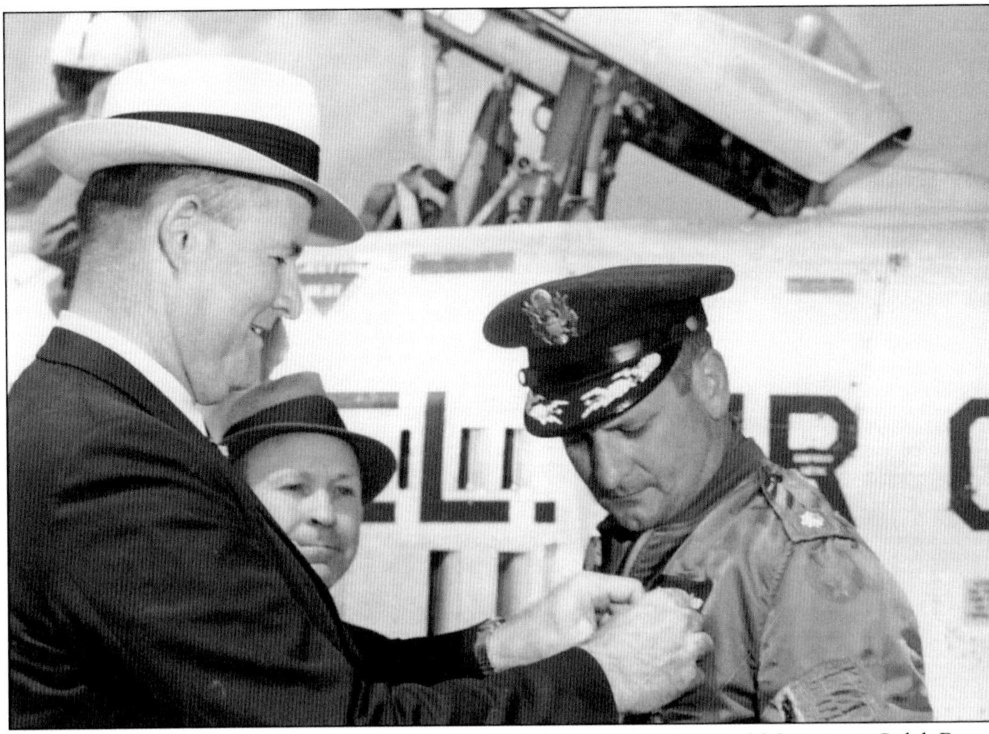

Around 1962, Gov. Elbert Carvel pins a device on Lt. Col. Ed Atkinson as U.S. senator Caleb Boggs (center) observes. (Courtesy of the Delaware Military Heritage and Education Foundation.)

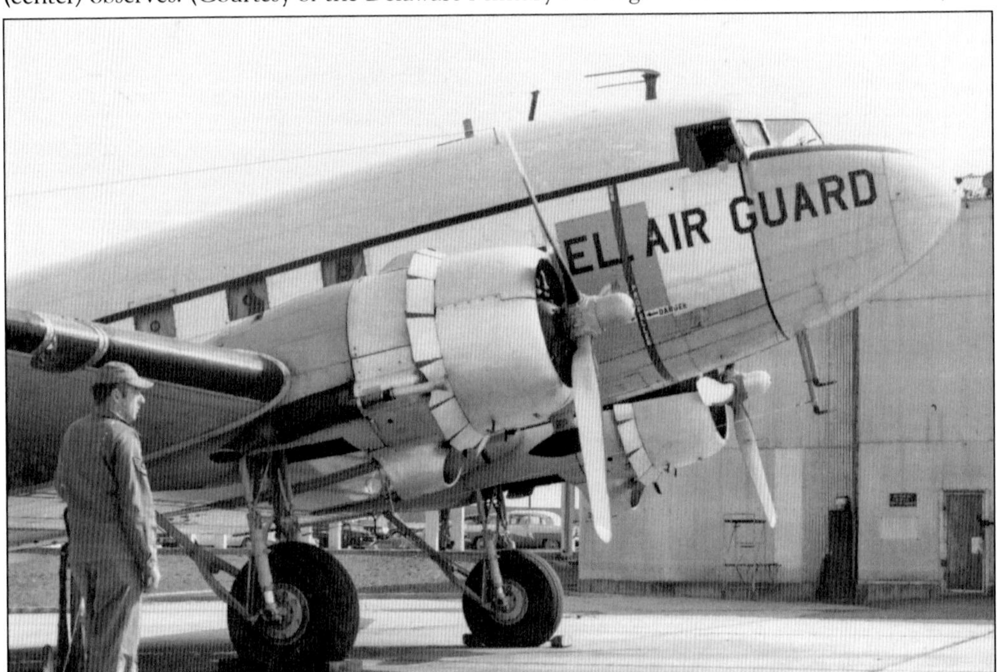

A C-47 transport perches with a painted "international orange" nose during the final days of the fighter mission. (Courtesy of the Delaware Military Heritage and Education Foundation.)

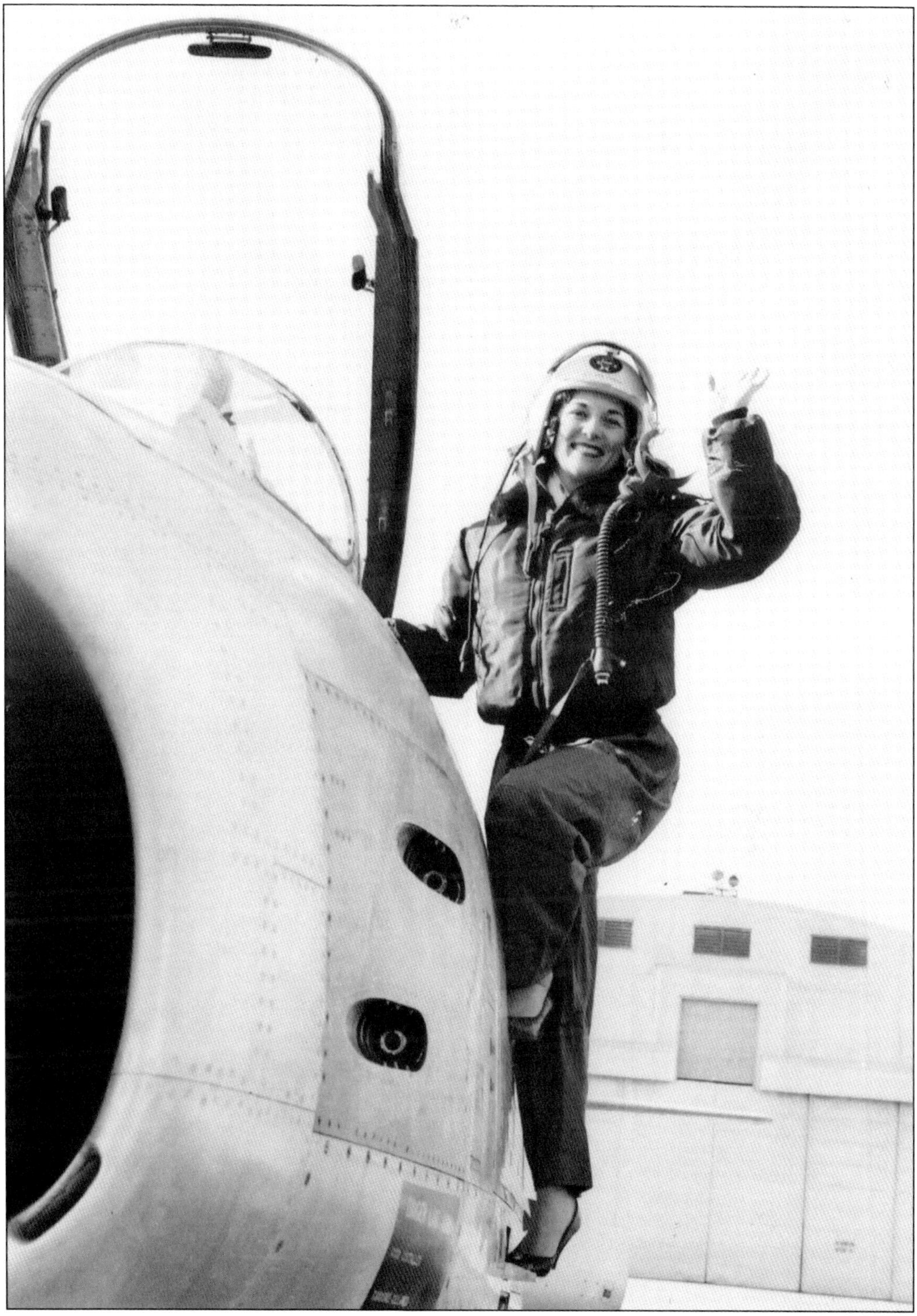

Playboy bunny and Delaware's Miss Universe contestant Michelle Voyer suits up and poses on a Delaware Air National Guard F-86 in 1973. (Courtesy of the Delaware Military Heritage and Education Foundation.)

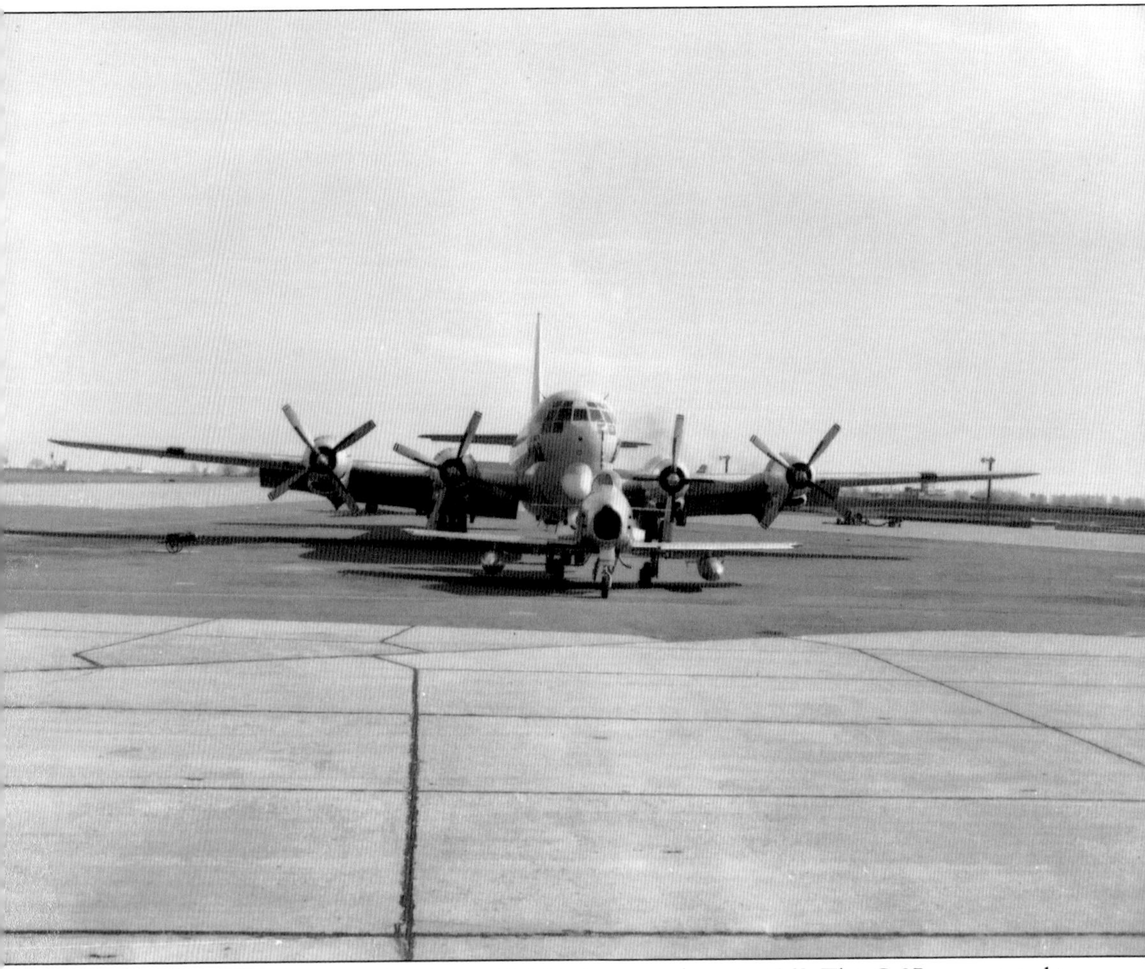

A C-97G in the background dwarfs the F-86H fighter it replaces in 1962. This C-97 was painted in a high-visibility livery with a bright "international orange" nose and a stripe on the tail. (Courtesy of the Delaware Military Heritage and Education Foundation.)

Four

STRATEGIC AIRLIFT

In March 1962, Lt. Colonel Clarence E. Atkinson was named commander of the 142nd Tactical Fighter Squadron. On April 7, 1962, the Delaware Air National Guard enlarged to "group status" as the 166th Air Transport Group and was reassigned to the Military Air Transport Service. The Delaware Air National Guard gave up its F-86 jets for the C-97 Boeing Stratofreighter, a strategic airlift plane. The 166th managed to transition to the C-97 and reach C-1 full-readiness status a full 21 months ahead of schedule. They were presented the prestigious Spaatz Trophy for this remarkable achievement.

In June 1962, the unit flew its first trans-Atlantic mission for the Military Airlift Command to Rhein-Main Air Base, Germany.

On October 22, 1962, a new unit—142nd Aeromedical Evacuation Flight—was added to the Delaware Air National Guard. In December 1963, Blue Hen planes and crews airlifted Bob Hope and his USO Christmas show on a mission to the Mediterranean area. In September 1965, only three years after receiving the C-97, the Delaware Air National Guard was awarded the McCallister Trophy as the Air National Guard Outstanding Transport Unit. In April 1966, the unit was awarded the Outstanding Unit Trophy based on its impressive achievements and safety record. On June 16, 1966, another unit, 166th Communications Flight, was added to the Delaware Air National Guard.

In July 1967, Garnell Purcell became the first African American man to enlist in the Delaware Air Guard.

In its first large-scale state activation, on April 9, 1968, the Delaware Air National Guard was called to state duty to quell civil disturbance and violence in the city of Wilmington, Delaware.

In January 1969, Colonel Atkinson became the adjutant general for Delaware. On November 8, 1969, the 166th Civil Engineering Flight organized as a separate unit of the Delaware Air National Guard.

During the period from 1964 to 1974, the 166th flew airlift missions to Vietnam with increasing tempo. While the unit was not mobilized and remained a part-time organization of reservists, it contributed a significant portion of the mission (an estimated 65 percent) it would have been expected to perform had it been fully activated.

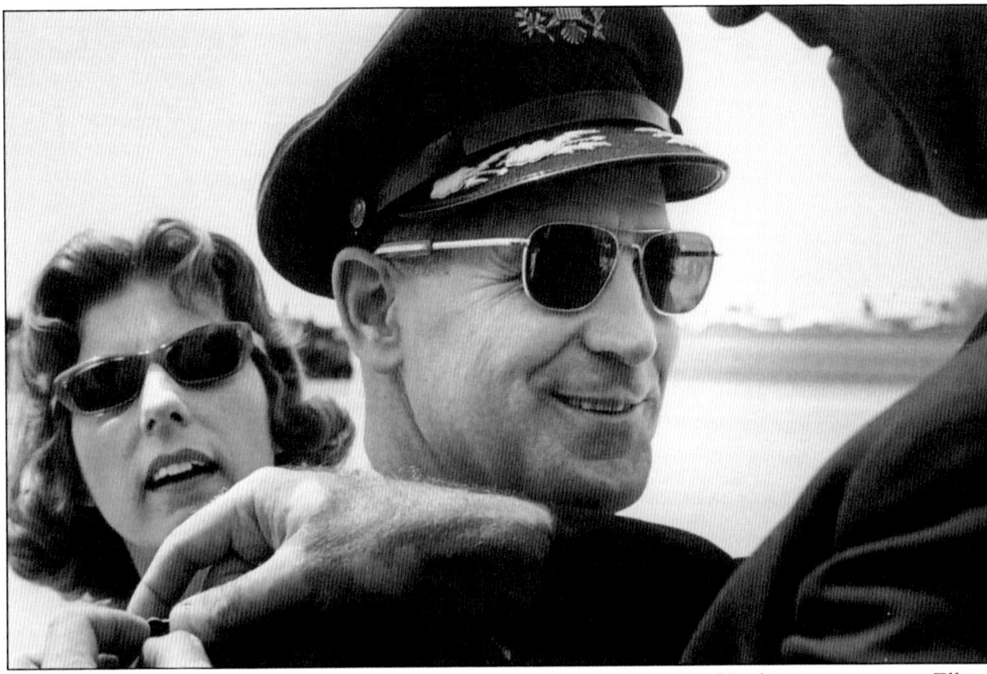

A pleased Colonel Atkinson receives his promotion at the hands of Delaware governor Elbert Carvel as his wife, Frances, looks on. In March 1962, Lt. Col. Clarence E. Atkinson was named commander of the 142nd Tactical Fighter Squadron. On April 7, 1962, the Delaware Air National Guard enlarged to "group status" as the 166th Air Transport Group and was reassigned from the Tactical Air Command to the Military Air Transport Service. (Courtesy of the Delaware Military Heritage and Education Foundation.)

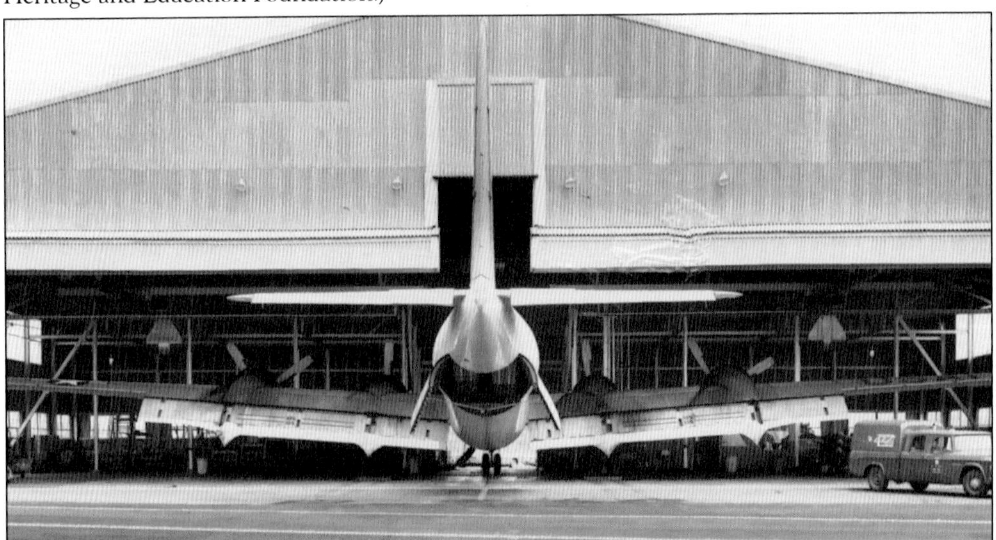

A ventral view shows the C-97, flaps down, demonstrating its clamshell cargo doors as it is parked in the "nose dock" hangar. The 166th managed to transition to the C-97 and reach C-1 full-readiness status 21 months ahead of schedule. They were presented the prestigious Spaatz Trophy for this remarkable achievement. (Courtesy of the Delaware Military Heritage and Education Foundation.)

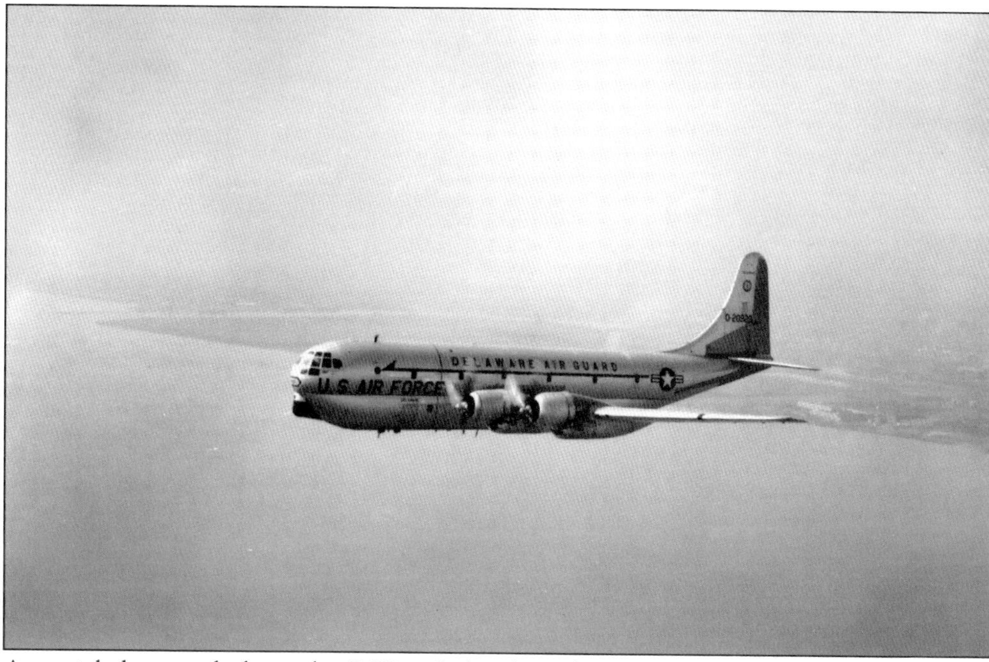

An aerial photograph shows the C-97 in flight. According to Roger Lambeth, during the shoot as a prank, the camera plane, piloted by Ernie Bossetti, passed the subject plane in a shallow dive with the two starboard engines (numbers 3 and 4) temporarily shut down. (Courtesy of the Delaware Military Heritage and Education Foundation.)

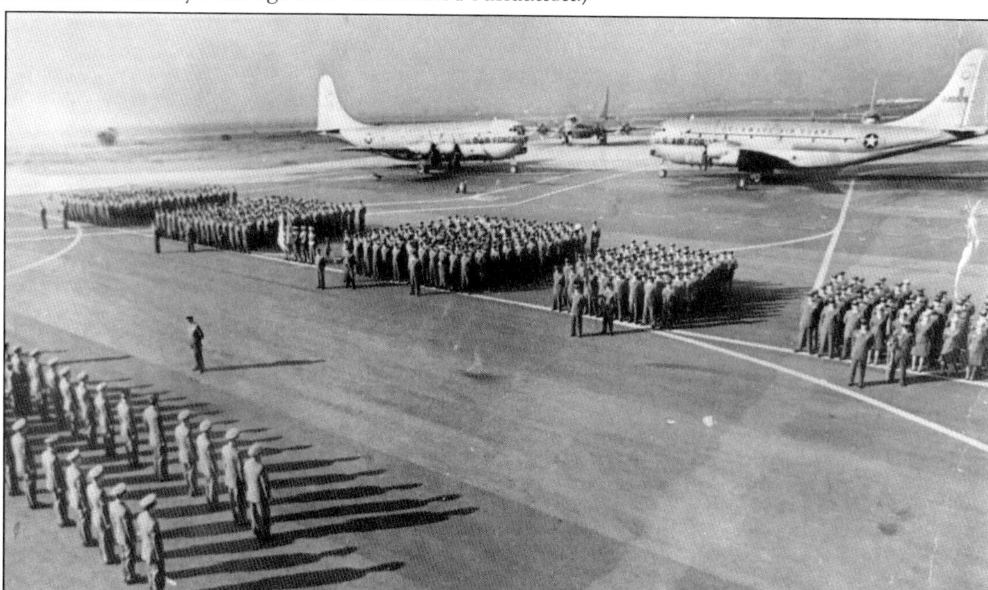

A formation and parade showcases the new airplane and the new strategic airlift mission of the Delaware Air National Guard. The Delaware Air National Guard gave up its F-86 jets for the four-engine C-97 Boeing Stratofreighter, a long-distance strategic airlift plane. The 166th Air Transport Group (Heavy) was enlarged to include the 166th Consolidated Aircraft Maintenance Squadron, the 166th Air Base Squadron, and the 166th USAF Dispensary. (Courtesy of the Delaware Military Heritage and Education Foundation.)

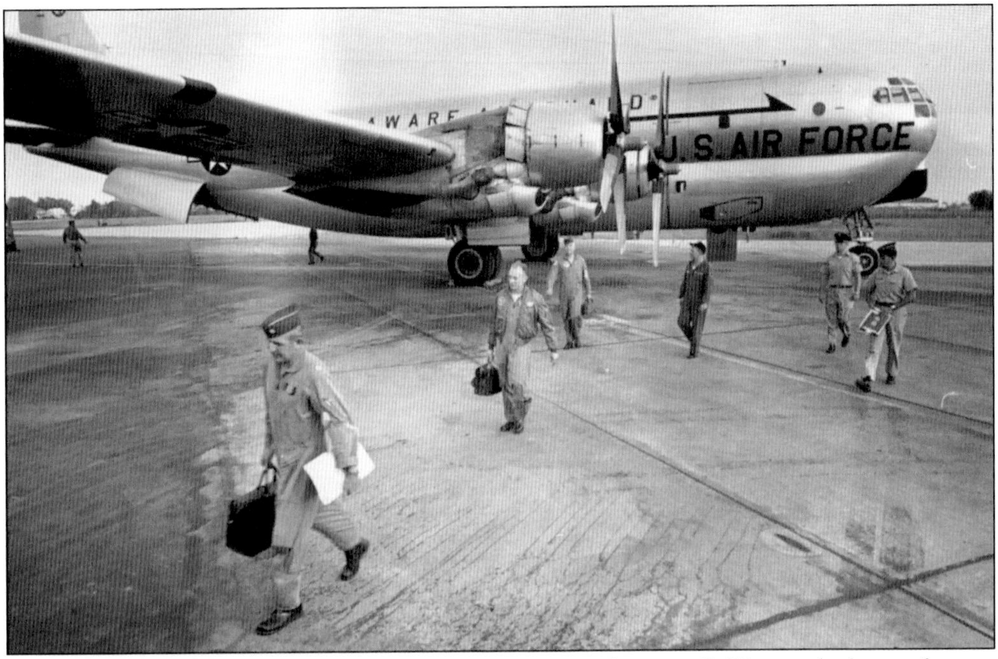

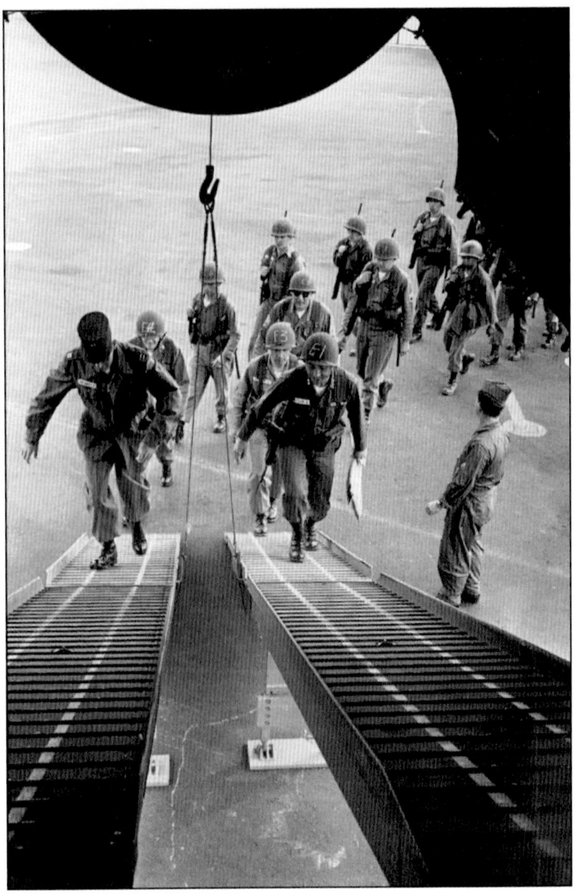

A weary C-97 crew deplanes after a mission led by Col. Charles Skinner, with Ernest Bossetti on the ramp at New Castle. A C-97 aircrew included a pilot, copilot, navigator, flight engineer, and loadmaster. This first significant shift in mission from fighter to transport allowed enlisted members to participate in the flying mission as engineers, loadmaster, crew chiefs, and aeromedical technicians. The mission also required additional officers, including flight nurses and navigators. (Courtesy of the Delaware Military Heritage and Education Foundation.)

U.S. Army troops board a C-97 through the rear clamshell doors. In December 1965, Operation Christmas Star took the Delaware ANG unit on its first cargo mission to Vietnam. Delaware ANG crews delivered gifts to the troops with regular flights continuing at the rate of four per month out of the total nationwide ANG pledge of 75 per month. (Courtesy of the Delaware Military Heritage and Education Foundation.)

Soldiers depart the C-97 "on the double" with their combat gear. (Courtesy of the Delaware Military Heritage and Education Foundation.)

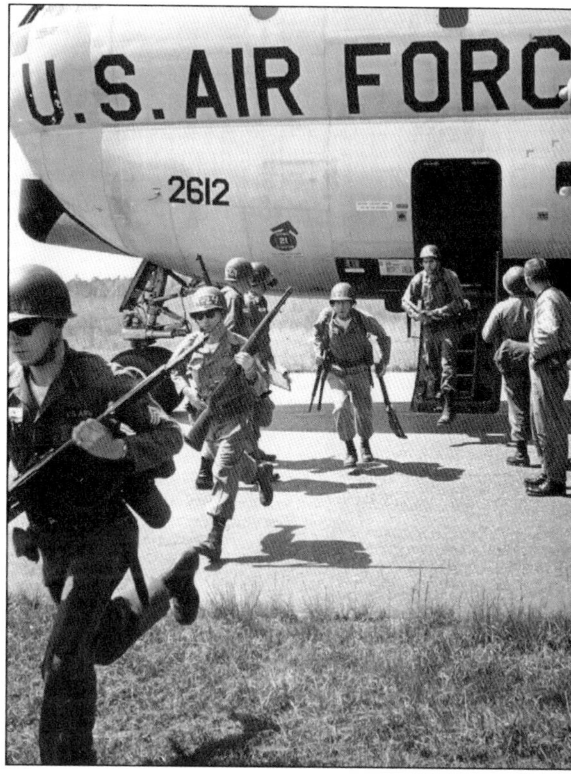

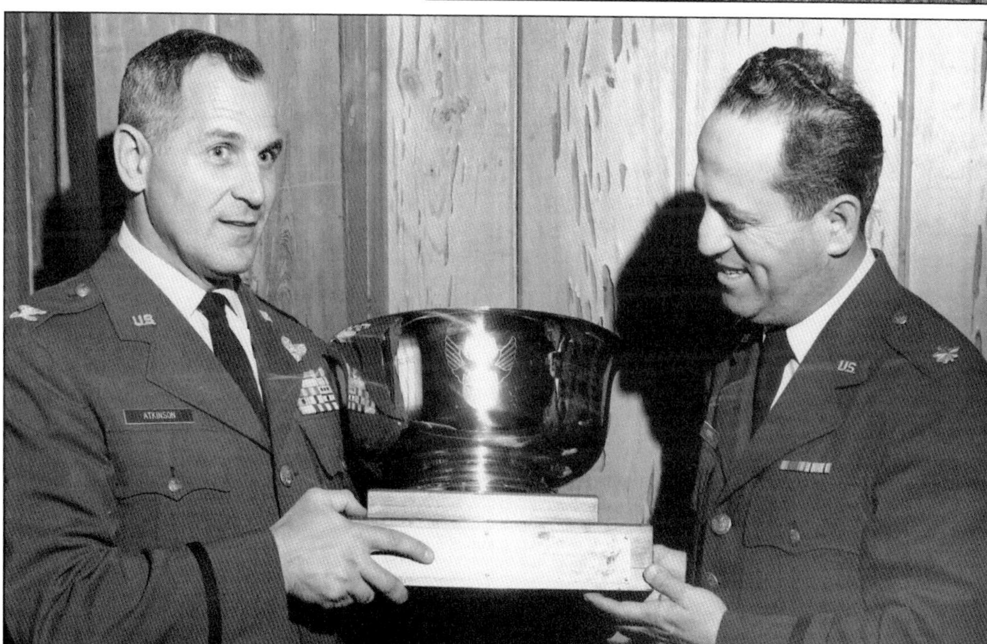

In April 1966, the unit was awarded the Outstanding Unit Trophy by the Air Force Association based on its impressive collection of achievements and its safety record. Air commander Colonel Atkinson (left) hefts the trophy with Lt. Col. Al Poppiti (right). (Courtesy of the Delaware Military Heritage and Education Foundation.)

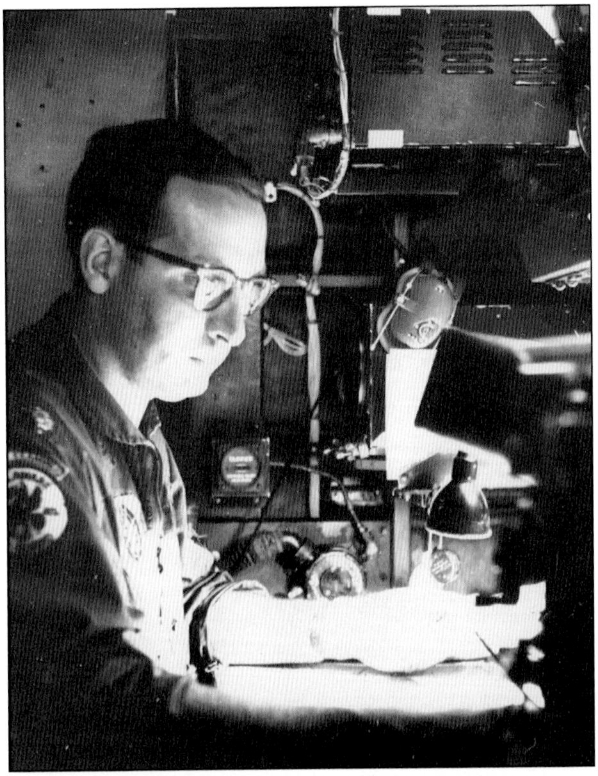

Maj. Phil Goettel sits at the navigator station on the C-97 flight deck. In September 1964, during Operation Ready Go, the Delaware ANG acted as back-up to ANG jets flying nonstop to Europe. (Courtesy of the Delaware Military Heritage and Education Foundation.)

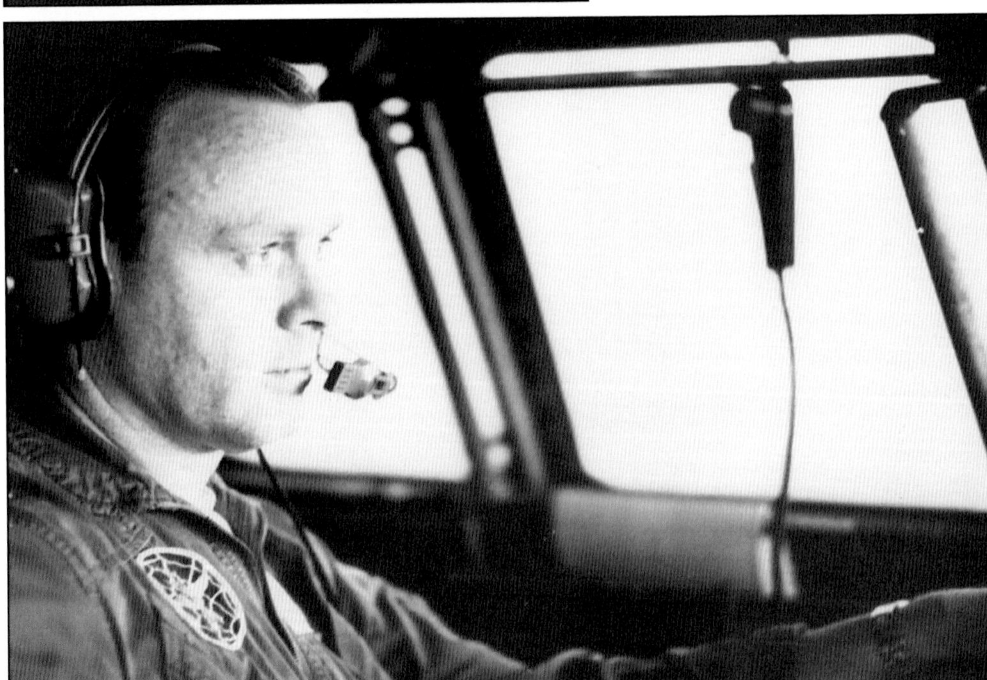

Aircraft commander Arthur Gorman is pictured at the controls of a C-97. In December 1963, Blue Hen planes and crews airlifted Bob Hope and his Christmas show on a goodwill mission to the Mediterranean area. (Courtesy of the Delaware Military Heritage and Education Foundation.)

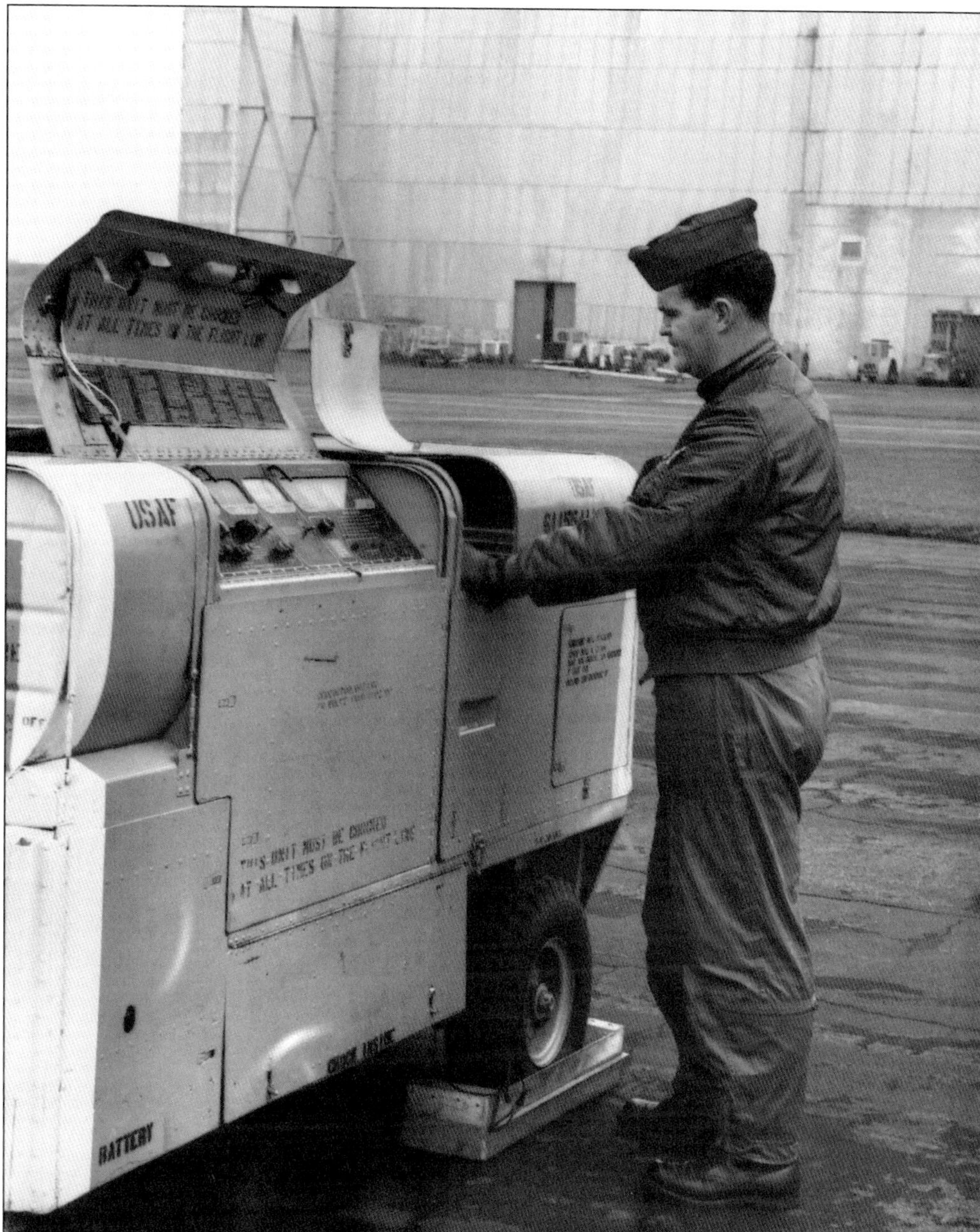

Flight engineer Roger Lambeth operates a "powercart" auxiliary power unit. In April 1966, in response to an earthquake, the Delaware ANG airlifted cattle, ducks, rabbits, and chickens to Lajes Air Base in the Azores. (Courtesy of the Delaware Military Heritage and Education Foundation.)

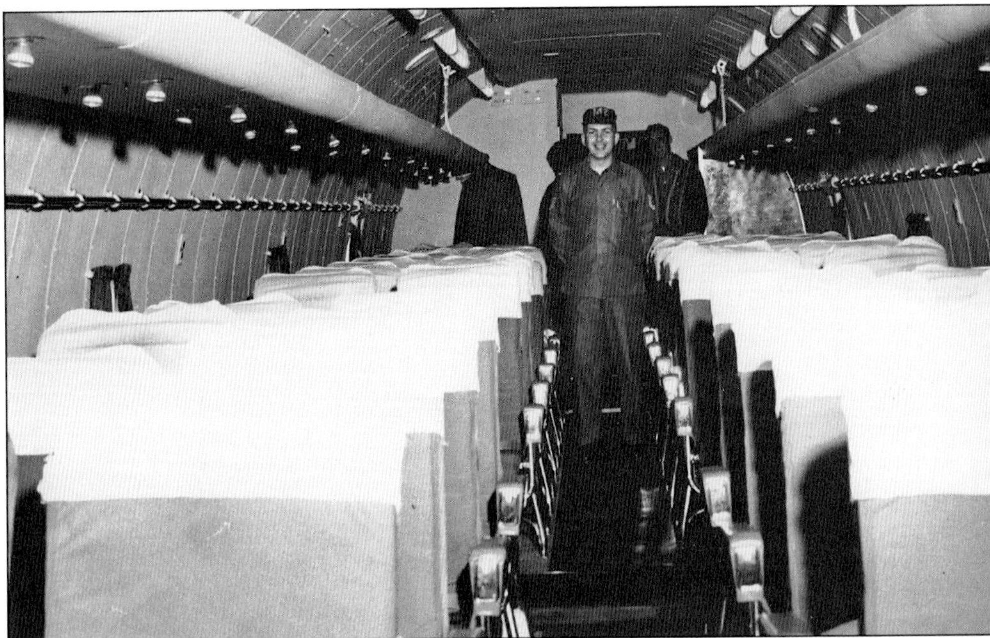

Jack Kunkle shows off his realm as loadmaster on the C-97, outfitted with airline-style seats. In July 1966, during Operation Combat Leave, the 166th supported airlifting military personnel during a commercial airline strike. (Courtesy of the Delaware Military Heritage and Education Foundation.)

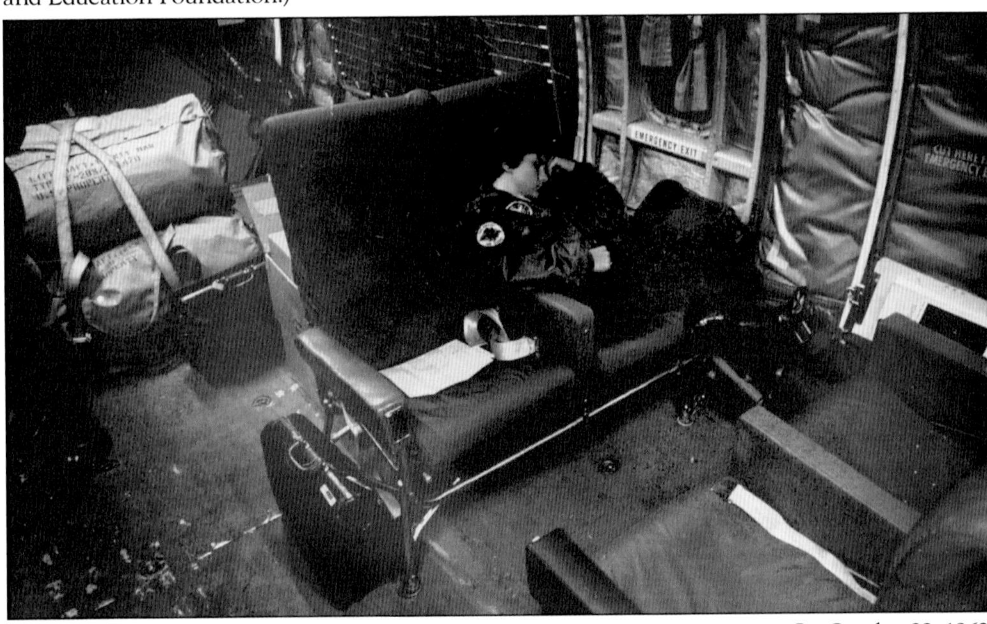

A flight nurse catches a catnap during an aeromedical evacuation training mission. On October 22, 1962, a new unit, the 142nd Aeromedical Evacuation Flight (AEF), was added to the Delaware Air National Guard. This unit initially consisted of only four personnel but had an authorized strength of 12 flight nurses and 36 aeromedical evacuation technicians qualified for the mission. Many 142nd AEF members augmented active-duty crews flying live missions to the United States from Europe and Japan. (Courtesy of the Delaware Military Heritage and Education Foundation.)

Linda Van Vechten, an aeromedical evacuation technician, was the first female enlisted in the Delaware Air National Guard in 1973. Capt. Carolyn Doolittle became the first female to command a unit in 1972, when she was appointed commander of the 142nd Aeromedical Evacuation Flight. (Courtesy of the Delaware Military Heritage and Education Foundation.)

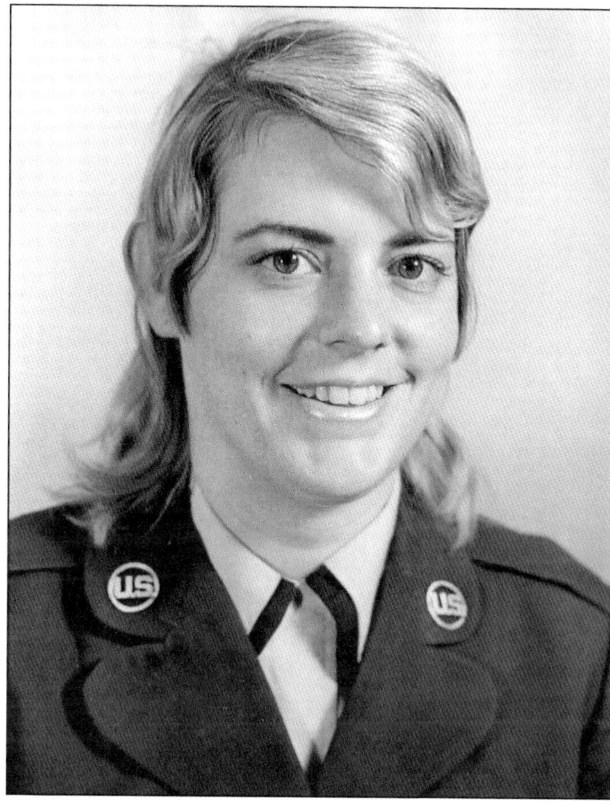

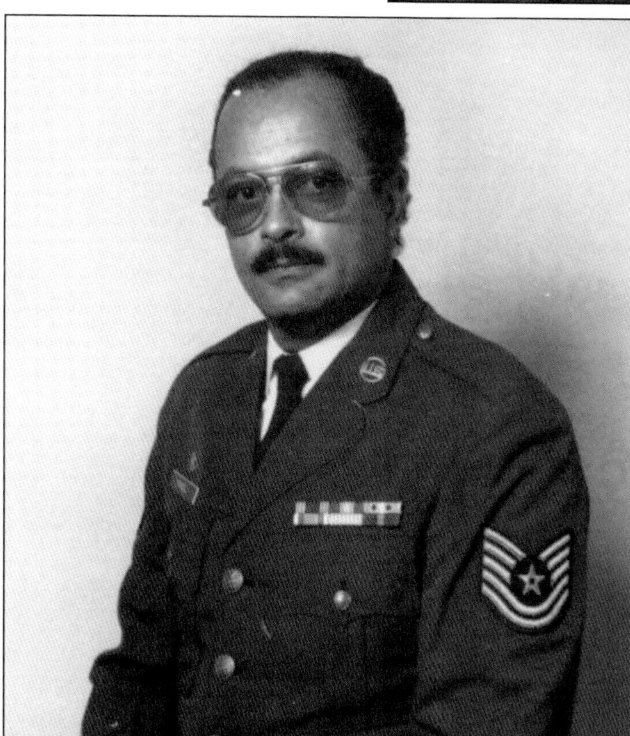

Garnell Purcell was the first African American enlistee in the Delaware Air Guard. He joined the unit in 1967 as a reciprocating aircraft engine mechanic. (Courtesy of the Delaware Military Heritage and Education Foundation.)

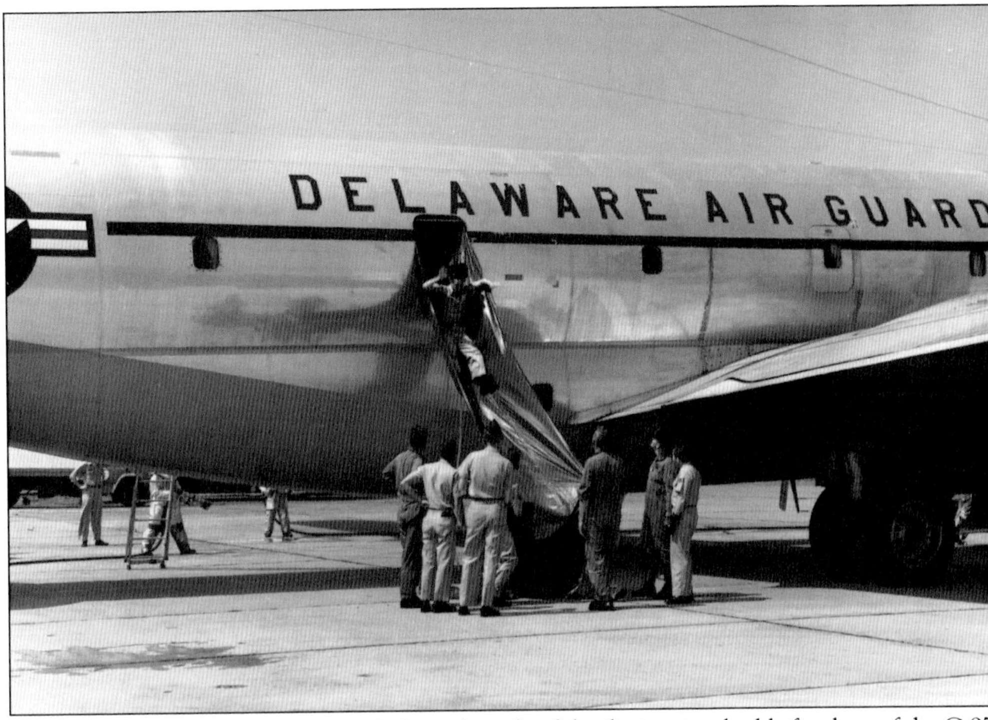

An emergency egress exercise extends from the side of the distinctive double fuselage of the C-97. (Courtesy of the Delaware Military Heritage and Education Foundation.)

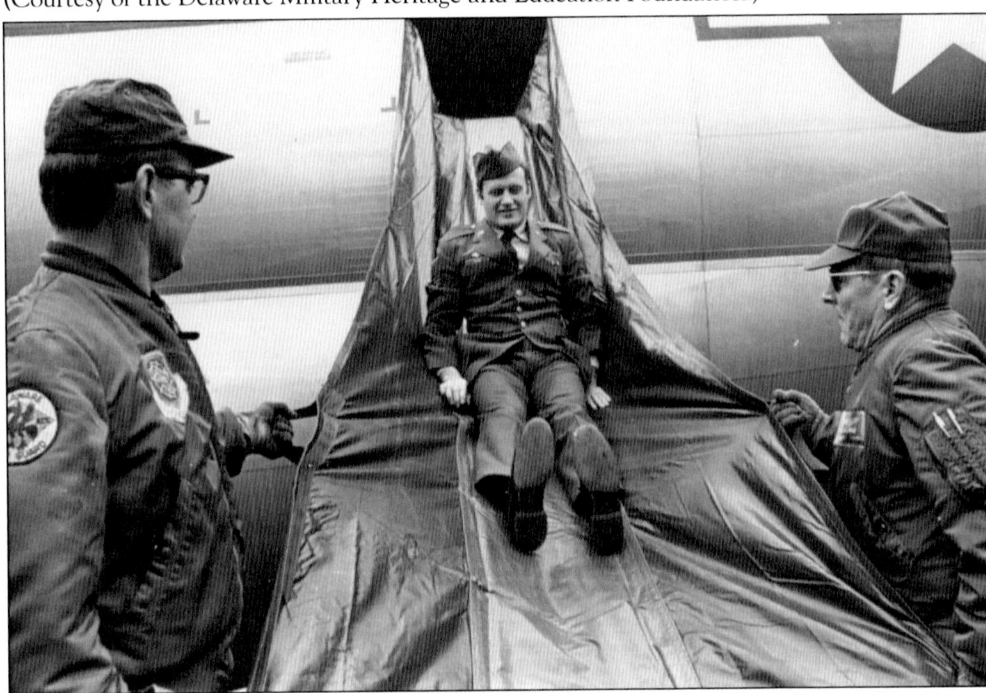

A1c. Chris Pechin demonstrates the emergency evacuation slide as Wilson Lysle (right) and an unidentified flight crewman assist. (Courtesy of the Delaware Military Heritage and Education Foundation.)

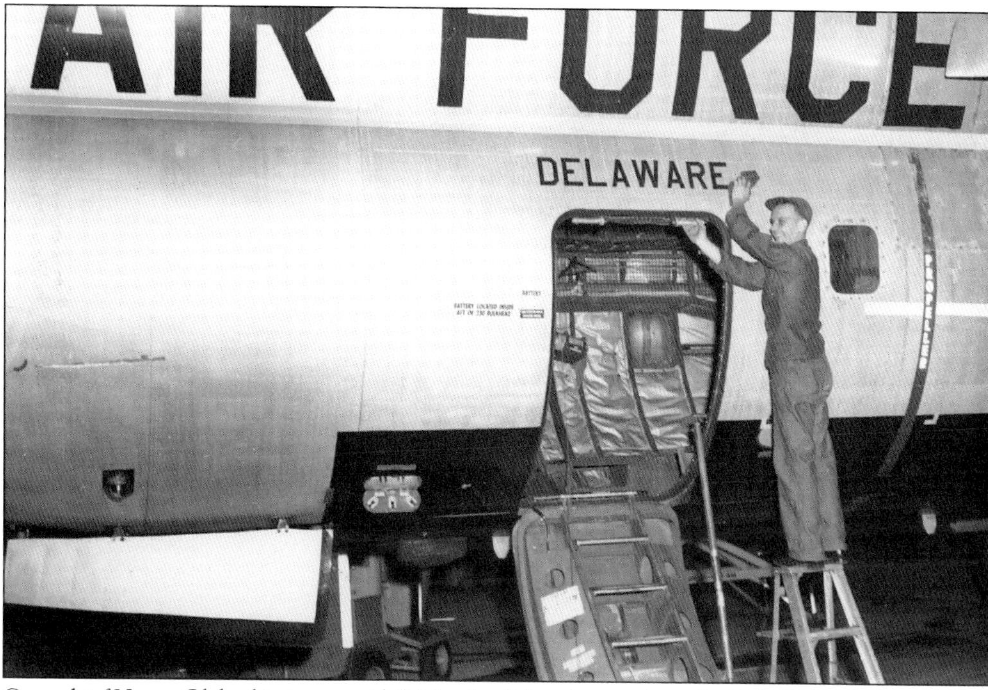

Crew chief Henry Olcheski gives a prideful final polish to his airplane. In 1967, Delaware ANG crews airlifted medical supplies to Vietnamese hospitals for a local Delaware group called Aid to International Medicine. (Courtesy of the Delaware Military Heritage and Education Foundation.)

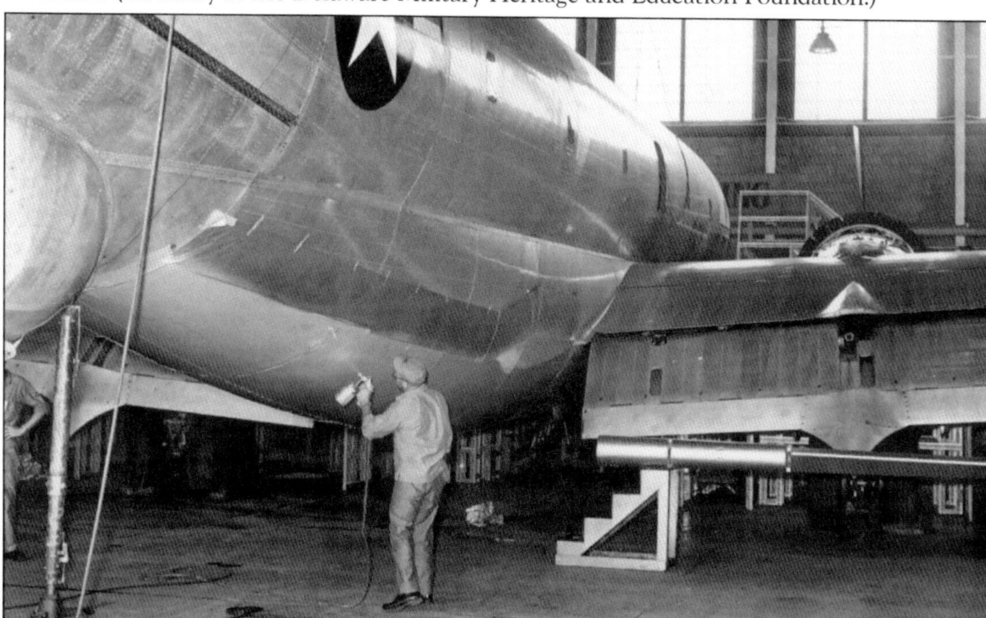
The belly of the C-97 gets a new coat of paint in the main maintenance hangar. In 1967, the Delaware ANG flew its first cargo mission to the Australian continent, and in May, the Blue Hens saved a NASA missile launch by rushing technicians to Ascension Island, in the South Atlantic between Brazil and West Africa, to repair a radar monitoring station. (Courtesy of the Delaware Military Heritage and Education Foundation.)

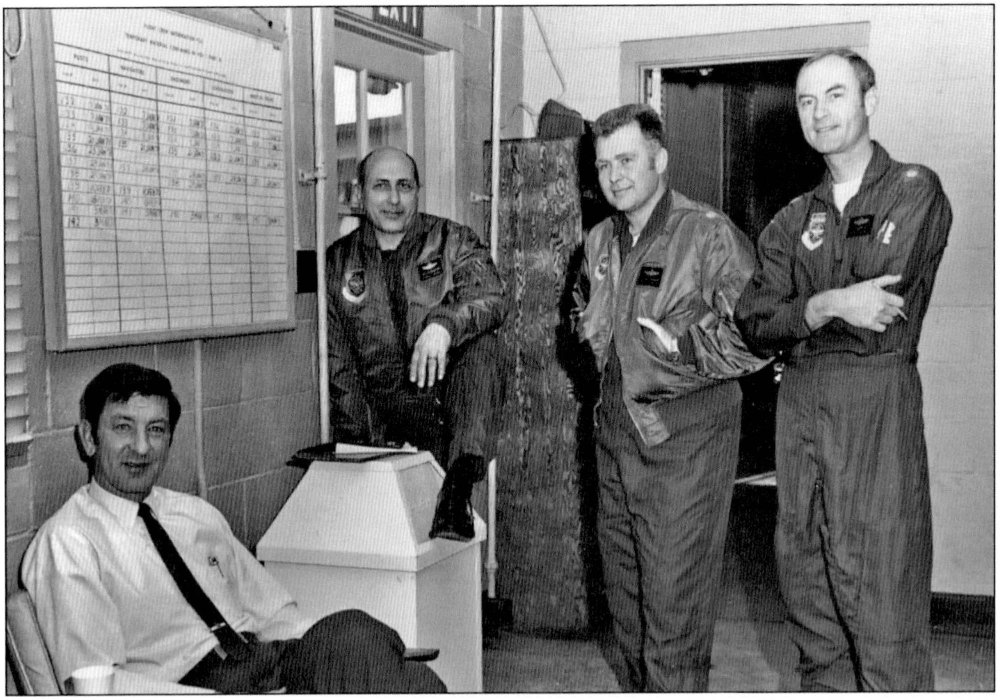

Flight Crew Operations in January 1971 include, from left to right, William Hutchison, Vito Panzarino, Judson Wooding, and James P. Scott II. (Courtesy of the Delaware Military Heritage and Education Foundation.)

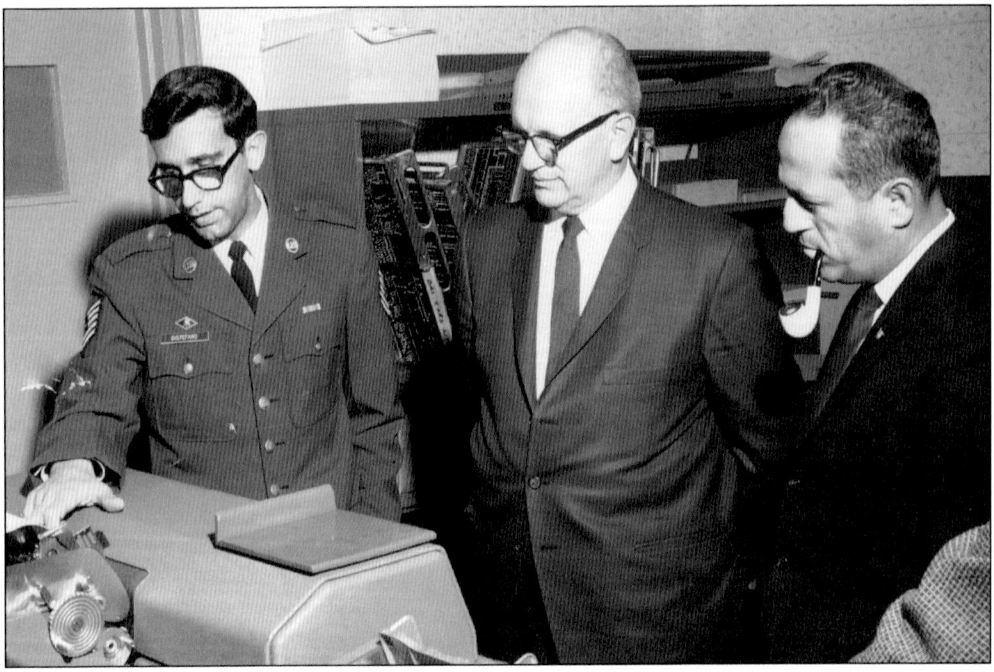

T.Sgt. Richard T. DiStefano (left) demonstrates data processing capability to Wilmington city mayor John Babiarz as a pipe-smoking Lt. Col. Albert Poppiti (Wilmington safety commissioner) looks on. (Courtesy of the Delaware Military Heritage and Education Foundation.)

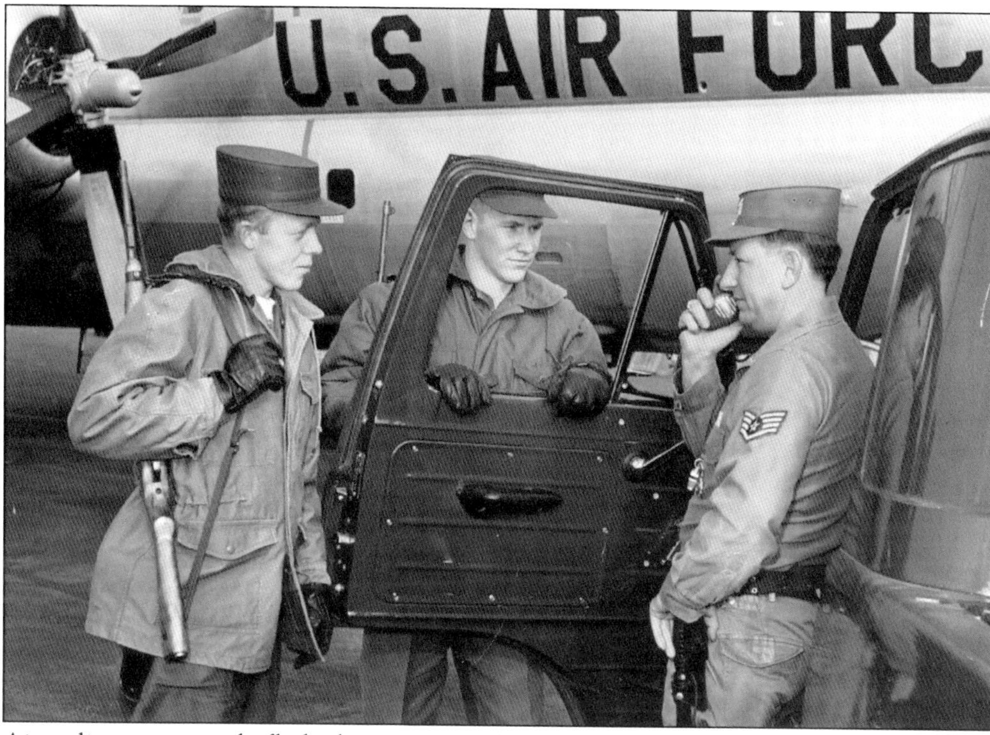

Air policemen provide flight line security. (Courtesy of the Delaware Military Heritage and Education Foundation.)

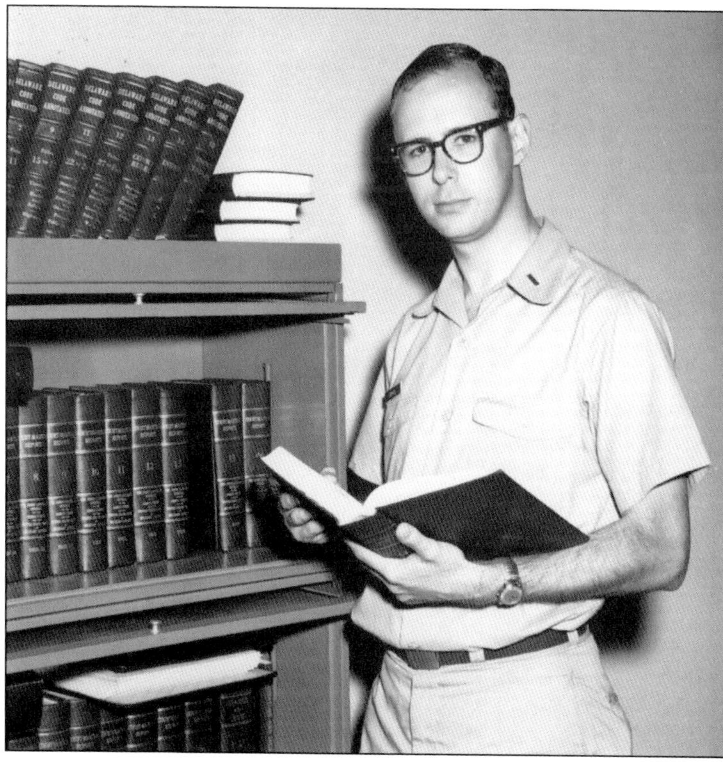

Lt. William Campbell was judge advocate for the Delaware Air National Guard in the early 1960s. (Courtesy of the Delaware Military Heritage and Education Foundation.)

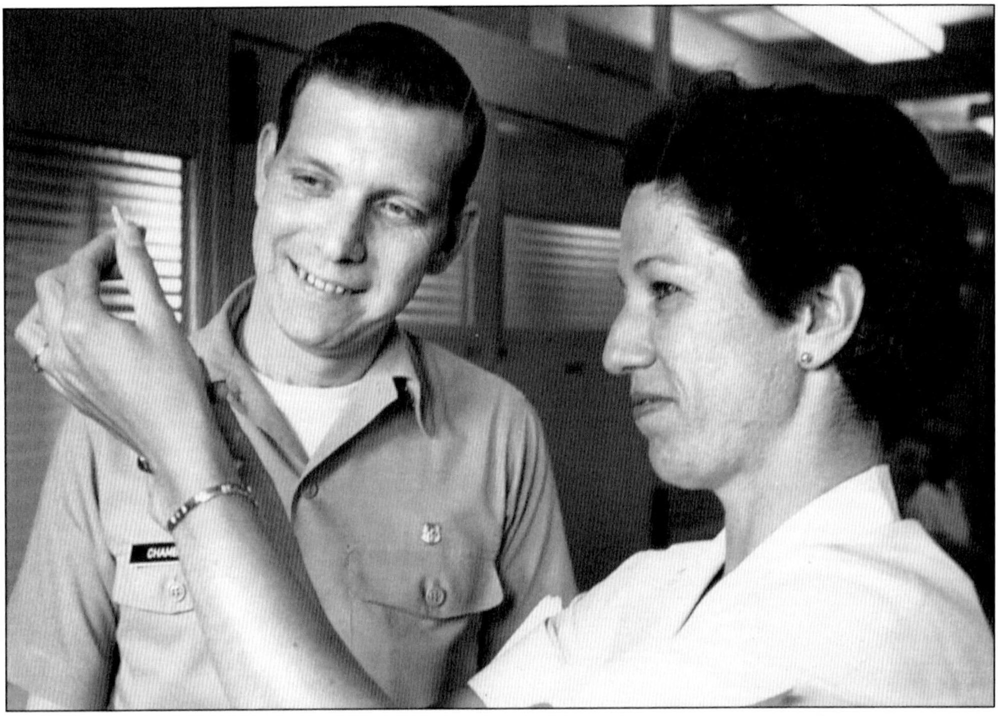

Lt. James L. Chambers and Capt. Patricia Brown, 166th dispensary nurses in 1964, are examining a medical syringe. (Courtesy of the Delaware Military Heritage and Education Foundation.)

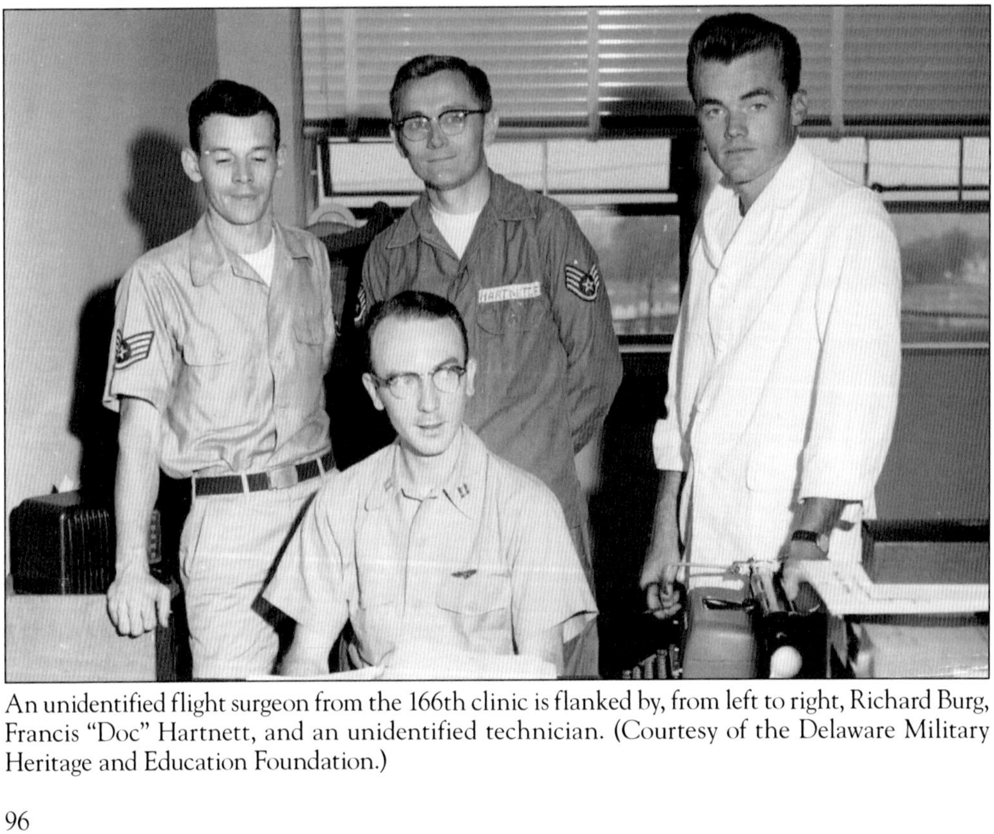

An unidentified flight surgeon from the 166th clinic is flanked by, from left to right, Richard Burg, Francis "Doc" Hartnett, and an unidentified technician. (Courtesy of the Delaware Military Heritage and Education Foundation.)

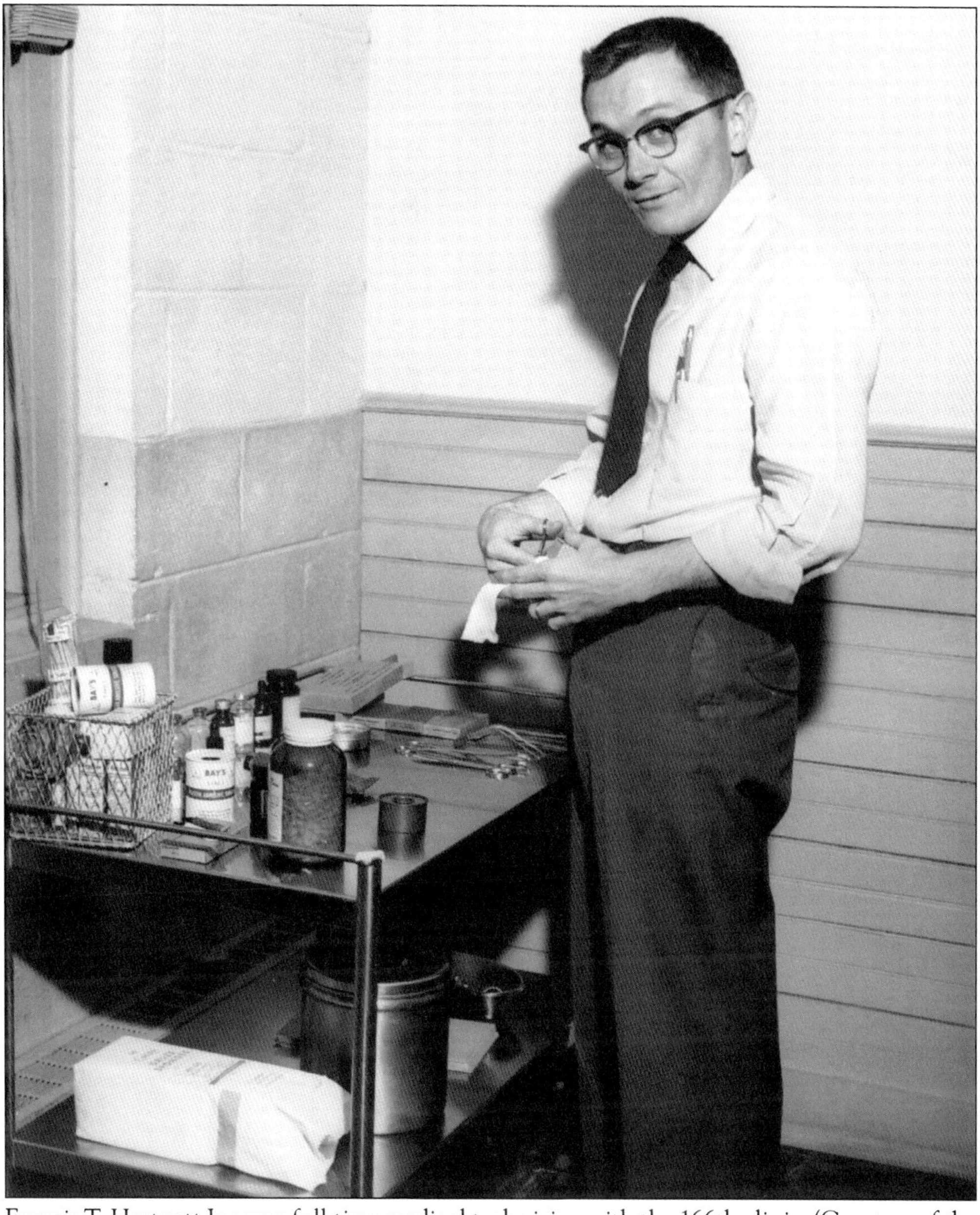

Francis T. Hartnett Jr. was a full-time medical technician with the 166th clinic. (Courtesy of the Delaware Military Heritage and Education Foundation.)

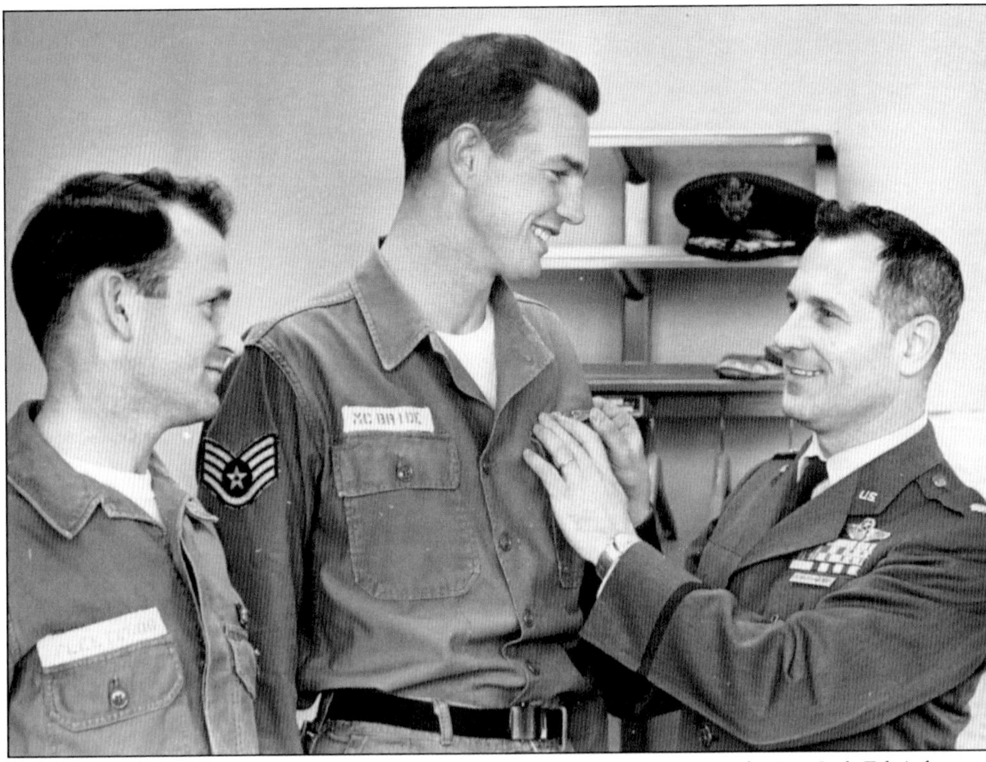

Loadmaster S.Sgt. Laurence McBride (center) is pinned with his wings by Lt. Col. Ed Atkinson as loadmaster James Fleetwood (left) looks on. The transition from fighters to transports widened the flying crew positions to include enlisted members as loadmasters, flight engineers, and medical technicians. In January 1969, Colonel Atkinson became the adjutant general for Delaware—the first Air National Guard member to do so. (Courtesy of the Delaware Military Heritage and Education Foundation.)

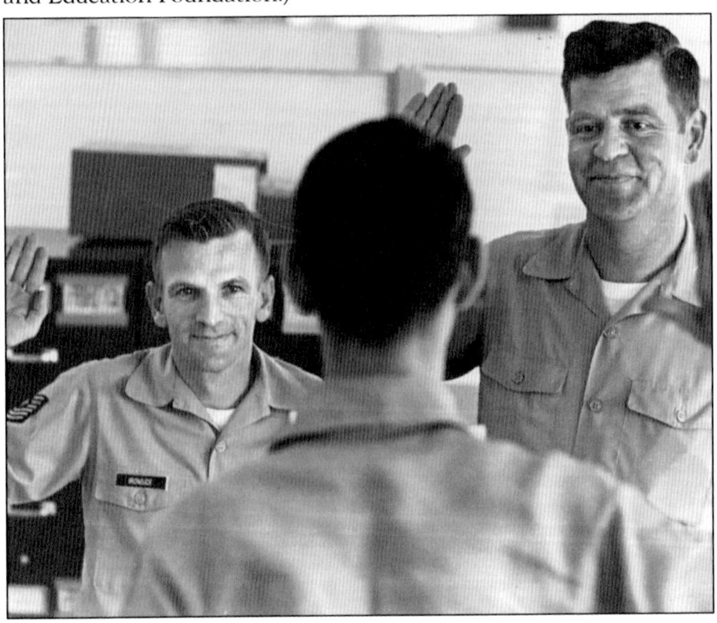

M.Sgt. Donald Ironside (left) and Amos Burke (right) take the reenlistment oath from Capt. Alan Murrayfield (center). The ANG had a high retention rate, losing only about 10 percent of its workforce annually, a historically low loss rate for a military organization. (Courtesy of the Delaware Military Heritage and Education Foundation.)

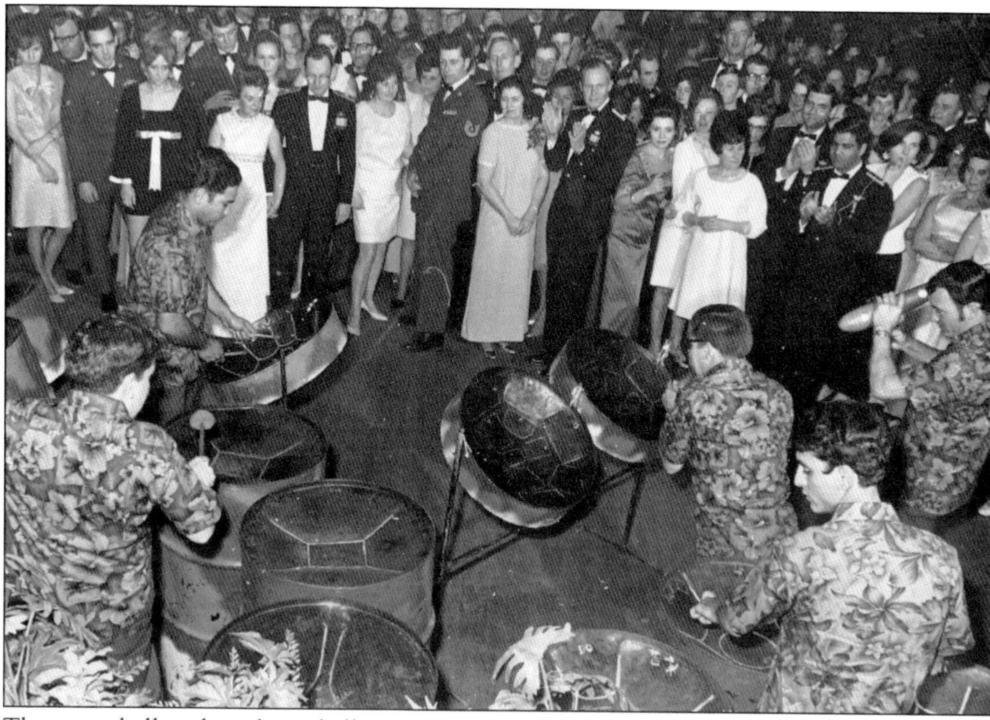

The annual all-ranks military ball, sometimes called the "Governor's Ball" when the governor attends, is held at the Wilmington Armory. Here a Puerto Rican steel band entertains the attendees, including Col. Charles Skinner (front center, behind woman in floor-length dress) and Col. Robert Fuller (center, right of woman in floor-length dress), the base detachment commander and group commander respectively. Skinner had the distinction of serving as a state police commander as well. (Courtesy of the Delaware Military Heritage and Education Foundation.)

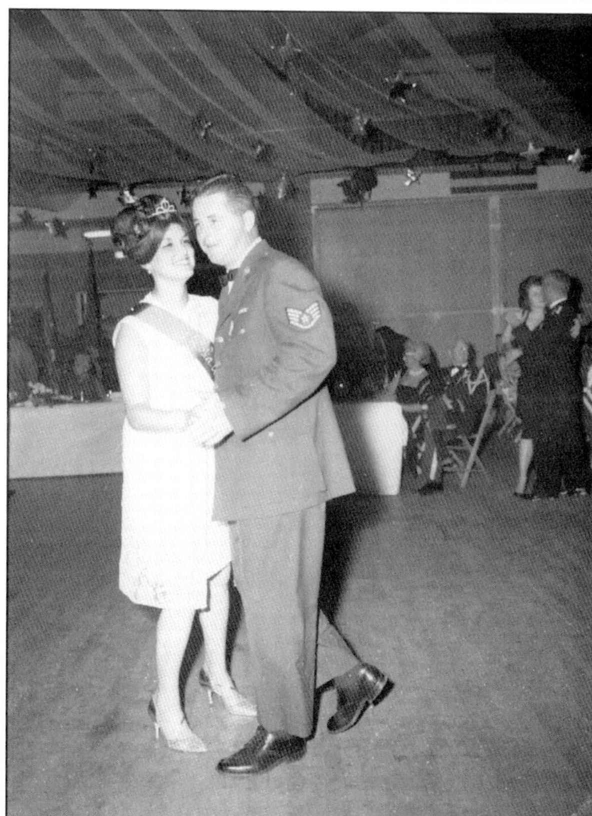

An airman takes a turn on the dance floor with honored guest Miss Delaware 1967 Mary Lee Mancini at the annual ball under a ceiling festooned with parachutes. (Courtesy of the Delaware Military Heritage and Education Foundation.)

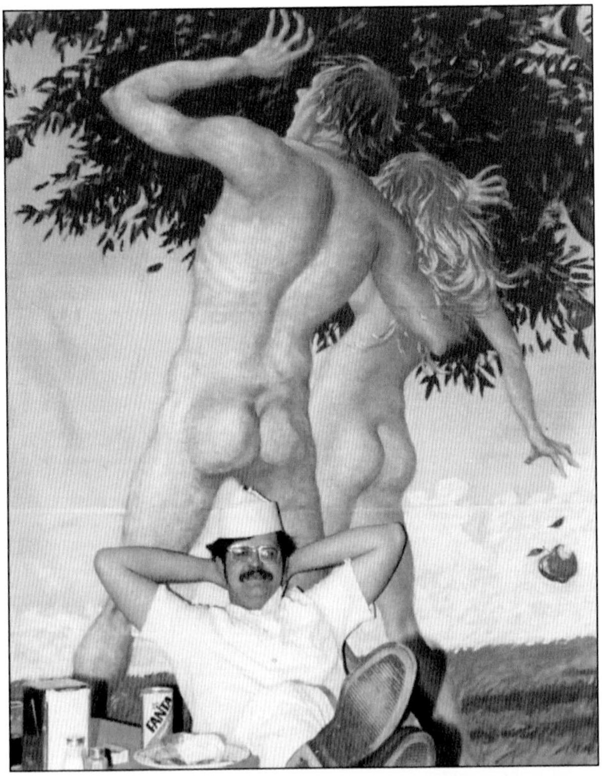

A cook from the dining facility relaxes before a mural painted by A1c. Jamie Wyeth with the help of Sgt. Larry "Sabre Sam" Vieth. The mural depicts Adam and Eve stunned at the sight of a C-97 in the sky (not visible here). It was originally installed as a backdrop for the annual ball and then placed in the dining hall for many years, before being moved to its place of honor in the new operations building. (Courtesy of the Delaware Military Heritage and Education Foundation.)

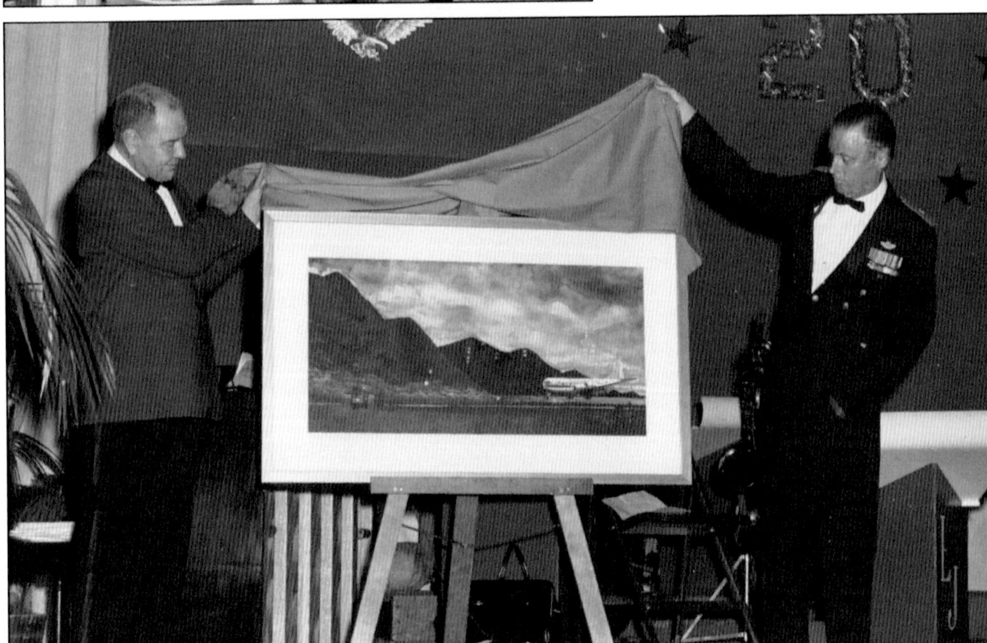

Another painting by A1c. Jamie Wyeth is unveiled depicting a unit C-97 landing at Cam Ranh Bay, Vietnam. It was commissioned to celebrate the unit's first 20 years in 1966. To the left is the adjutant general, Maj. Gen. Joseph Scannell, and to the right is Brig. Gen. William Spruance. (Courtesy of the Delaware Military Heritage and Education Foundation.)

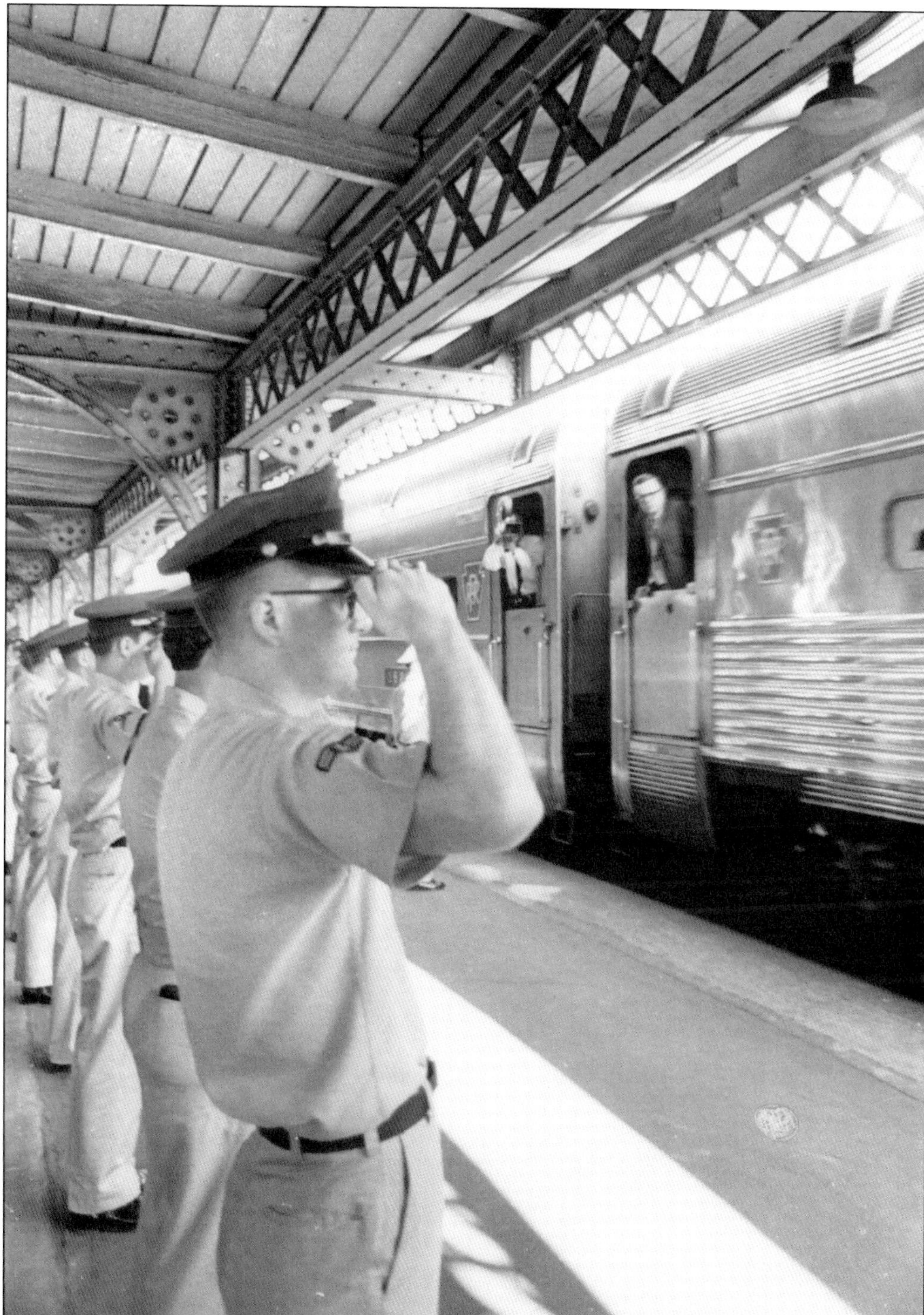

In the aftermath of the Robert Kennedy assassination in 1968, his body was taken by train to Washington, D.C. An honor guard of Delaware Air Guardsmen saluted as the train passed through the Wilmington train station. (Courtesy of the Delaware Military Heritage and Education Foundation.)

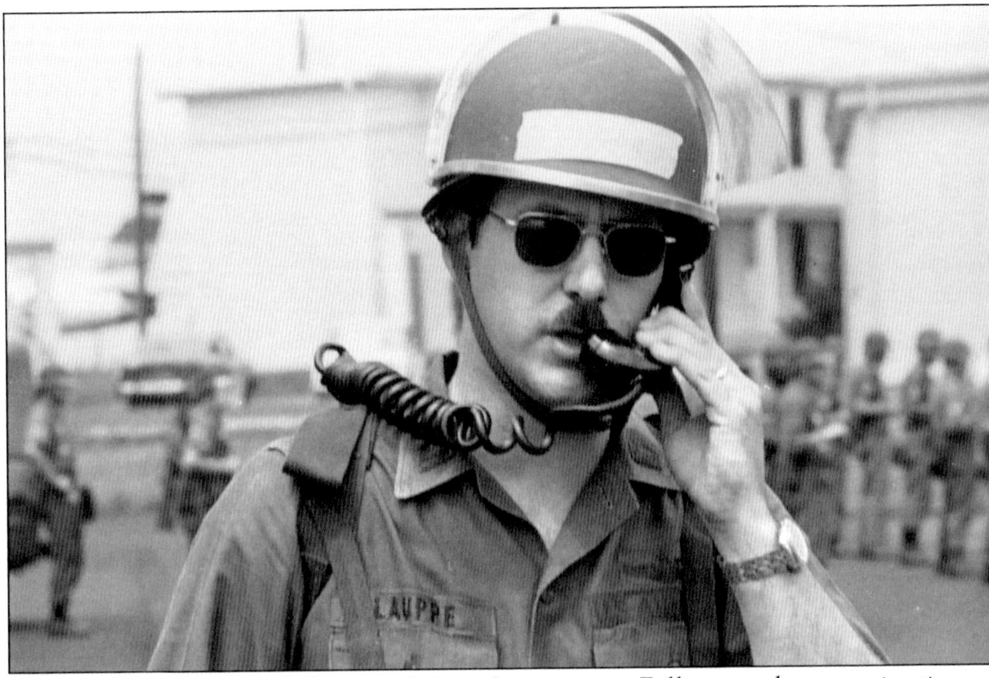

Capt. Tom Lauppe is clad in civil disturbance gear. Following the assassination of Rev. Martin Luther King Jr. in Memphis, Tennessee, riots broke out in 19 major American cities. Some 68,000 National Guardsmen and 22,600 U.S. Army troops were called upon to suppress the outbreaks. (Courtesy of the Delaware Military Heritage and Education Foundation.)

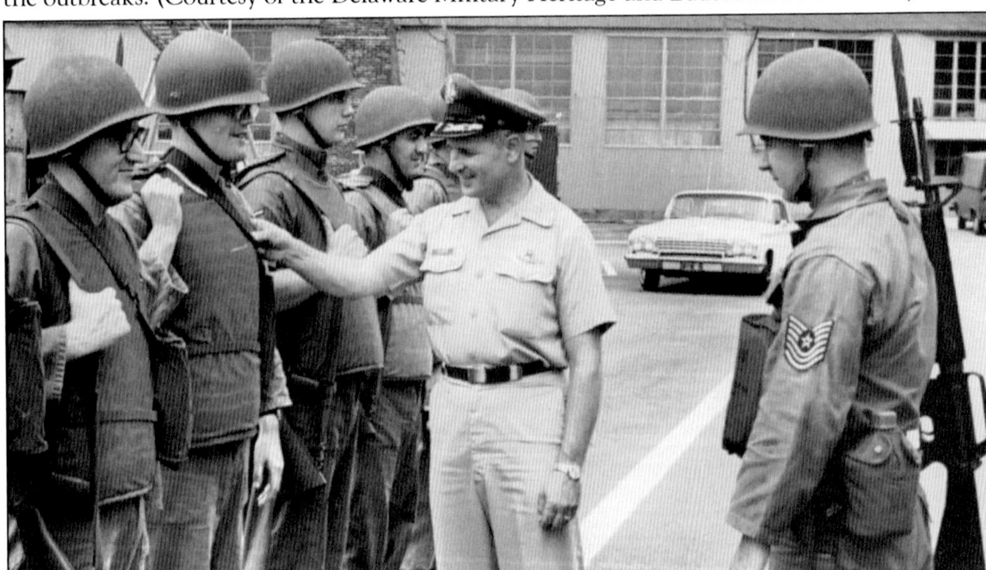

Atkinson inspects the bulletproof vests of members of the Air Police Flight clad in their riot control garb, as noncommissioned officer in charge Sgt. John Clancy looks on. In its first large-scale state activation, on April 9, 1968, the Delaware Air National Guard was called to state duty to quell civil disturbance and violence in the city of Wilmington, Delaware. The unit was released from state duty after several weeks. However, many individuals remained on state duty through January 20, 1969. (Courtesy of the Delaware Military Heritage and Education Foundation.)

Lt. Col. Frank Welch demonstrates proper use of the riot baton. (Courtesy of the Delaware Military Heritage and Education Foundation.)

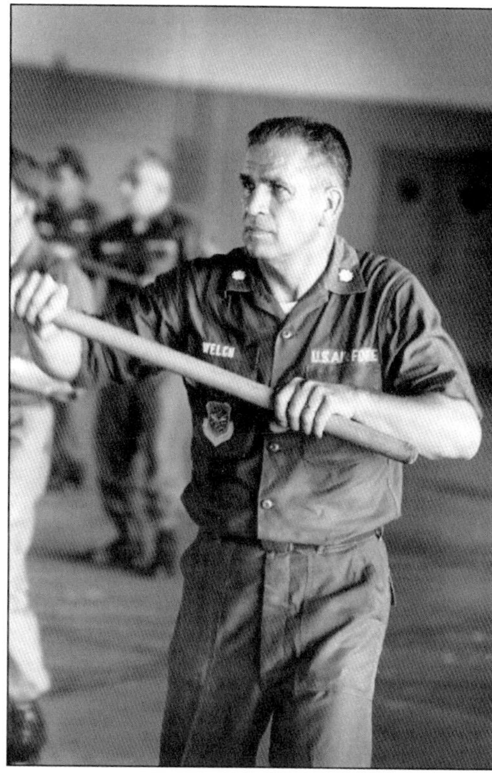

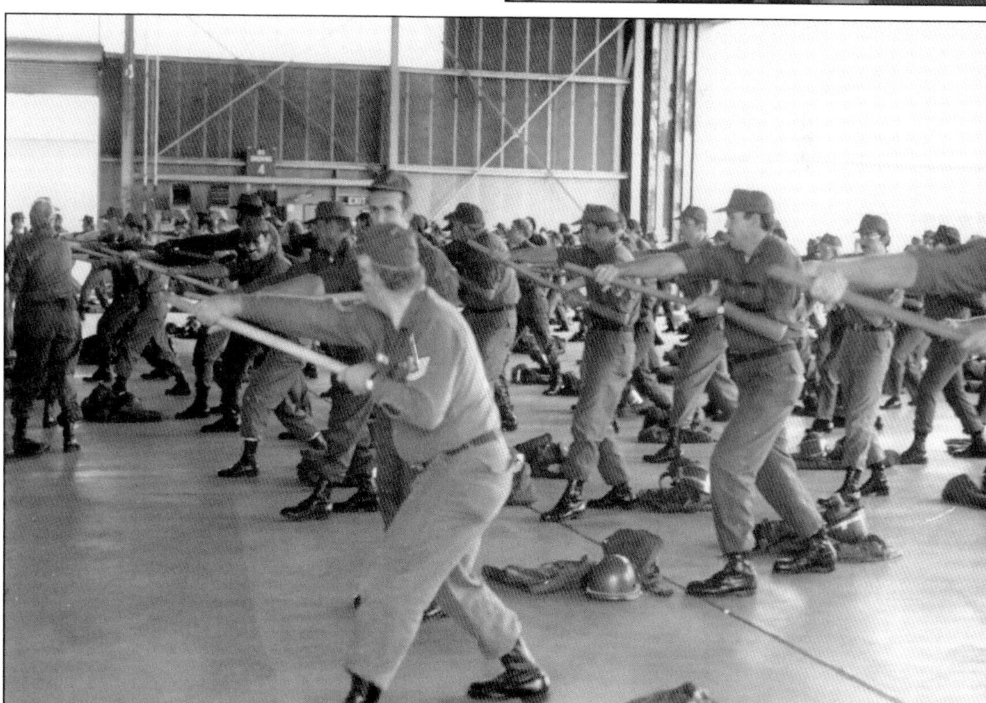

Formation civil disturbance training was held in the Nose Dock maintenance hangar on a hot summer day. (Courtesy of the Delaware Military Heritage and Education Foundation.)

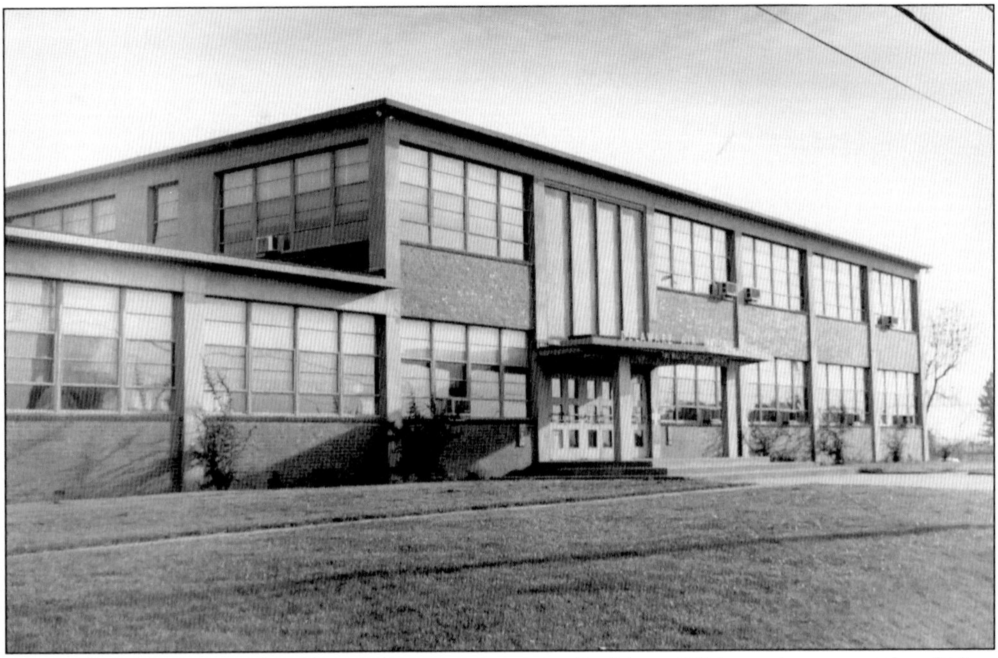

The original Delaware Air Guard Headquarters was Building 1504 on the west side of New Castle County Airport. It contained a dining facility, a clinic, an auditorium, and administrative offices for state staff and group headquarters. (Courtesy of the Delaware Military Heritage and Education Foundation.)

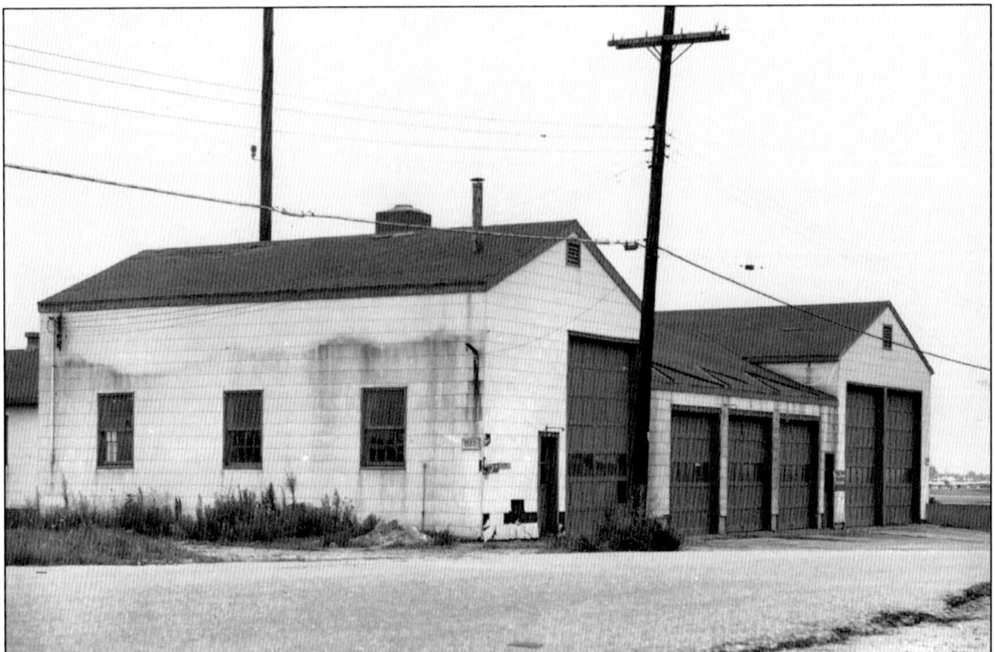

This firehouse was the original home of the 142nd squadron firefighters. On November 8, 1969, the 166th Civil Engineer Flight organized as a separate unit in the Delaware Air National Guard. (Courtesy of the Delaware Military Heritage and Education Foundation.)

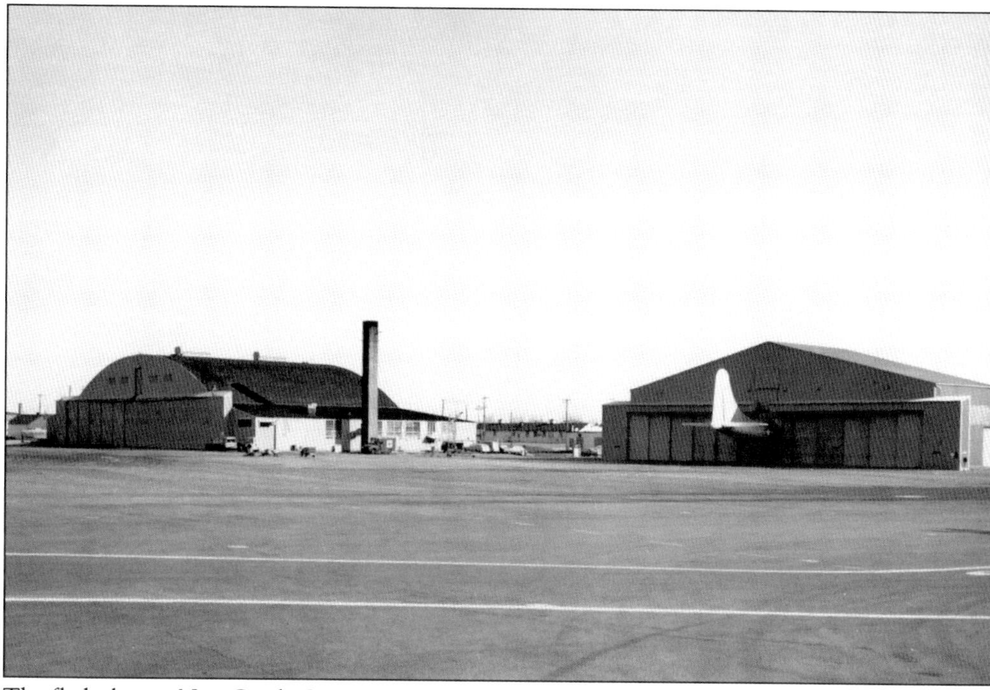

The flight line at New Castle County Airport is shown at its present location on the east side of the base. On the left is the main hangar, and to the right is the Nose Dock, containing all but the tail of a C-97 around 1968. (Courtesy of the Delaware Military Heritage and Education Foundation.)

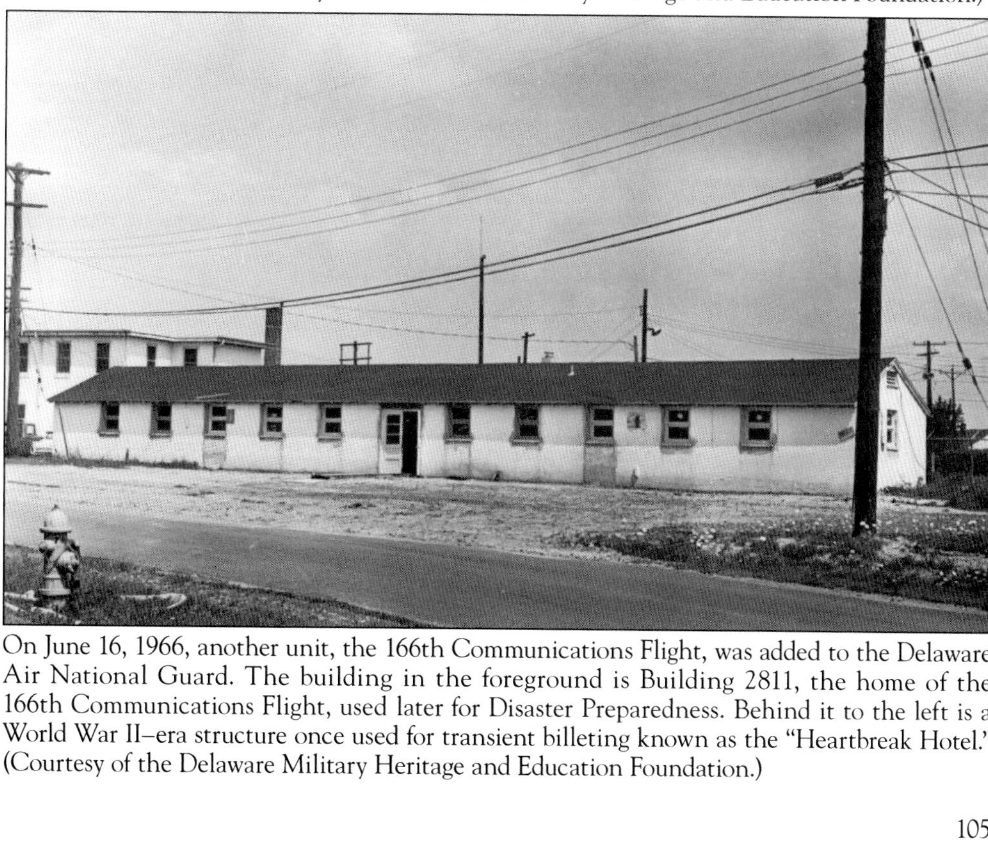

On June 16, 1966, another unit, the 166th Communications Flight, was added to the Delaware Air National Guard. The building in the foreground is Building 2811, the home of the 166th Communications Flight, used later for Disaster Preparedness. Behind it to the left is a World War II–era structure once used for transient billeting known as the "Heartbreak Hotel." (Courtesy of the Delaware Military Heritage and Education Foundation.)

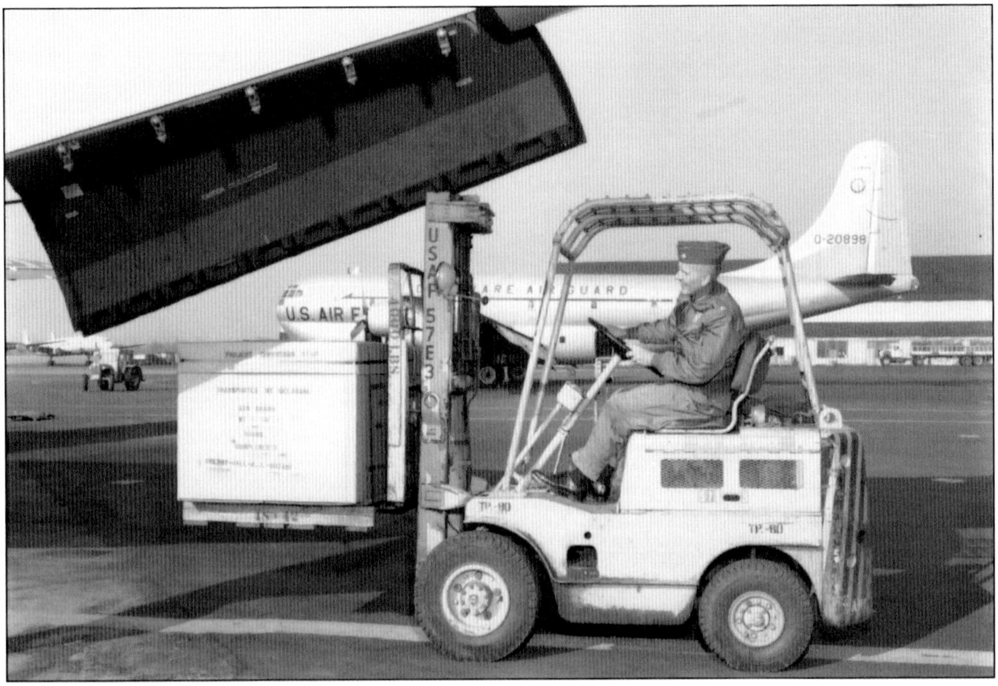

Col. Ralph A. Skowron guides a forklift of donated supplies into a C-97 bound for Vietnam during Operation Christmas Airlift in December 1965. (Courtesy of the Delaware Military Heritage and Education Foundation.)

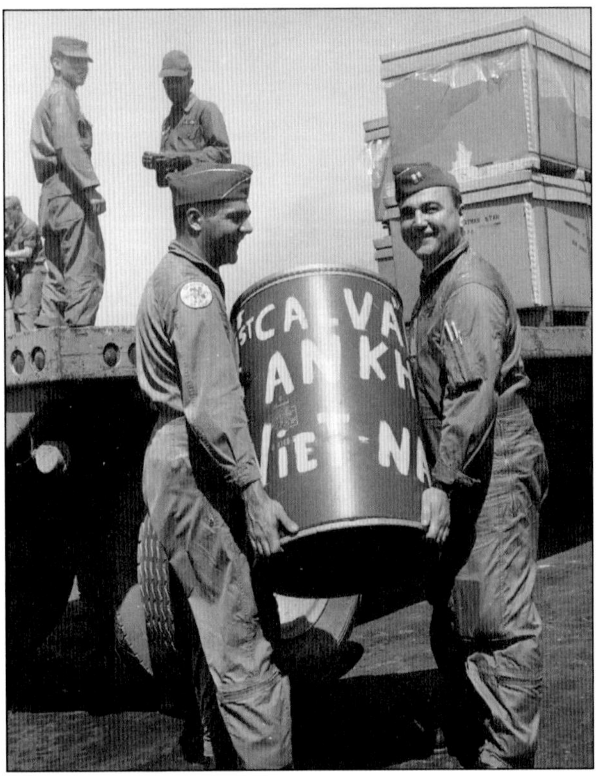

Capt. Bruno Muzzi (right) and Capt. Jack Bal load cargo bound for the 1st Cavalry in Vietnam. During the period from 1964 to 1974, the Delaware Air National Guard flew airlift missions to Vietnam with increasing tempo. The organization made an impact on the war effort by voluntarily contributing a significant portion of the mission (an estimated two-thirds) it would have performed had it been fully activated. (Courtesy of the Delaware Military Heritage and Education Foundation.)

Five

Tactical Airlift

In September 1972, Col. William F. Hutchison Jr. was named commander of the 166th Tactical Airlift Group, a position he held for 11 years.

In October 1977, Operation Volant Oak was launched from Howard Air Base, Panama, with 15-day rotations of ANG personnel providing military airlift by four to six C-130s for U.S. Southern Command.

On October 16, 1985, the Delaware Air National Guard began replacing its aging C-130As with the delivery of a brand-new C-130H.

During the Persian Gulf War, the Delaware Air Guard flew 487 missions in 2,140 sorties for a total of 2,942.2 flying hours. They moved 15,985 passengers, including evacuating about 4,500 refugees, and 5,952.8 tons of cargo.

From September 1993 through the spring of 1994, unit members voluntarily deployed to aid in Operation Restore Hope in Somalia.

In 1998, the 142nd Airlift Squadron journeyed across the Atlantic to Germany in support of Operation Joint Forge in the Balkans.

On October 1, 2001, the first Delaware Air Guard unit was called up in response to the events of 9/11. The Delaware Air National Guard 166th Security Forces Squadron, part of the 166th Airlift Wing, reported for a one-year mobilization. On October 23, members of the 142nd Aeromedical Evacuation Squadron were called up and airlifted overseas.

On October 31, another 67 members of the Delaware Air National Guard were called to active duty. Members of three units—the 142nd Aeromedical Evacuation Squadron, the 142 Airlift Squadron, and the 166th Airlift Wing—were placed on active duty.

Kathleen L. Eastburn was the first woman promoted to colonel by the Delaware Air National Guard, on April 13, 2002.

In March 2003, six aircraft and 103 mechanics were deployed to a classified air base in the Arabian Gulf region, just in time for the official start of the war in Iraq.

One year later, on March 17, 2004, Lt. Col. Carol A. Timmons was added to the Hall of Fame of Delaware Women. She was the first female pilot in the Delaware Air National Guard and was inducted into the Delaware Aviation Hall of Fame in 2007.

In 2004, Brig. Gen. Hugh Broomall, a former enlisted airman, became the first general officer appointed to the Delaware ANG who was not a rated aviator.

Double calamities struck the Delaware Air National Guard when a tornado swept through the flight line and severely damaged four of the C-130H aircraft in September 2004. Months later, in the spring of 2005, the organization barely escaped folding its flag as a result of the BRAC (base realignment and closing) Congressional initiatives.

Brig. Gen. Ernie Talbert became the first black general officer in the Delaware ANG in 2005.

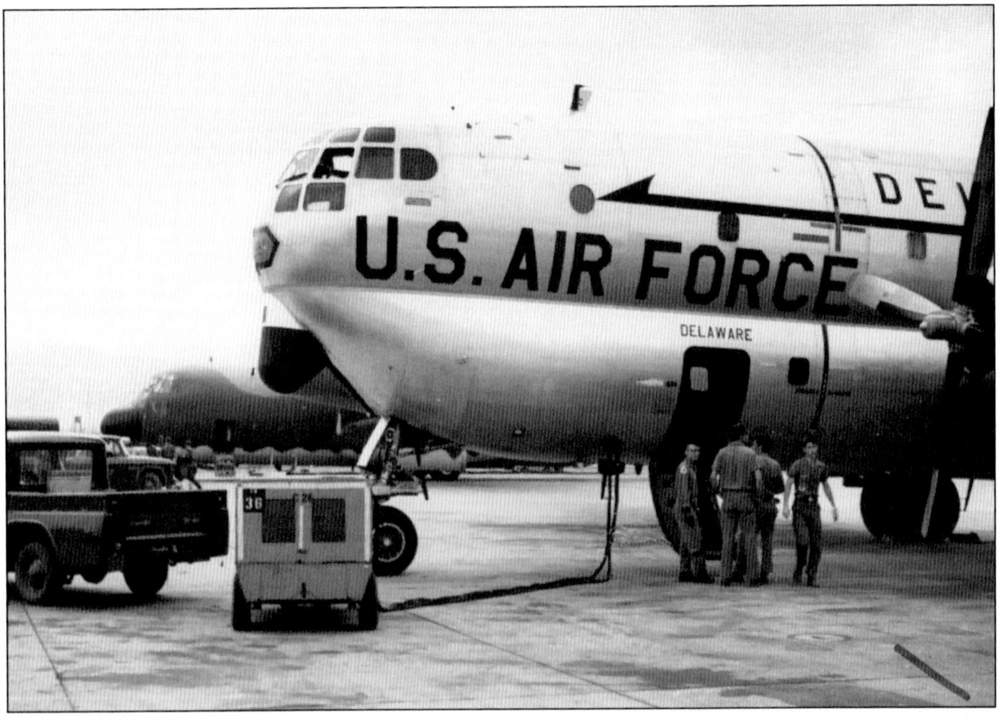

The unit's C-97G is shadowed in the background with its future destiny, the C-130 Hercules. (Courtesy of the Delaware Military Heritage and Education Foundation.)

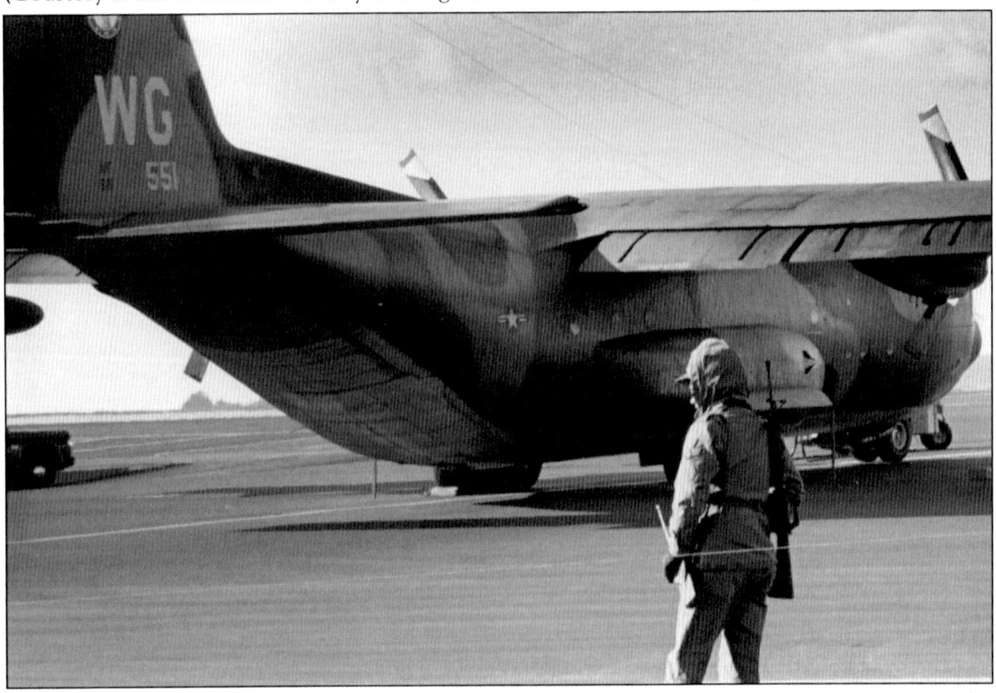

A lonely sentinel from the Air Police Squadron provides ramp security for the C-130A. The marking on the tail, WG, signifies this aircraft was from Wilmington (no longer used). (Courtesy of the Delaware Military Heritage and Education Foundation.)

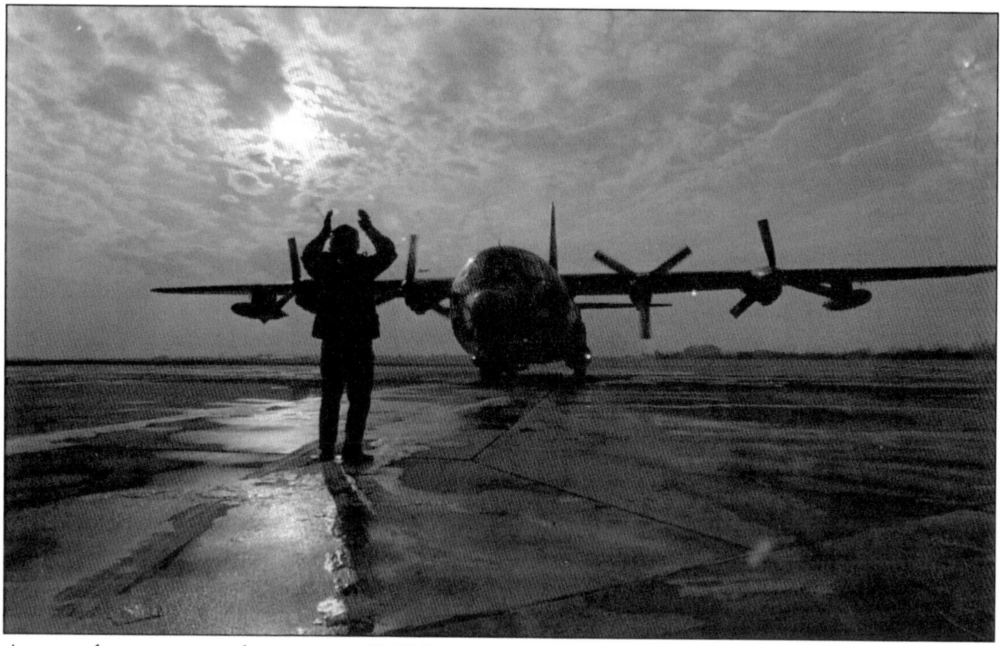

A ground crewman guides a taxiing C-130A to its icy spot on the New Castle flight line. (Courtesy of the Delaware Military Heritage and Education Foundation.)

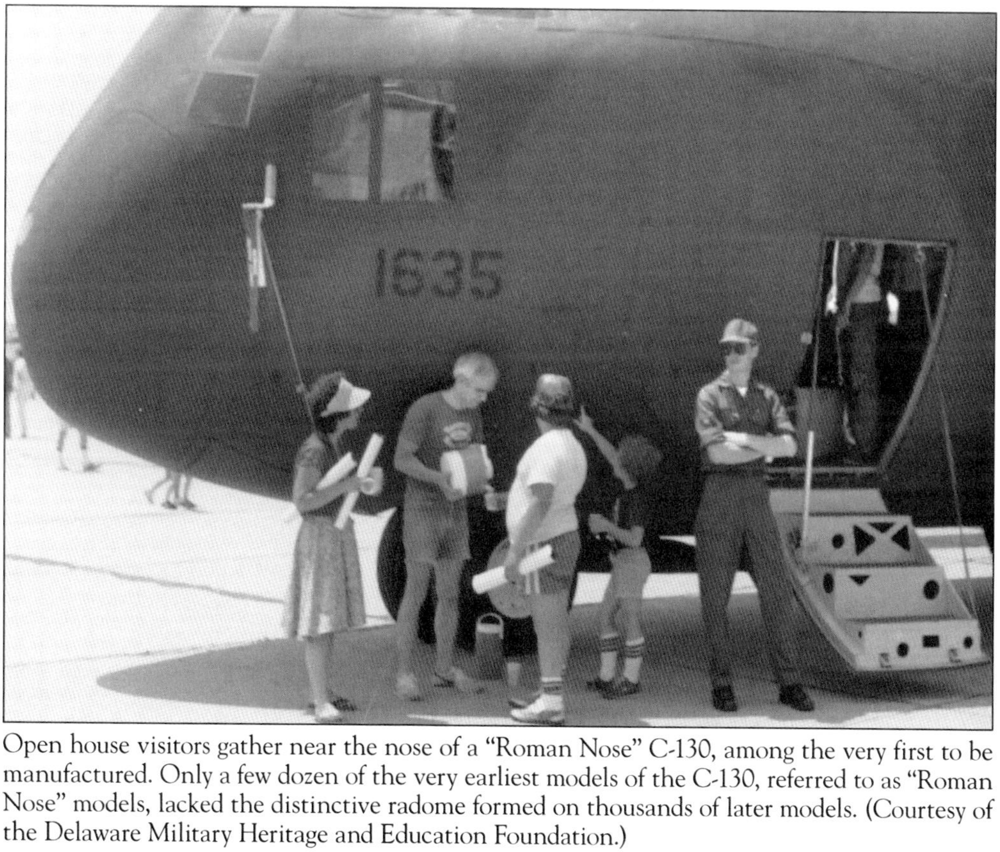

Open house visitors gather near the nose of a "Roman Nose" C-130, among the very first to be manufactured. Only a few dozen of the very earliest models of the C-130, referred to as "Roman Nose" models, lacked the distinctive radome formed on thousands of later models. (Courtesy of the Delaware Military Heritage and Education Foundation.)

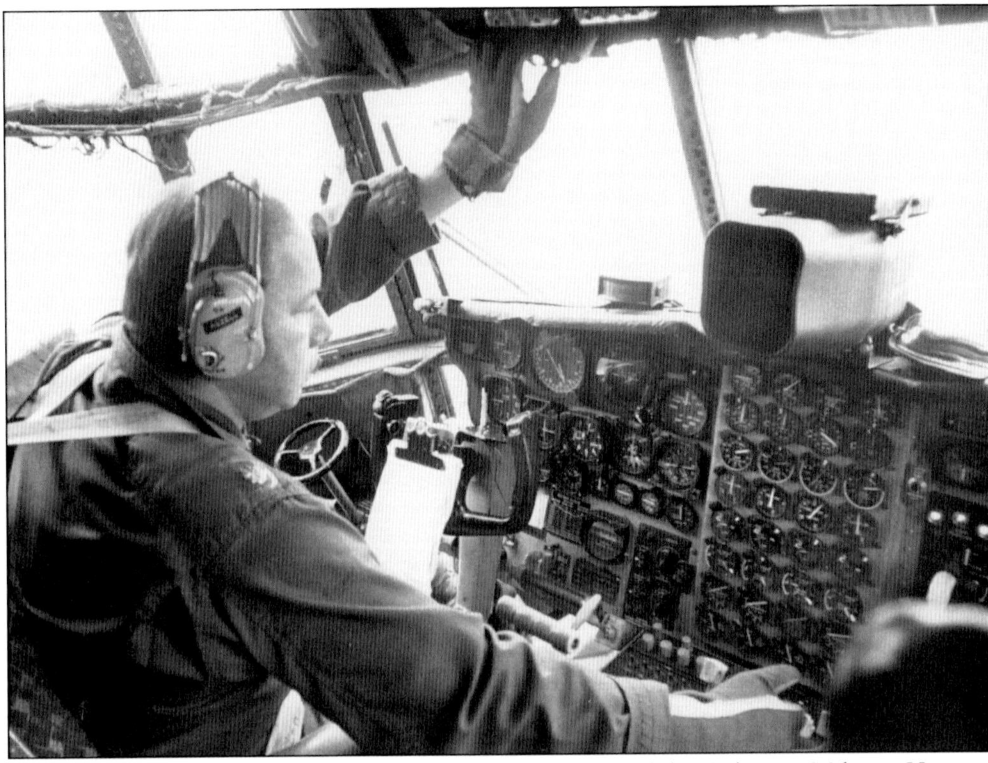

Maj. Richard Hazel is at the yoke of a C-130A. (Courtesy of the Delaware Military Heritage and Education Foundation.)

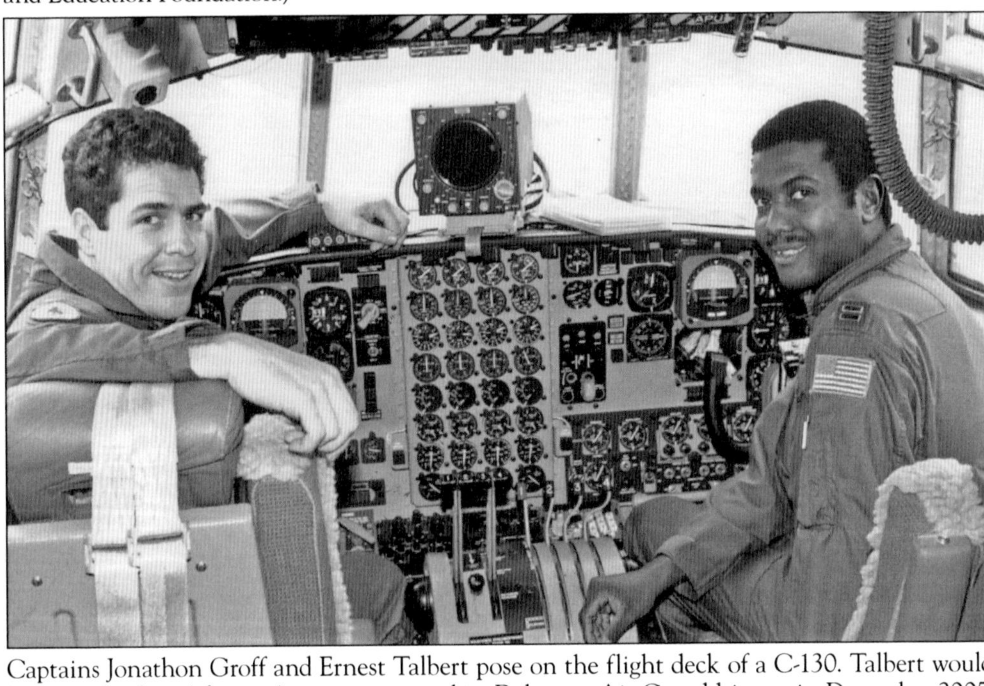

Captains Jonathon Groff and Ernest Talbert pose on the flight deck of a C-130. Talbert would become the first African American general in Delaware Air Guard history in December 2005. (Courtesy of the Delaware Military Heritage and Education Foundation.)

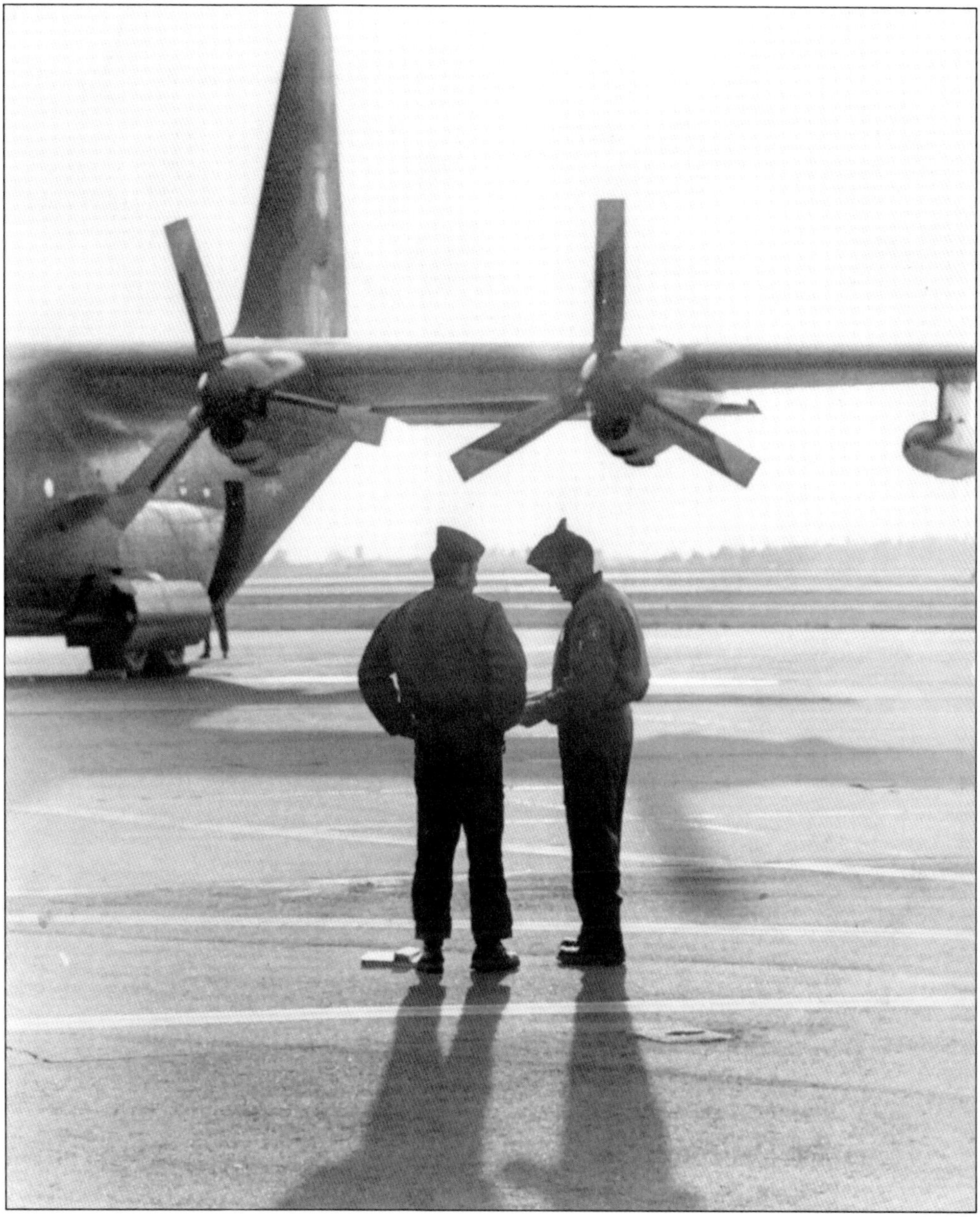

An unidentified flight crew confers before a C-130A. This airplane was the "sport model" with three-bladed propellers. It was among the lightest and fastest versions. Later versions would add weight and a four-bladed propeller. (Courtesy of the Delaware Military Heritage and Education Foundation.)

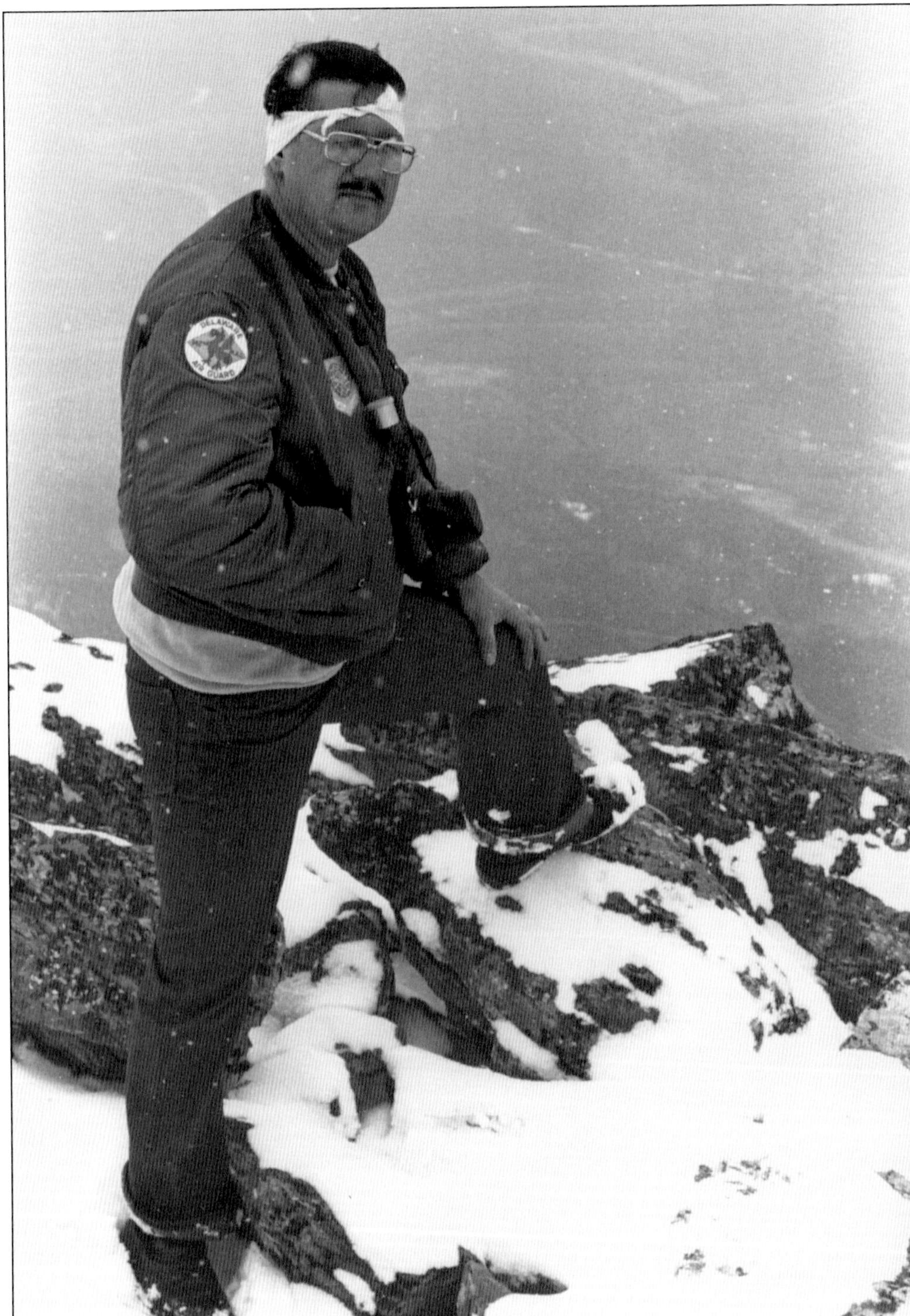

Richard Stell, a loadmaster deployed to Alaska during an exercise, climbs a mountain in Denali National Park. (Courtesy of the Delaware Military Heritage and Education Foundation.)

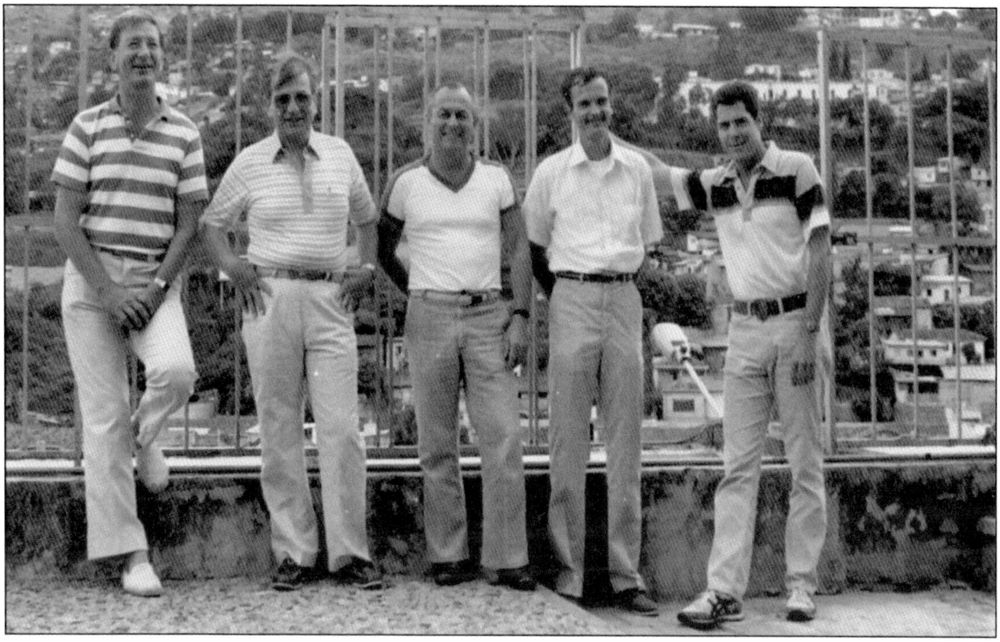

A crew deployed to Tegucigalpa, Honduras, during the Volant Oak rotation poses in mufti. From left to right are William Hutchison, aircraft commander; William Buoni, navigator; John Quigley, flight engineer; Charles Jackson, loadmaster; and Jonathon Groff, copilot. In October 1977, Operation Volant Oak was launched from Howard Air Base, Panama, with 15-day rotations of ANG and Air Force Reserve units providing military airlift by four to six C-130s for U.S. Southern Command, replacing a former active component organization. (Courtesy of the Delaware Military Heritage and Education Foundation.)

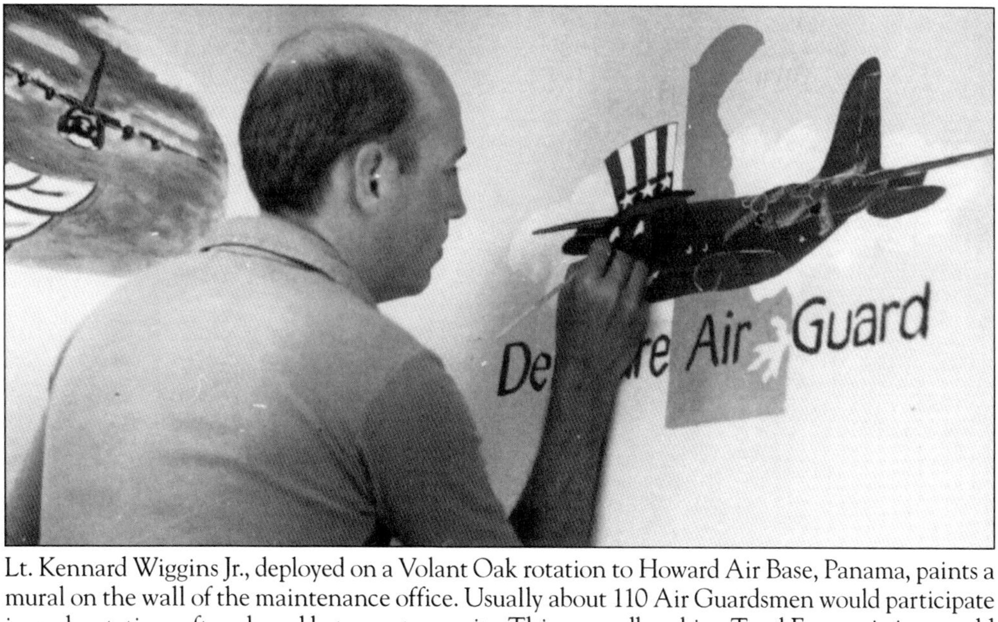

Lt. Kennard Wiggins Jr., deployed on a Volant Oak rotation to Howard Air Base, Panama, paints a mural on the wall of the maintenance office. Usually about 110 Air Guardsmen would participate in each rotation, often shared between two units. This groundbreaking Total Force mission would continue to be based in Panama under a different name (Coronet Oak) until December 1999, when the mission moved to Puerto Rico. (Courtesy of Kennard Wiggins.)

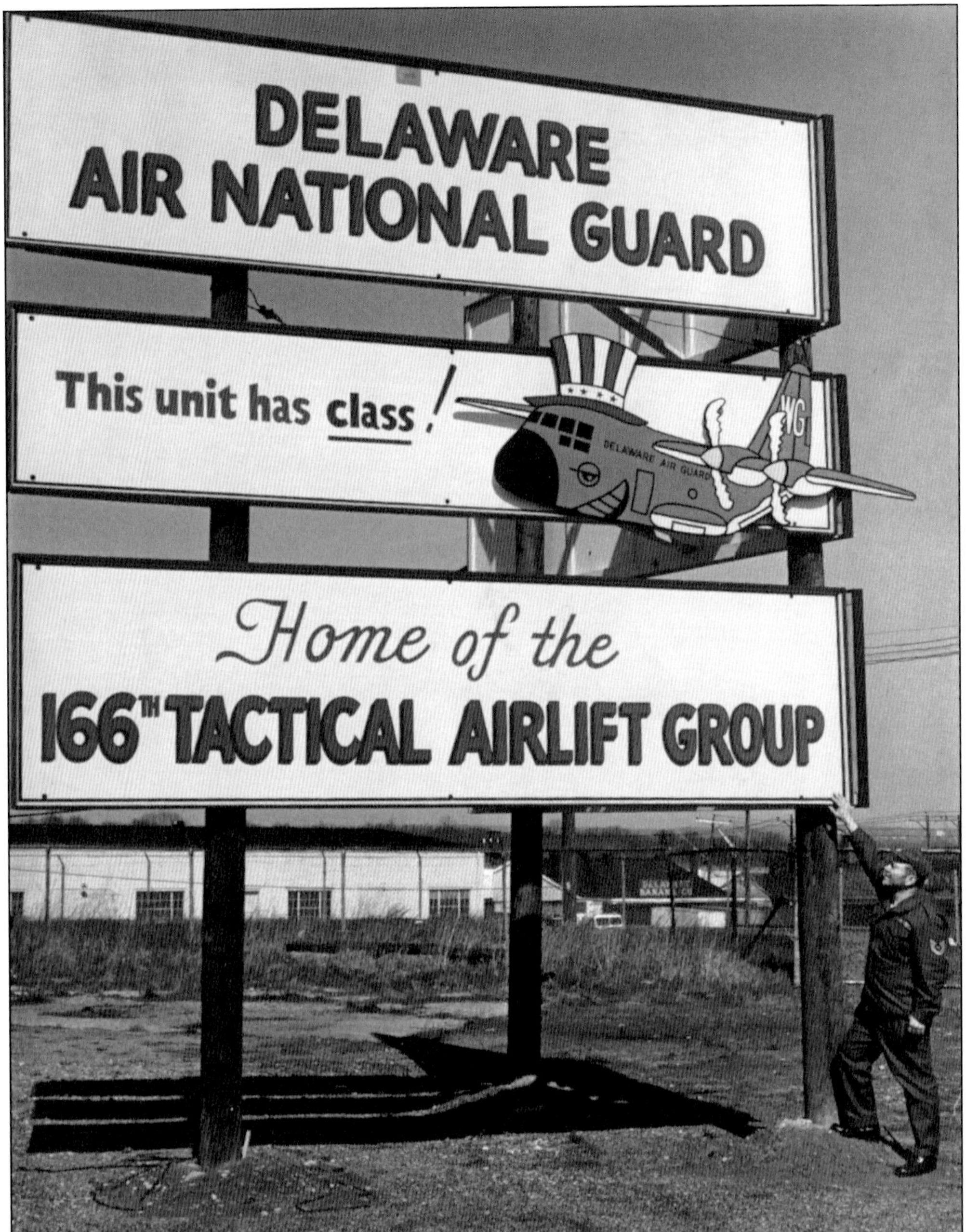

A billboard-sized sign on Basin Road (Route 141) near the Air Guard alert hangars has a slogan by William Hutchison, design by Kennard Wiggins, and execution by sign painter T.Sgt. Robert Jenkins, pictured at lower right. (Courtesy of the Delaware Military Heritage and Education Foundation.)

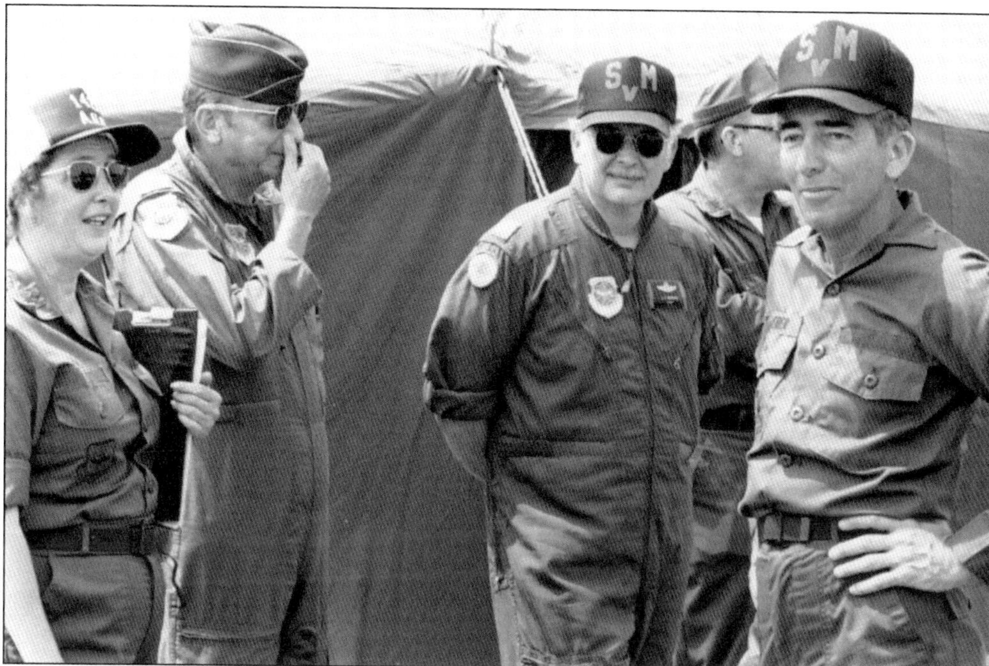

From 1980 to 1985, the 142nd Aeromedical Evacuation Flight hosted Operation Sentry Medic, which involved other Air National Guard units and was one of the first field training exercises ever planned and executed by an aeromedical evacuation unit. From left to right are Maj. Carolyn Doolittle, 142nd AEF commander; Colonel Coch; Col. Judson Wooding; and C.M.Sgt. Clark Weber. (Courtesy of the Delaware Military Heritage and Education Foundation.)

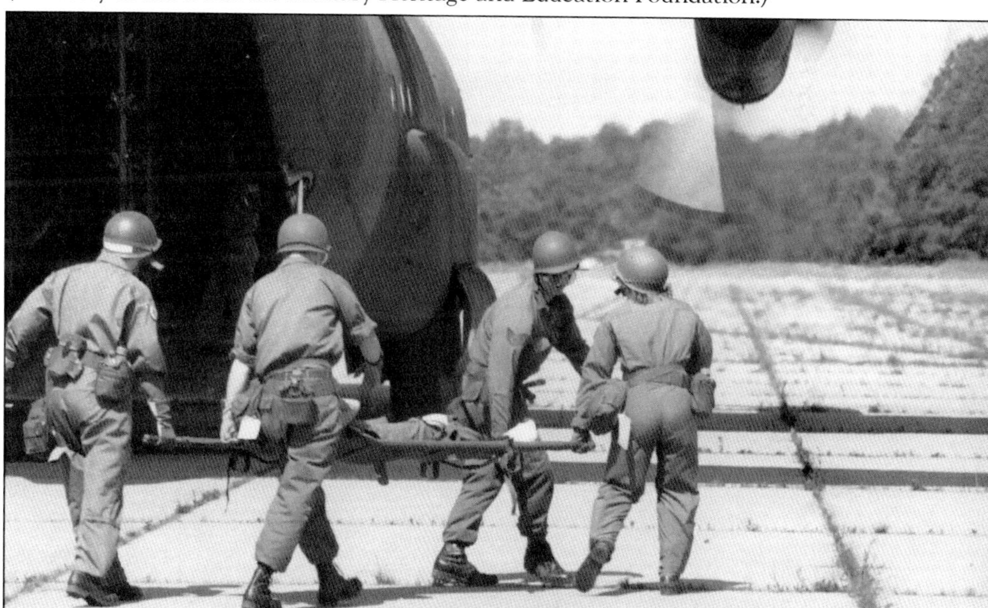
Aeromed technicians offload medical evacuees from a C-130 with engines running during an exercise in the mid-1970s. (Courtesy of the Delaware Military Heritage and Education Foundation.)

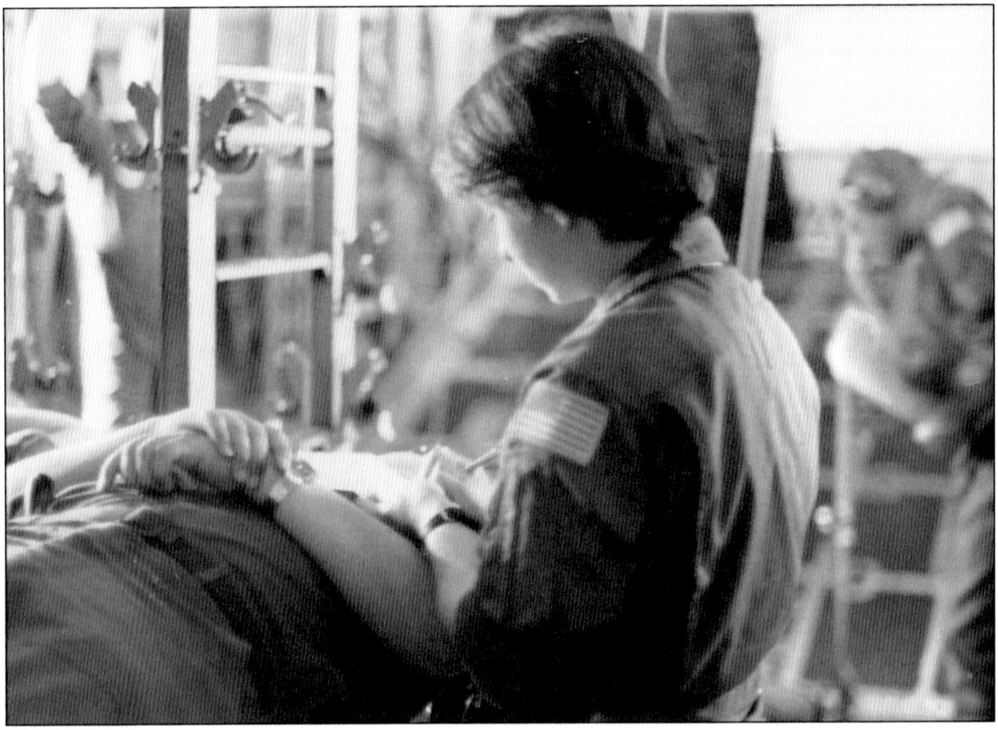

A flight nurse tends a patient during an in-flight medical evacuation exercise. (Courtesy of the Delaware Military Heritage and Education Foundation.)

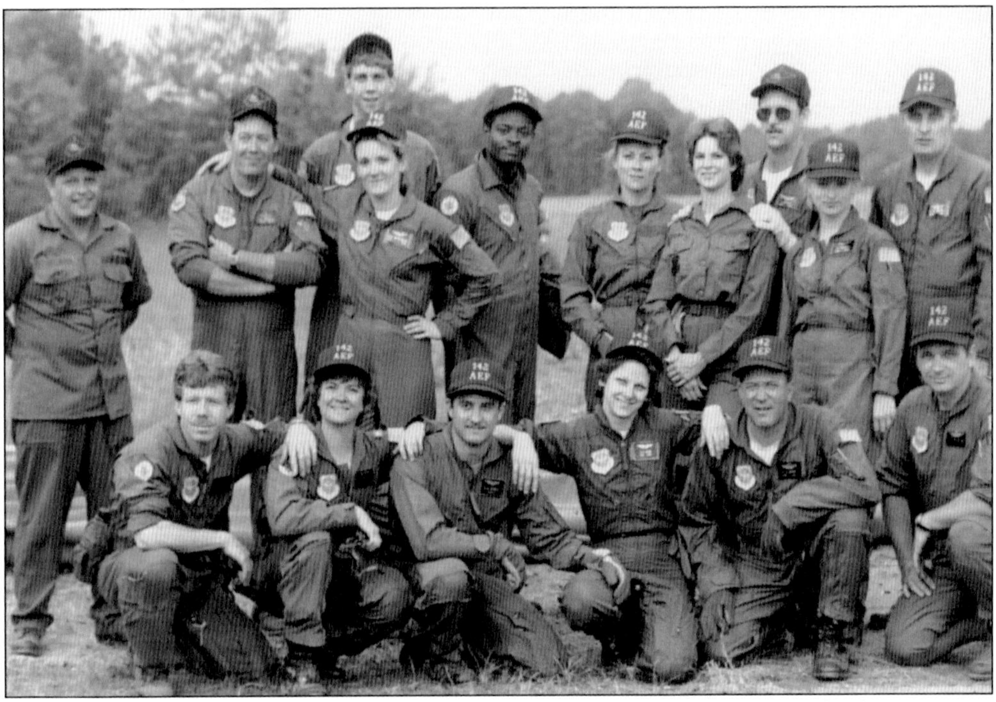

An affectionate "family portrait" was taken of members of the 142nd Aeromedical Evacuation Flight. (Courtesy of the Delaware Military Heritage and Education Foundation.)

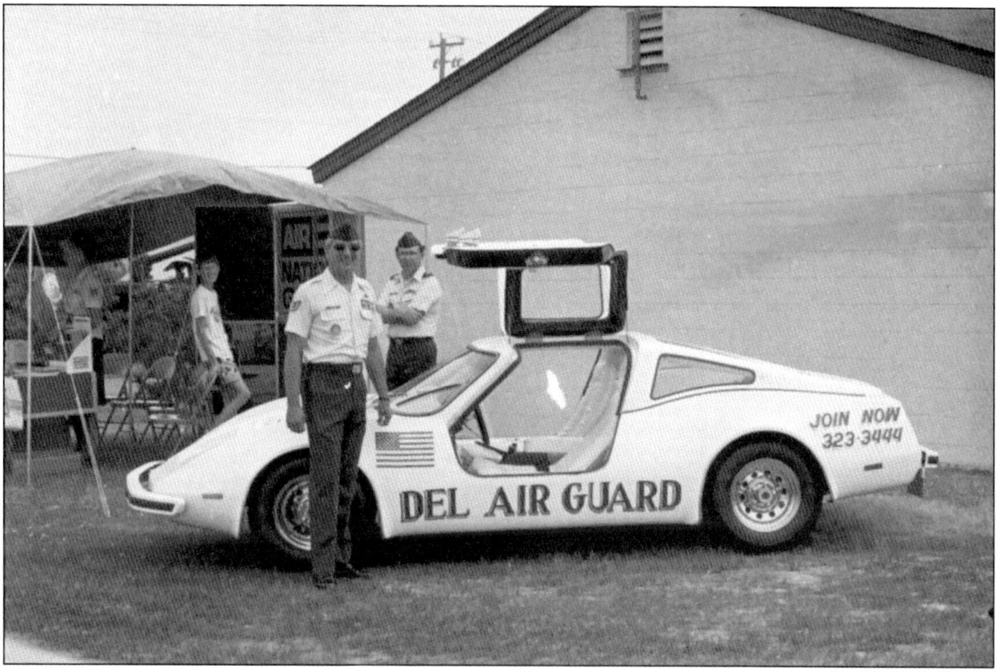

A kit car painted in Delaware Air Guard livery was used as a recruiting advertisement. T.Sgt. Lee Wiseman, a Delaware ANG recruiter, poses by front wheel; Eric Loveless is to the right behind the car. (Courtesy of the Delaware Military Heritage and Education Foundation.)

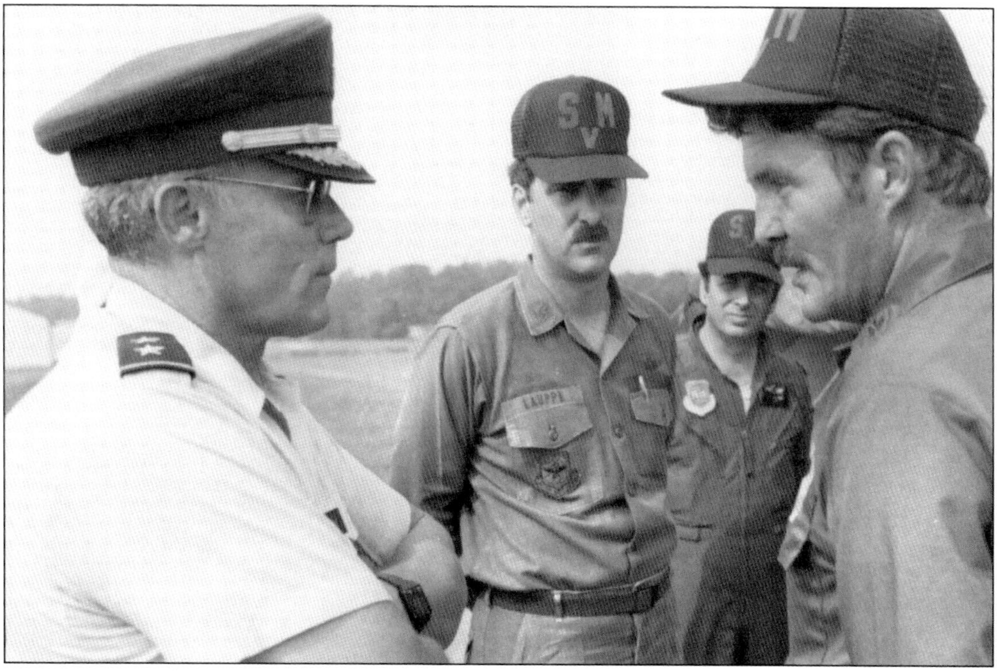

Maj. Gen. Joseph Lank, the adjutant general, (left) listens to a briefing by Maj. Hugh Broomall (right) as Maj. Tom Lauppe (center) and Maj. Stanley Bastien observe. Lauppe was a future general officer, and Broomall was destined to be the first non-rated general officer in Delaware Air Guard history when he was appointed assistant adjutant general in December 2004.

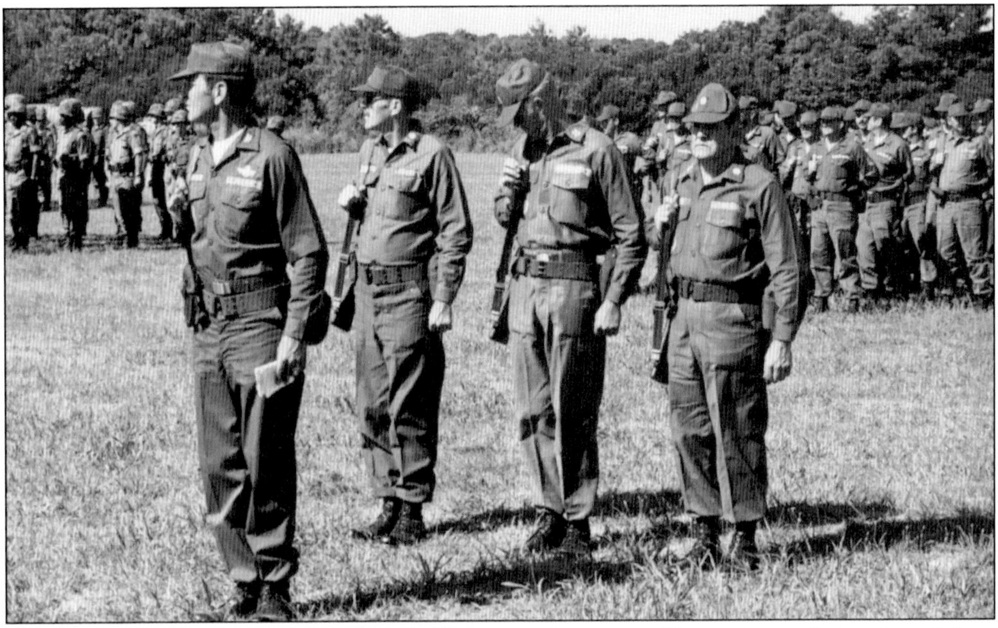

The Delaware Air National Guard leadership team during a field exercise includes, from left to right, Col. William Hutchison, group commander; Lt. Col. Max Beheler; Capt. Robert Garvey; and Lt. Col. Ralph Piazza. (Courtesy of the Delaware Military Heritage and Education Foundation.)

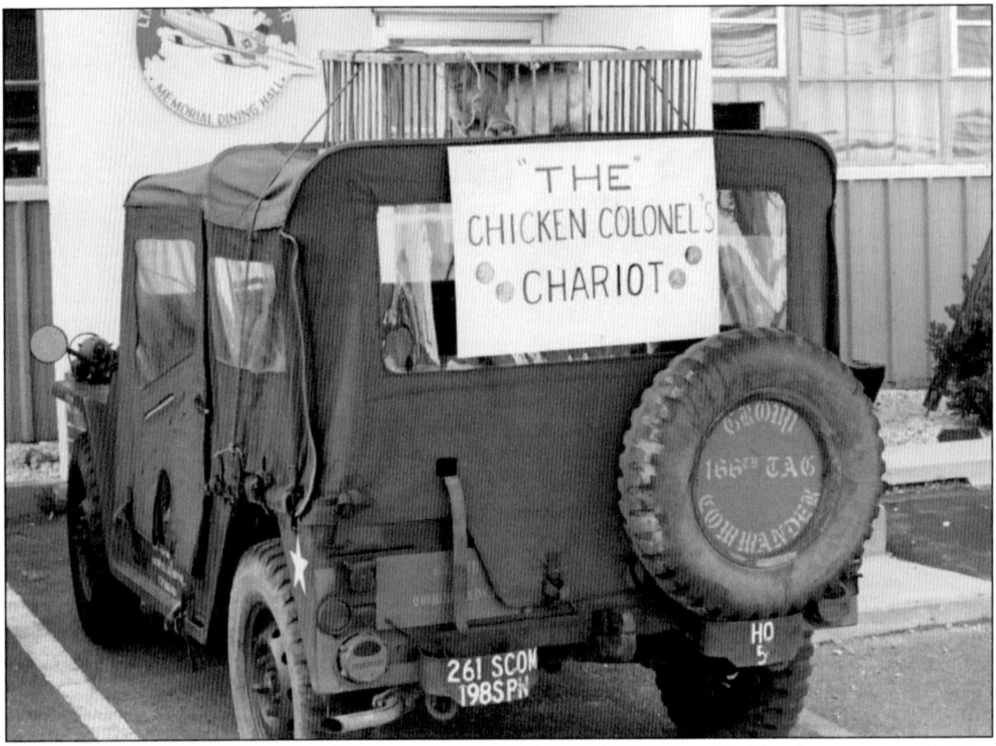

The luxurious staff car driven by group commander Col. William F. Hutchison is parked in front of the McCallister Memorial Dining Hall. (Courtesy of the Delaware Military Heritage and Education Foundation.)

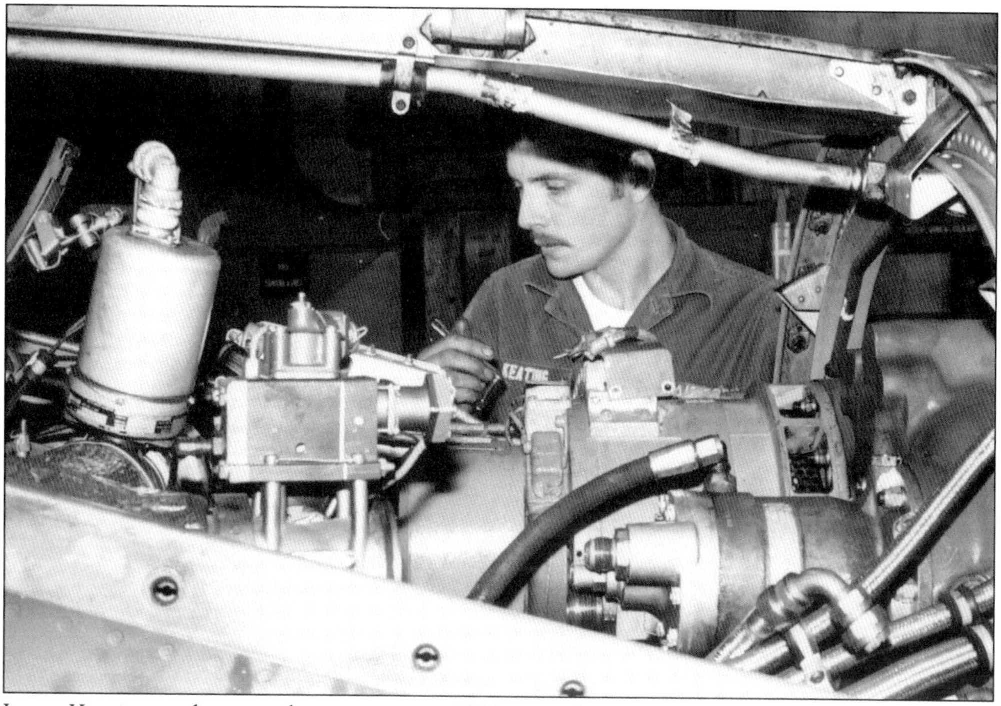

Larry Keating makes an adjustment on a T-56 jet turbine engine in the 166th Consolidated Aircraft Maintenance Squadron engine shop. (Courtesy of the Delaware Military Heritage and Education Foundation.)

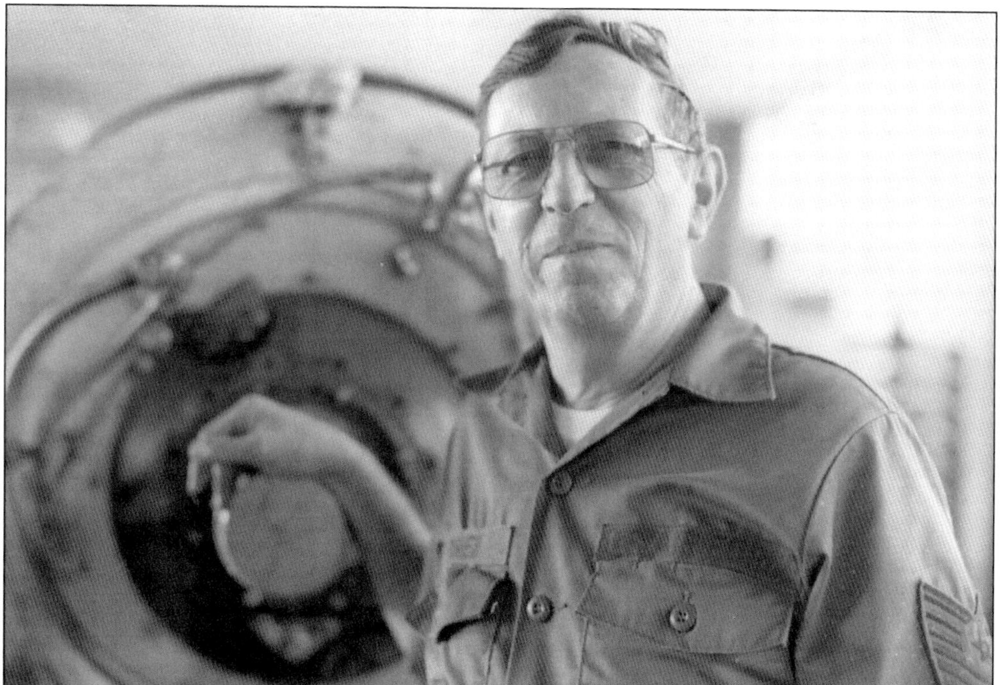

M.Sgt. Thomas Fisher poses by the nose section of a jet turbine engine. (Courtesy of the Delaware Military Heritage and Education Foundation.)

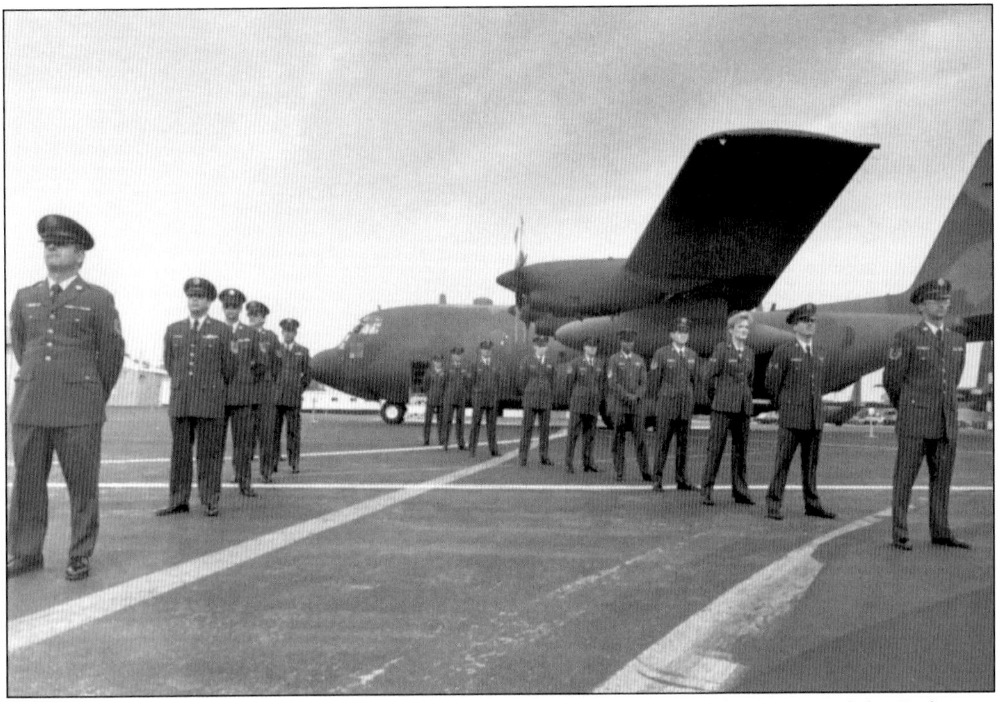

A parade and review are held on the flight line in Class A uniform. (Courtesy of the Delaware Military Heritage and Education Foundation.)

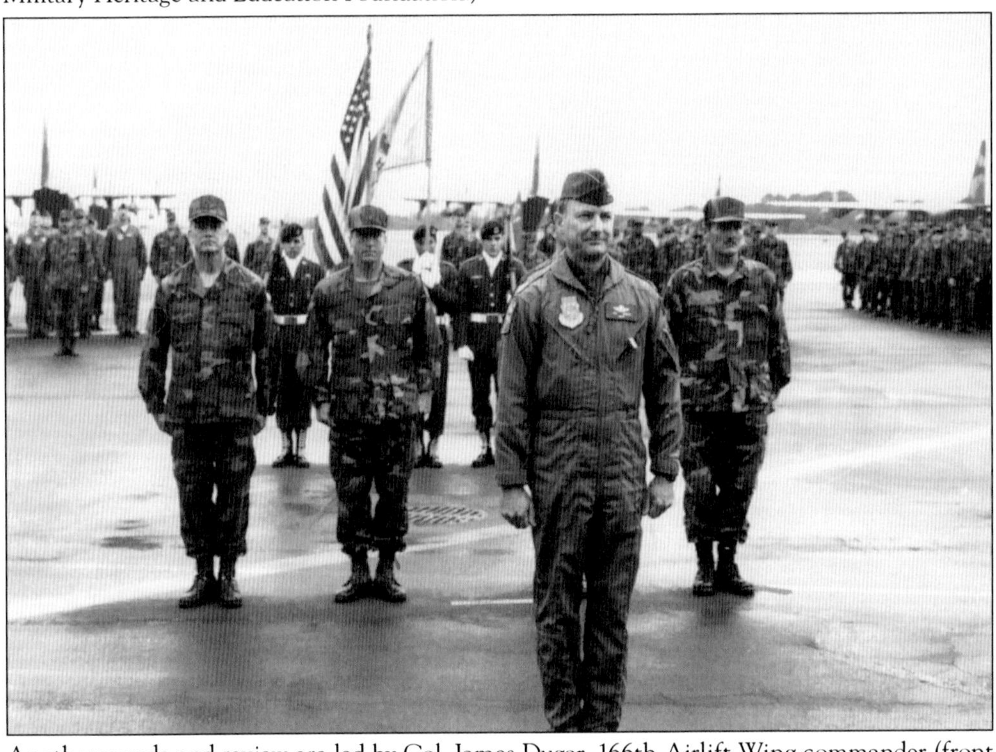

Another parade and review are led by Col. James Dugar, 166th Airlift Wing commander (front center). (Courtesy of the Delaware Military Heritage and Education Foundation.)

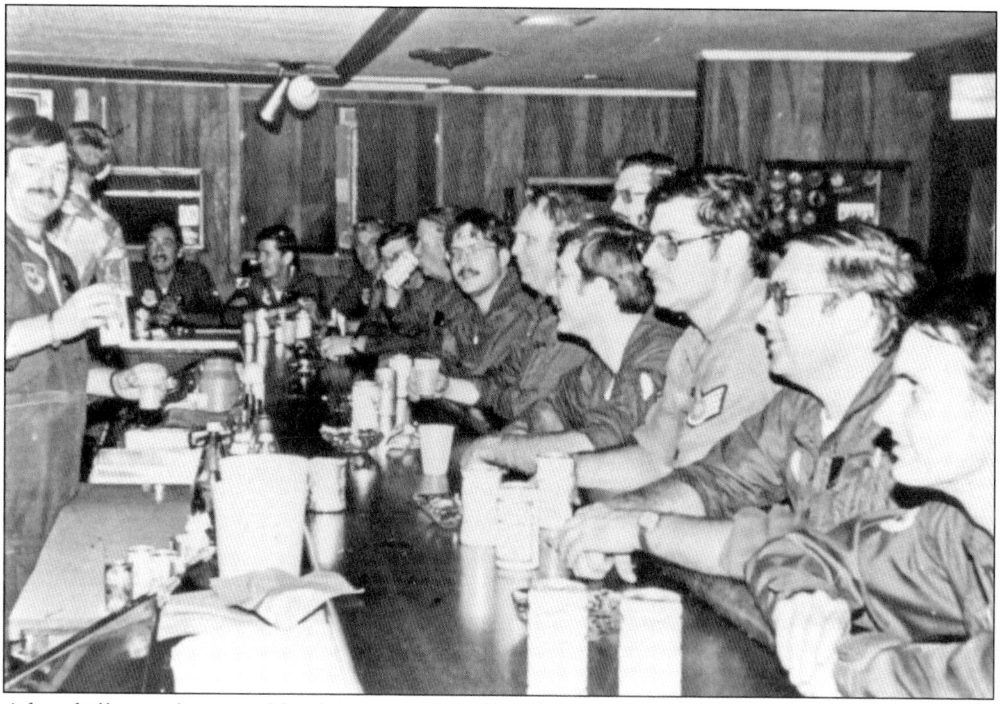

After drill, members would celebrate at the all-ranks club, formerly the New Castle Army Air Base Officers Club. (Courtesy of the Delaware Military Heritage and Education Foundation.)

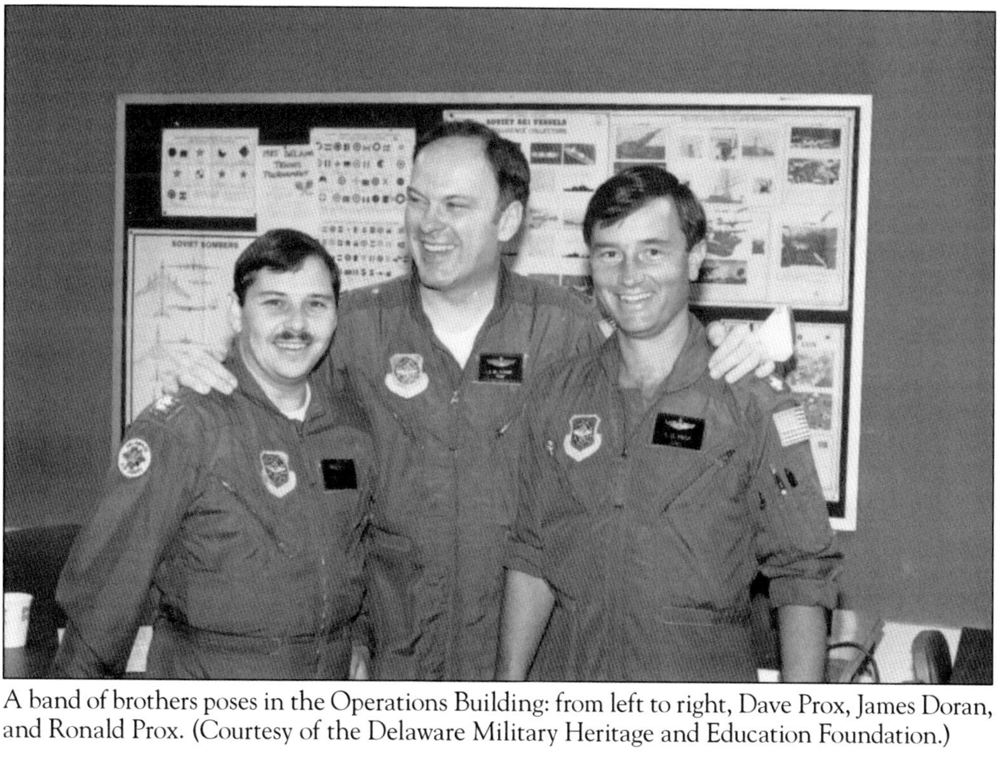

A band of brothers poses in the Operations Building: from left to right, Dave Prox, James Doran, and Ronald Prox. (Courtesy of the Delaware Military Heritage and Education Foundation.)

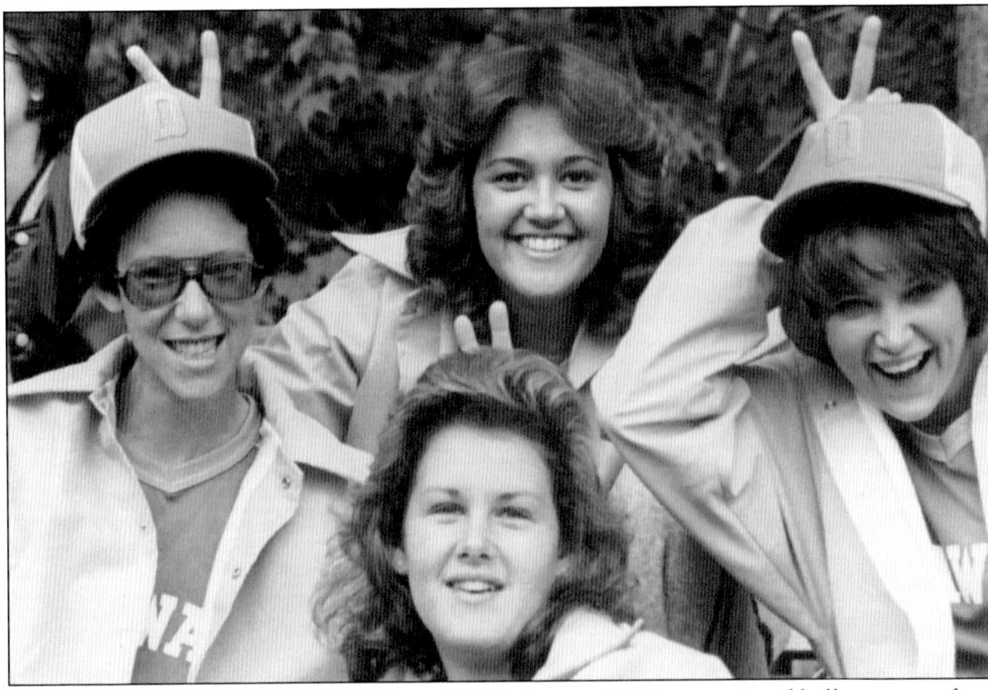

Some members of the first-place-winning 1978 Delaware ANG women's softball team are, from left to right, Jane Lerch, Sandy McDowell (bottom), Kathy Navitsky, and Kathy Kearns. (Courtesy of the Delaware Military Heritage and Education Foundation.)

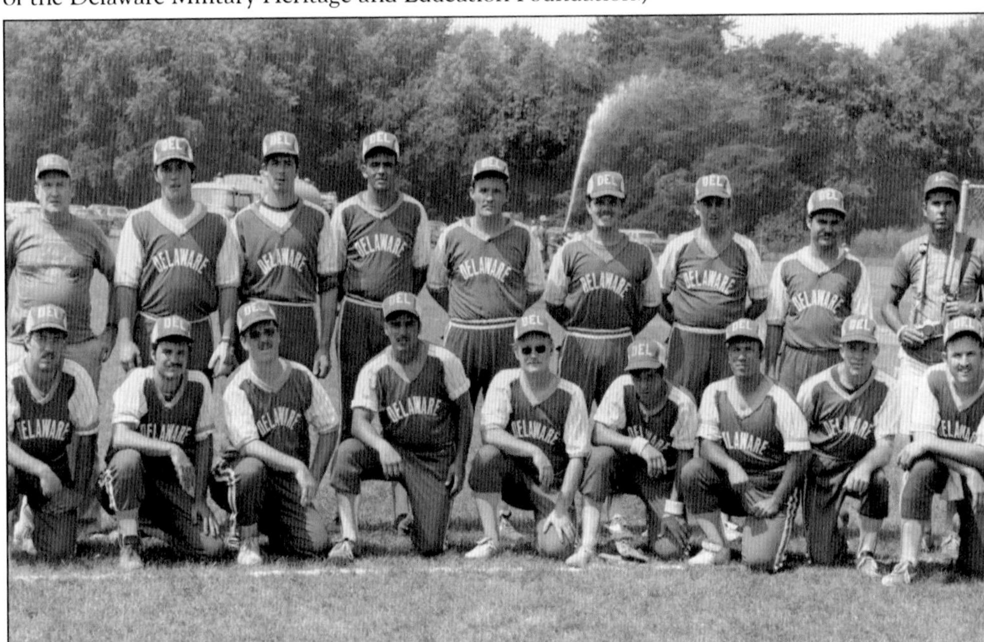

A Delaware Air Guard men's softball team had been formed as early as 1961. They were national champions in 1978, 1982, 1983, 1988, 1989, 1990, and 1995. There were bowling teams, volleyball teams, and a basketball team as well. (Courtesy of the Delaware Military Heritage and Education Foundation.)

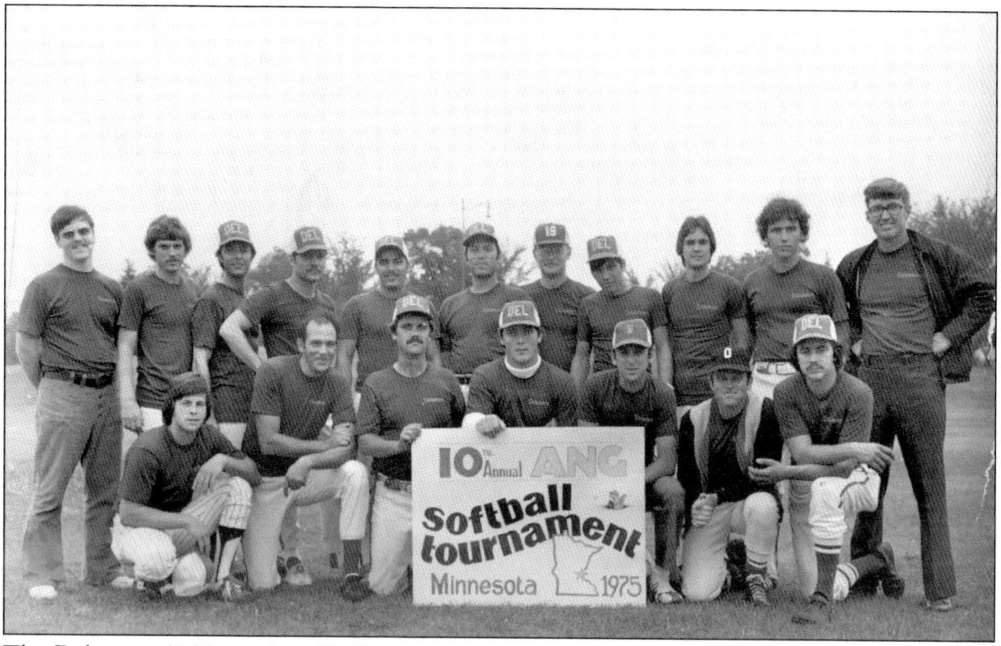

The Delaware ANG men's softball team is pictured at a 1975 tournament in Minnesota. They placed second that year. From left to right are (first row) Mike Cleary, Glen Hefner, Larry Dugan, Kenny Thompkins, Don Goldstein, Willis Grier, and Kenny Scott; (second row) Pete Clarkin, Tim Bennett, Mark Moldoff, Jerry "Doc" Dougherty, Dave Crescenzo, Nick Nesci, Bob McVaugh, Paul Crescenzo, Lee Hagenbach, Paul Thorson, and Joe Pfister; absent is Larry Wiggins. (Courtesy of the Delaware Military Heritage and Education Foundation.)

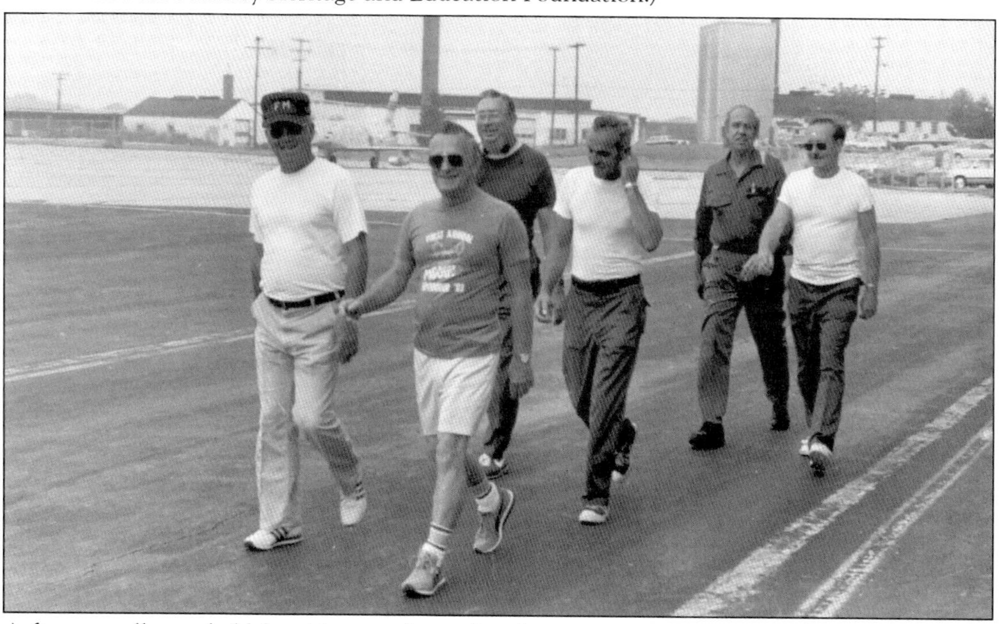
A fitness walk was held for older members who chose not to participate in the running fitness initiative of the 1970s. From left to right are S.M.Sgt. Victor Macy, C.M.Sgt. Donald Ironside, M.Sgt. George Gooden, M.Sgt. Ernie Antes, M.Sgt. Roger Demers, and M.Sgt. Horchler. (Courtesy of the Delaware Military Heritage and Education Foundation.)

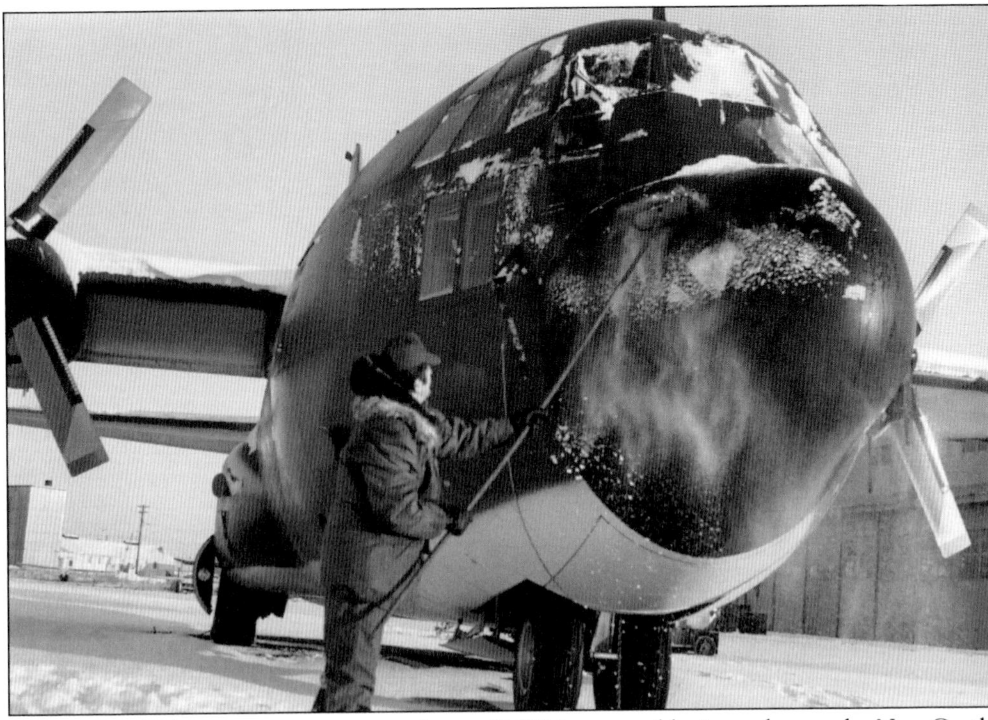

An unidentified airman removes snow from a C-130A on a cold winter day on the New Castle flight line. (Courtesy of the Delaware Military Heritage and Education Foundation.)

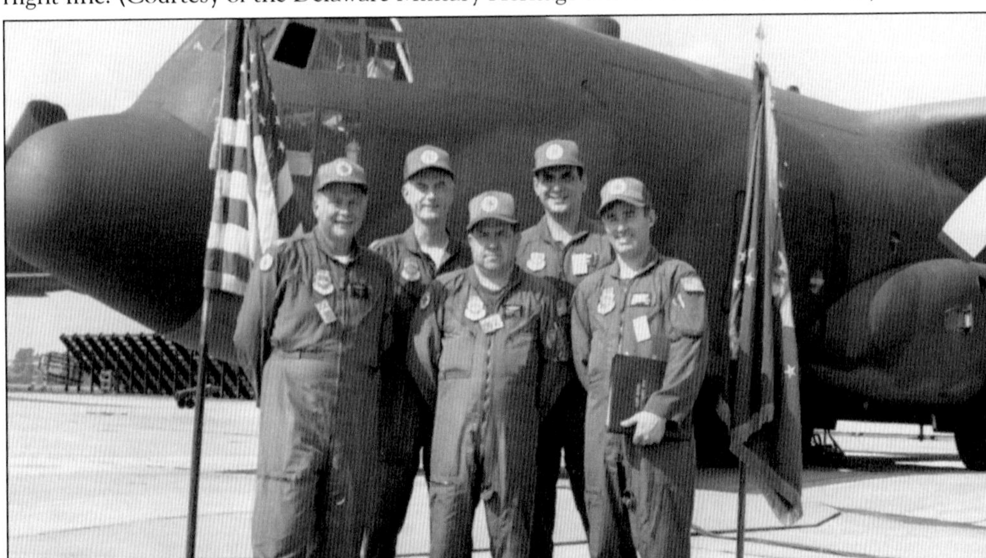

The Delaware Air Guard takes delivery on October 16, 1985, of the first C-130H–model aircraft at Lockheed-Marietta Plant, Georgia, after a vigorous effort by Delaware's congressional delegation on October 16, 1985. In January 1986, the unit received the last of eight C-130H aircraft. From left to right are Col. Judson Wooding, 166th Tactical Airlift Group commander; Col. James P. Scott II; S.M.Sgt. James Boyce, loadmaster; Col. Phil Goettel; and M.Sgt. Ray Holder, flight engineer. (Courtesy of the Delaware Military Heritage and Education Foundation.)

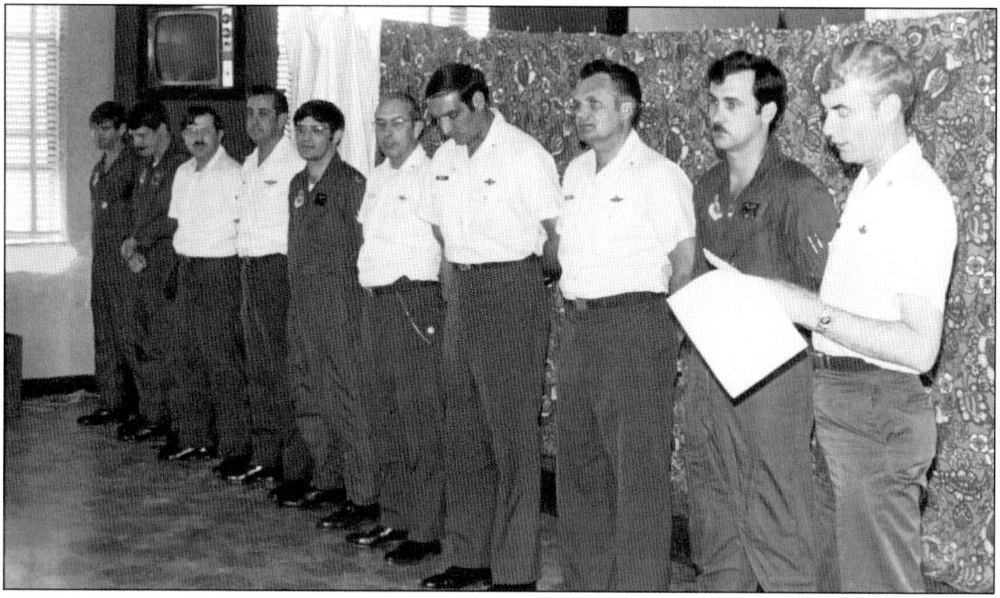

An aircrew is cited by Col. Jim Scott (far right) for exceptional service. Pictured from left to right are A1c. Ron Roark, loadmaster; S.Sgt. Wayne R. Wolfe, loadmaster; S.Sgt. John L. Valentine, loadmaster; M.Sgt. Don Galbraith, flight engineer; Capt. William Schell, navigator; Maj. Joseph Lanahan, navigator; Lt. Col. Hugh Goettel, navigator; Maj. Frank Wooten, copilot; and Capt. Thomas Lauppe, aircraft commander. (Courtesy of the Delaware Military Heritage and Education Foundation.)

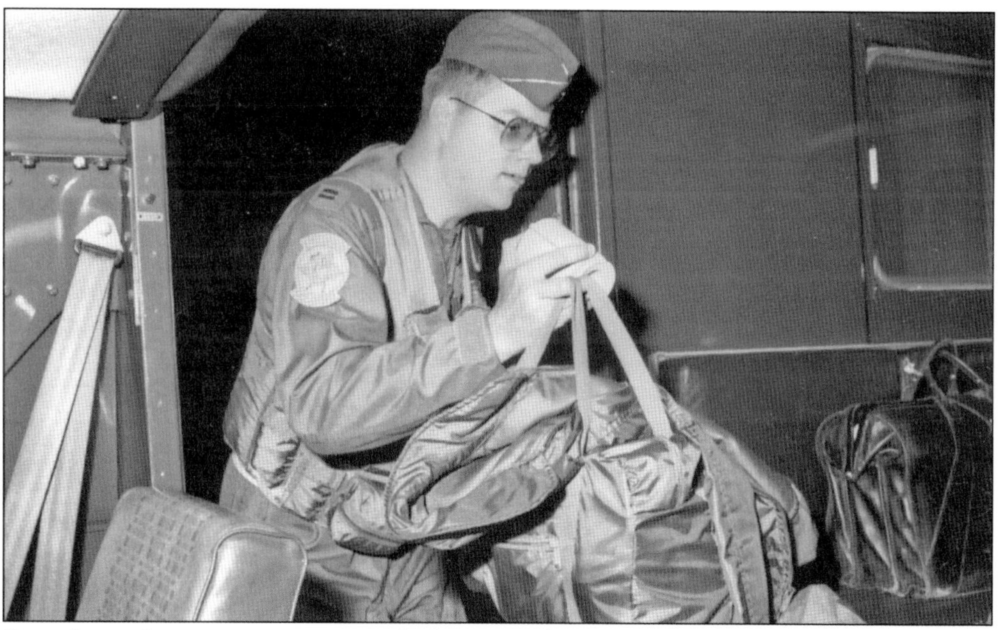

Capt. James Stewart is preparing to deploy to Saudi Arabia for Operation Desert Storm. On January 25, 1991, selected units of the Delaware Air National Guard were activated for the Persian Gulf War, known as Operation Desert Storm (Delaware ANG sent eight planes with crews and maintenance and support personnel). A majority of the unit was stationed at Al Kharj Air Base, Saudi Arabia. (Courtesy of the Delaware Military Heritage and Education Foundation.)

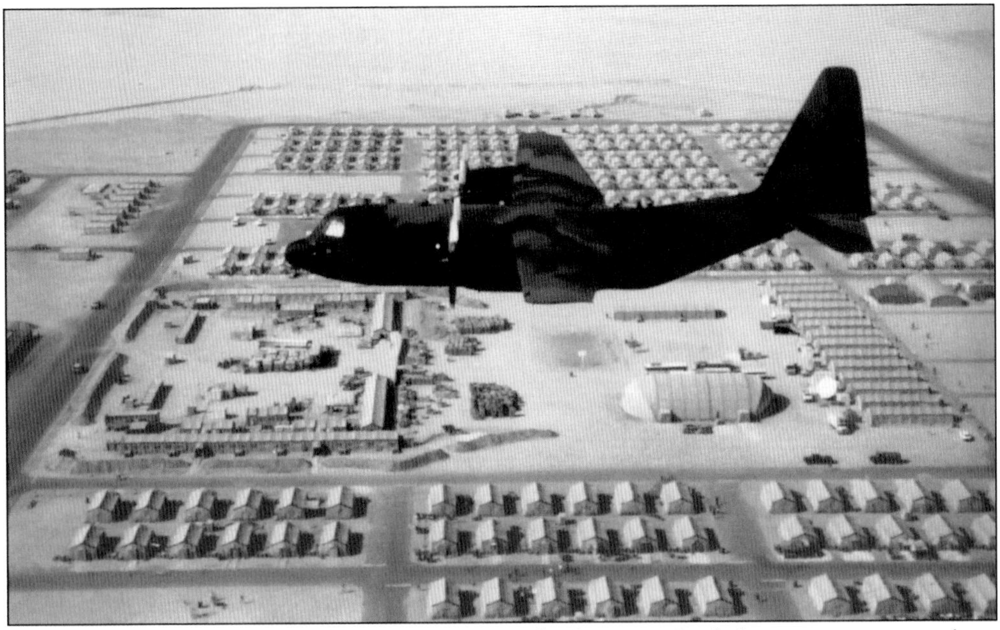

A Delaware Air National Guard C-130H soars over the desert sands of a large tent city somewhere in Saudi Arabia. During the period of August 16, 1990, through October 1990, three aircraft, with supporting crews and many volunteers of the Delaware Air National Guard, participated in Operation Desert Shield based in Al Ain, United Arab Emirates. (Courtesy of the Delaware Military Heritage and Education Foundation.)

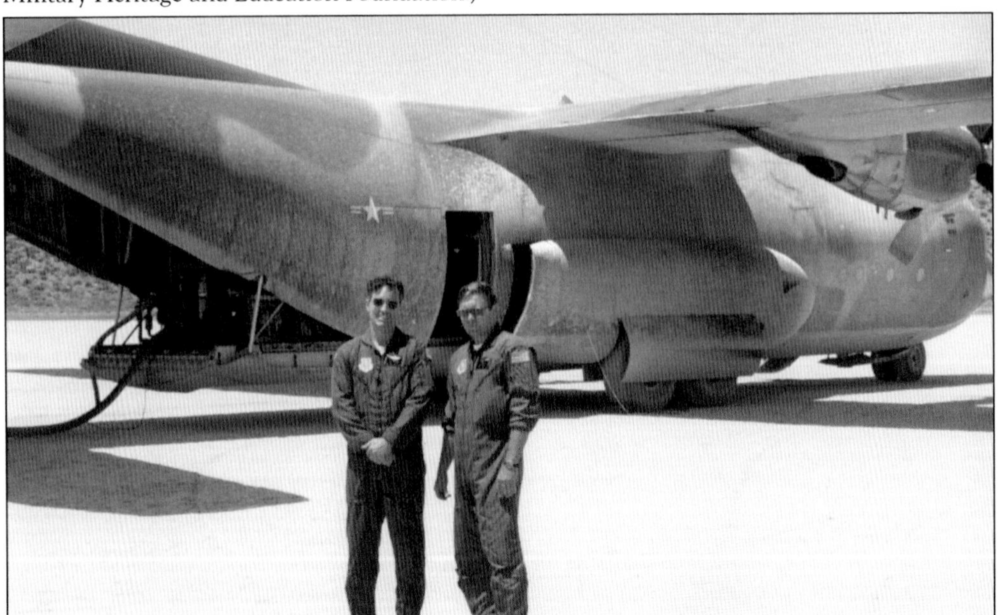

Flight engineer Ray Holder (left) and loadmaster Mike Perry (right) pose in front of a very dirty Delaware C-130 under a desert sky. By the end of the Gulf War, the Delaware Air Guard had made a significant contribution to the effort, flying thousands of sorties on hundreds of operations. They delivered the goods, flying almost 6,000 tons of supplies to the troops on the ground. (Courtesy of the Delaware Military Heritage and Education Foundation.)

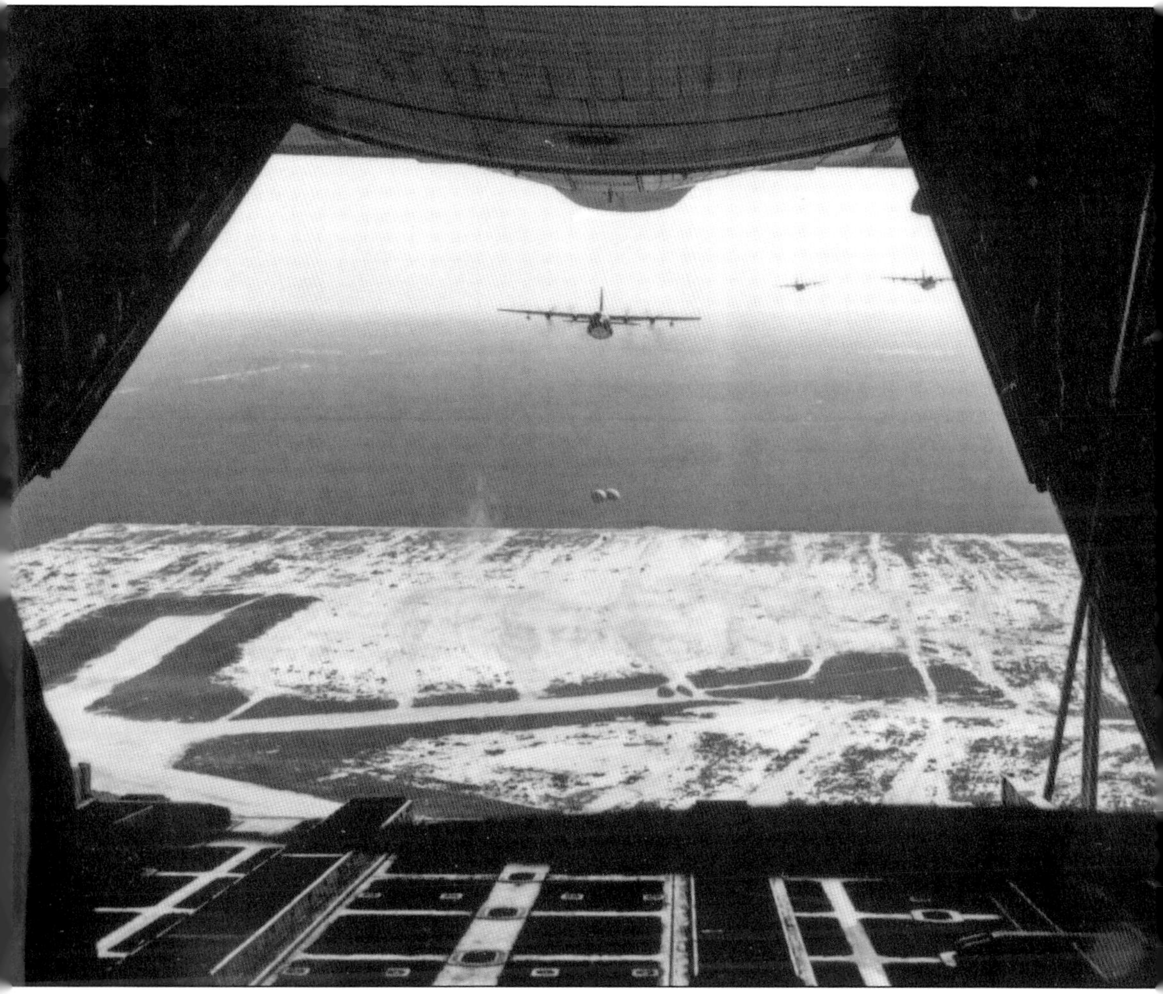

The business end of the tactical airlift mission is demonstrated here. An aerial drop of cargo is shown over the Coyle, New Jersey, drop zone, photographed by T.Sgt. Paul Marsico. (Courtesy of the Delaware Military Heritage and Education Foundation.)